Contents

CONTENTS

STUDIES IN THE DEAD SEA SCROLLS AND RELATED LITERATURE

Peter W. Flint, Martin G. Abegg Jr., and Florentino García Martínez

GENERAL EDITORS

The Dead Sea Scrolls have been the object of intense interest in recent years, not least because of the release of previously unpublished texts from Qumran Cave 4 since the fall of 1991. With the wealth of new documents that have come to light, the field of Qumran studies has undergone a renaissance. Scholars have begun to question the established conclusions of the last generation; some widely held beliefs have withstood scrutiny, but others have required revision or even dismissal. New proposals and competing hypotheses, many of them of an uncritical and sensational nature, vie for attention. Idiosyncratic and misleading views of the Scrolls still abound, especially in the popular press, while the results of solid scholarship have yet to make their full impact. At the same time, the scholarly task of establishing reliable critical editions of the texts is nearing completion. The opportunity is ripe, therefore, for directing renewed attention to the task of analysis and interpretation.

STUDIES IN THE DEAD SEA SCROLLS AND RELATED LITERATURE is a series designed to address this need. In particular, the series aims to make the latest and best Dead Sea Scrolls scholarship accessible to scholars, students, and the thinking public. The volumes that are projected — both monographs and collected essays — will seek to clarify how the Scrolls revise and help shape our understanding of the formation of the Bible and the historical development of Judaism and Christianity. Various offerings in the series will explore the reciprocally illuminating relationships of several disciplines related to the Scrolls, including the canon and text of the Hebrew Bible, the richly varied forms of Second Temple Judaism, and the New Testament. While the Dead Sea Scrolls constitute the main focus, several of these studies will also include perspectives on the Old and New Testaments and other ancient writings — hence the title of the series. It is hoped that these volumes will contribute to a deeper appreciation of the world of early Judaism and Christianity and of their continuing legacy today.

PETER W. FLINT
MARTIN G. ABEGG JR.
FLORENTINO GARCÍA MARTÍNEZ

RELIGION
in the
DEAD SEA SCROLLS

Edited by

JOHN J. COLLINS
and
ROBERT A. KUGLER

WILLIAM B. EERDMANS PUBLISHING COMPANY
GRAND RAPIDS, MICHIGAN / CAMBRIDGE, U.K.

Wm. B. Eerdmans Publishing Co.

255 Jefferson Ave. S.E., Grand Rapids, Michigan 49503 /
P.O. Box 163, Cambridge CB3 9PU U.K.

Printed in the United States of America

05 04 03 02 01 00   5 4 3 2 1

Library of Congress Cataloging-in-Publication Data

Religion in the Dead Sea scrolls /
edited by John J. Collins and Robert A. Kugler.
  p.   cm. — (Studies in the Dead Sea scrolls and related literature)
Includes bibliographical references.
ISBN 0-8028-4743-9 (alk. paper)
1. Dead Sea scrolls. 2. Qumran community. 3. Judaism — History —
Post-exilic period, 586 B.C.–A.D. 210.   I. Collins, John Joseph, 1946–
II. Kugler, Robert A.   III. Series.

BM487.A785 2000
296.1′55 — dc21
00-035470

www.eerdmans.com

Contributors

JOHN J. COLLINS, Holmes Professor of Old Testament, Yale University, New Haven, Connecticut

EILEEN SCHULLER, Department of Religious Studies, McMaster University, Hamilton, Ontario

MARTIN HENGEL, Professor Emeritus, Eberhard-Karls-Universität, Tübingen

TIMOTHY H. LIM, Department of Hebrew and Old Testament, The University of Edinburgh, New Haven, Mound Place, Edinburgh

HANNAH K. HARRINGTON, Biblical and Theological Studies, Patten College, Oakland, California

ROBERT A. KUGLER, Department of Religious Studies, Gonzaga University, Spokane, Washington

JAMES C. VANDERKAM, John A. O'Brien Professor of Old Testament, Department of Theology, University of Notre Dame, Notre Dame, Indiana

CRAIG A. EVANS, Trinity Western University, Langley, British Columbia

Diacritical Marks, Sigla,
and Abbreviations

Abbreviations of journals, reference works, and other secondary sources generally conform to the "Instructions for Contributors" in the *Membership Directory and Handbook* of the Society of Biblical Literature (1994) 223-40. For abbreviations of Qumran sigla, see J. A. Fitzmyer, *The Dead Sea Scrolls: Major Publications and Tools for Study,* rev. ed. (SBLRBS 20; Atlanta: Scholars Press, 1990) 1-8.

Diacritical Marks and Sigla

(?)	Doubt exists as to the identification of a verse or reading.
[Daniel]	The bracketed word is no longer extant but has been restored.
Da[niel]	The bracketed part of the word has been restored.
דני[אל]	As above
to (his) throne	The parenthetical word has been added to improve the English translation.
[ ] or [. . .]	There is a space between fragments or the surface of the leather is missing.
]. . .[	Letters (in this case three) with ink traces remaining cannot be identified.
frg. 10 ii 4-5	Fragment 10, column 2, lines 4-5

Abbreviations

AB	Anchor Bible
ABD	D. N. Freedman (ed.), *Anchor Bible Dictionary*
AbrN	*Abr-Nahrain*
ABRL	Anchor Bible Reference Library
ASOR	American Schools of Oriental Research
BARev	*Biblical Archaeology Review*
BibOr	Biblica et orientalia
BJS	Brown Judaic Studies
BN	*Biblische Notizen*
BO	*Bibliotheca orientalis*
CBQ	*Catholic Biblical Quarterly*
CBQMS	Catholic Biblical Quarterly — Monograph Series
CJA	Christianity and Judaism in Antiquity
ConBOT	Coniectanea biblica, Old Testament
CRINT	Compendia rerum iudaicarum ad novum testamentum
DJD	Discoveries in the Judaean Desert
DSD	*Dead Sea Discoveries*
DSRL	Studies in the Dead Sea Scrolls and Related Literature
Ebib	Etudes bibliques
GTA	Göttinger theologische Arbeiten
HAR	*Hebrew Annual Review*
HSM	Harvard Semitic Monographs
HUCA	*Hebrew Union College Annual*
IEJ	*Israel Exploration Journal*
IBL	*Journal of Biblical Literature*
JBT	*Jahrbuch für biblische Theologie*
JJS	*Journal of Jewish Studies*
JQR	*Jewish Quarterly Review*
JQRMS	Jewish Quarterly Review Monograph Series
JSJ	*Journal for the Study of Judaism in the Persian, Hellenistic and Roman Period*
JSJSup	Journal for the Study of Judaism in the Persian, Hellenistic and Roman Period, Supplements
JSQ	*Jewish Studies Quarterly*
JSOT	*Journal for the Study of the Old Testament*
JSOTSup	Journal for the Study of the Old Testament, Supplements
JSP	*Journal for the Study of the Pseudepigrapha*
JSPSup	Journal for the Study of the Pseudepigrapha, Supplements

JTS	*Journal of Theological Studies*
LXX	Septuagint
MH	Mishnaic Hebrew
MT	Masoretic Text
NCB	New Century Bible
NRSV	New Revised Standard Version
NTS	*New Testament Studies*
OG	Old Greek
OTL	Old Testament Library
RB	*Revue biblique*
RevQ	*Revue de Qumran*
RSV	Revised Standard Version
SBLDS	SBL Dissertation Series
SBLEJL	SBL Early Judaism and Its Literature
SBLMS	SBL Monograph Series
SBLRBS	SBL Resources for Biblical Study
SBLSS	SBL Semeia Studies
SIJD	Schriften des Institutum Judaicum Delitzschianum
SJLA	Studies in Judaism in Late Antiquity
SNTSMS	Society for New Testament Studies Monograph Series
SR	*Studies in Religion/Sciences religieuses*
STDJ	Studies on the Texts of the Desert of Judah
SUNT	Studien zur Umwelt des Neuen Testaments
TDNT	*Theological Dictionary of the New Testament*
TSAJ	Texte und Studien zum antiken Judentum
VT	*Vetus Testamentum*
WUNT	Wissenschaftliche Untersuchungen zum Neuen Testament
ZNW	*Zeitschrift für die neutestamentliche Wissenschaft*

For abbreviations of Dead Sea Scrolls and other ancient sources, see Patrick H. Alexander et al., ed., *The SBL Handbook of Style* (Peabody, Mass.: Hendrickson: 1999).

Introduction

JOHN J. COLLINS

Helmer Ringgren's book, *The Faith of Qumran: Theology of the Dead Sea Scrolls*, first appeared in English in 1963.[1] (The Swedish original appeared in 1961.) Like Józef T. Milik's *Ten Years of Discovery in the Wilderness of Judaea*,[2] and Frank Moore Cross's *The Ancient Library of Qumran and Modern Biblical Studies*,[3] it represented a synthesis of the first phase of the study of the Dead Sea Scrolls. It differed from these other books insofar as it concentrated entirely on issues of religion and theology. All these books assumed that the Scrolls represented the writings of a community that had resided at Qumran, and that they gave expression to a coherent set of religious and theological ideas. These ideas were found above all in the *Rule of the Community,* the *Damascus Document,* the *Hodayot,* the *Pesharim,* and the *War Scroll,* although the *Genesis Apocryphon* and "miscellaneous fragments" were also acknowledged. These core documents, with the exception of the *Damascus Document,* had been found in Cave 1, were relatively well preserved, and were the first published and best-known texts from Qumran.

Thirty years later, Ringgren felt justified in reissuing the book unchanged. He granted that texts published since 1963 "would obviously enable me to add interesting details," but he felt that they would not change his basic

---

1. H. Ringgren, *The Faith of Qumran: Theology of the Dead Sea Scrolls* (Philadelphia: Fortress, 1963); reprinted with an introduction by J. H. Charlesworth (New York: Crossroad, 1995).

2. J. T. Milik, *Ten Years of Discovery in the Wilderness of Judaea* (London: SCM, 1959).

3. F. M. Cross, *The Ancient Library of Qumran and Modern Biblical Studies* (Garden City: Doubleday, 1958; 2nd ed., 1961; 3rd ed., Sheffield: Sheffield Academic Press, 1995).

1

ideas substantially. Insofar as Ringgren's book is a synthesis of the texts available in 1963, it has in fact held up quite well, but no scholar engaged in the study of the Scrolls in the 1990s would agree with his assessment of the significance (or relative insignificance) of the texts that have become available since that time.

The view that Qumran was a sectarian settlement, and that the Scrolls constituted its library, remains standard, despite the vociferous advocacy of alternative interpretations in recent years.[4] It also remains highly probable that the settlement pertained to the Essene sect.[5] Two factors, however, have altered the landscape of Scrolls scholarship since the early 1960s. The first pertains to the number of scrolls, and the second to the content of some of the texts that were published after Ringgren wrote.

Only when the full corpus became available in the early 1990s did scholars generally become aware of the sheer number of texts that were hidden in the caves near Qumran. Hartmut Stegemann estimates that approximately 1,000 scrolls were hidden; fragments of 900 were preserved, and it is possible to determine the content of some 660.[6] It is now generally admitted that this collection included many texts that were not products of the Qumran community. This point has long been granted with regard to biblical texts, and to the books of *Enoch* and *Jubilees,* which were known before the discovery of the Scrolls and are generally agreed to have been written before the establishment of the settlement at Qumran. In recent years, it is recognized that even previously unknown works are not necessarily peculiar to the Qumran sect. Neither can we assume that all nonsectarian works were "pre-Qumran," in the sense that they were composed before the emergence of the Qumran sect. Moreover, the Essene sect was not confined to Qumran, and the *Damascus Document* envisages "camps" scattered throughout the land. The relation of the scrolls found at Qumran to the other sectarian settlements is uncertain. It is possible that sectarians from several settlements hid their scrolls in the wilderness, in proximity to the Qumran community. We cannot assume a unified theological vision in all this literature. There remains, however, a core corpus of texts that is recognized as sectarian because of references to the Teacher, or to the community, or to some distinctive themes and motifs. This corpus corresponds essentially to the texts on which Ringgren based his book, but with some significant additions from later publications.

4. For a lucid, balanced review, see J. C. VanderKam, *The Dead Sea Scrolls Today* (Grand Rapids: Eerdmans, 1994) 2-27. The most vocal critic of this consensus is N. Golb, *Who Wrote the Dead Sea Scrolls?* (New York: Scribner, 1995).

5. VanderKam, *The Dead Sea Scrolls Today,* 71-98.

6. H. Stegemann, *The Library of Qumran* (Grand Rapids: Eerdmans, 1998) 79.

In his introduction to the reprint of Ringgren's book, James H. Charlesworth asserts that "numerous theologies were found at Qumran."[7] This remark referred not only to the differences between sectarian texts and those composed elsewhere, but also to the corpus of texts that were presumably composed at Qumran. We should indeed expect that beliefs and practices changed over a period of some two hundred years. As yet, however, no satisfactory way has been found to trace chronological development within the sectarian scrolls. Hartmut Stegemann has claimed that the sectarian scrolls were composed within a short time frame and that no distinctively sectarian (Essene) text can be dated later than the middle of the first century BCE.[8] Differences can certainly be detected within the sectarian scrolls. Whether these constitute different "theologies" is debatable. Even Charlesworth goes on to describe common trends that cut across the supposed "theologies" of Qumran. In any case, the more urgent question in the study of the religion of the Scrolls concerns the degree to which the sectarians shared beliefs and practices with other Jews of the time. It is now clear that the Qumran community was not as isolated as has often been assumed. The question arises whether works and traditions that were not peculiar to the sect were nevertheless influential factors in their religious thinking. The religion of the Qumran sect was constituted not only by their distinctive ideas and beliefs, but also by those that they shared with other Jews.

The second factor that has changed the landscape of Qumran studies also concerns relations with other strands of Judaism, especially with those strands later represented by the rabbinic literature. The first phase of scholarship on the Dead Sea Scrolls, reflected in the books of Milik, Cross, and Ringgren, was predominantly the work of Christian scholars, who quite naturally viewed the texts through the filter of their own interests and expectations. The use of the words "Faith" and "Theology" in the title of Ringgren's book speaks volumes for its Christian perspective. There is little in his book to suggest to the reader that halakah, the life of obedience to divine commandments, was a significant factor in the spirituality of the Scrolls. This is not to suggest that Ringgren, or other Scrolls scholars of his generation, wanted to subordinate the Scrolls to Christian interests. Ringgren very explicitly insisted that the Jewish literature must be understood in its own right before it can be compared or contrasted with the New Testament. However, the questions and categories he brought to the text were distinctly Christian. They were not necessarily invalid for that reason, but

---

7. Ringgren, *The Faith of Qumran*, xix.

8. Stegemann, *The Library of Qumran*, 137. Some of these texts were still copied in the first century CE.

their perspective was partial and incomplete and suffered from the lack of dialogue with Jewish scholars.

Ringgren's perspective was also limited by lack of access to some important legal texts. This situation began to change after 1967, when Qumran and the Scrolls came under Israeli control. A major watershed was reached with the acquisition of the *Temple Scroll*. The publication of this scroll by Yigael Yadin drew attention to the central importance of legal, halakic issues for the people of the Scrolls.[9] There is still dispute as to whether the *Temple Scroll* should be considered a sectarian composition, but it enabled scholars to see the prominence of halakic issues in an indisputably sectarian text, the *Damascus Document*. Then in 1984 John Strugnell and Elisha Qimron presented a paper in Jerusalem on "An Unpublished Halakhic Letter from Qumran."[10] This text, dubbed by Strugnell "a letter from the Teacher of Righteousness to the Wicked Priest" and now known as 4QMMT,[11] appeared to give the reasons for the separation of the Dead Sea sect from the rest of Judaism. These reasons were halakic in nature and were largely concerned with issues of purity. A section of the text, perhaps an addition to the original composition, was devoted to the cultic calendar. These reasons were similar in kind to the concerns discussed in connection with the origin of the sect in the *Damascus Document*. Earlier scholarship on the Scrolls had argued that the separation of the sect was due to disputes over the high priesthood. It now appeared to be due primarily to disagreement over the correct calendar and over several technical points of Jewish law. The eyes of scholars had been opened to the importance of halakic considerations in the Scrolls, and these interests have been highlighted in more recent studies. The change in perspective is perhaps most clearly evident in Lawrence Schiffman's book, *Reclaiming the Dead Sea Scrolls*, where the section "To Live as a Jew" deals with issues of law, prayer, and ritual.[12] It is ironic that 4QMMT had been known to the editors since the 1950s as a "proto-Mishnaic" text, but its importance had not been recognized.

---

9. Y. Yadin, *The Temple Scroll* (3 vols.; Jerusalem: Israel Exploration Society, 1983).

10. E. Qimron and J. Strugnell, "An Unpublished Halakhic Letter from Qumran," in *Biblical Archaeology Today: Proceedings of the International Congress on Biblical Archaeology, Jerusalem, April 1984*, ed. J. Amitai (Jerusalem: Israel Exploration Society, 1985) 400-407. For the official publication of the text see E. Qimron and J. Strugnell, *Qumran Cave 4, V: Miqṣat Maʿase Ha-Torah* (DJD 10; Oxford: Clarendon 1994).

11. That is, *Miqṣat Maʿase Ha-Torah* (= Some of the Works of the Law) from Qumran Cave 4.

12. L. H. Schiffman, *Reclaiming the Dead Sea Scrolls* (New York: Jewish Publication Society, 1994) 243-312.

It is now readily granted that scholarship on the Dead Sea Scrolls in Helmer Ringgren's generation failed to perceive a very important aspect of the religion of the Scrolls, the continuity of the Scrolls with rabbinic Judaism. Even though the rabbis often adopt positions contrary to those of Qumran, they are frequently concerned with similar issues.[13] We should not, however, jump to the conclusion that all that was written on the Scrolls and the New Testament, or the Scrolls and Christian origins, was invalid. The "faith of Qumran" described by Ringgren is generally well founded in the texts, even though "faith" may not be the best rubric to categorize it. Issues such as messianic expectation and judgment after death, which became central in Christianity but less prominent in rabbinic Judaism, are also important in the Scrolls. The Qumran community, like early Christianity, was informed by a lively belief that the "end of days" was at hand. We know of no comparable community in Judaism in the rabbinic period. At the same time, the religious ideals and ethical values of the Scrolls are in sharp contrast to the New Testament and closer to the world of the rabbis. In fact, the Scrolls are older than, and independent of, both Christianity and rabbinic Judaism. The catastrophic Jewish revolt against Rome, which incidentally brought about the destruction of Qumran, was to some degree the ashes from which both rabbinic Judaism and Christianity (as a predominantly Gentile religion) emerged. The Dead Sea sect was a product of the Hellenistic age and bears the imprint of that age in many ways. To appreciate it, we must do justice both to its continuity with Jewish tradition and to its distinctive innovations; both to the centrality of halakah and to the importance of eschatology; to its affinities both with early Christianity and with rabbinic Judaism.

Now that the project of editing the entire corpus of Dead Sea Scrolls is nearing completion, the time is perhaps ripe to undertake a new synthetic treatment of the religion of Qumran. We do not pretend, however, to provide such a treatment in this volume. All but one of the articles in this book originated in a conference at Trinity Western University in Langley, B.C., on April 24, 1999. Since the target audience of the conference required that it be held on a Saturday, it was not possible to include Jewish speakers. Hannah Harrington's article, which was not presented at the conference, compensates partially for this omission, but Jewish perspectives are admittedly underrepresented. Moreover, a collection of conference papers is not a systematic treatment, but rather a series of probes that uncover aspects of the re-

---

13. L. H. Schiffman, "The Qumran Scrolls and Rabbinic Judaism," in *The Dead Sea Scrolls after Fifty Years: A Comprehensive Assessment*, ed. P. W. Flint and J. C. VanderKam (2 vols.; Leiden: Brill, 1998, 1999) 2.552-72.

ligion of Qumran rather than the whole structure. This volume, then, has the character of a prolegomenon to the study of the religion of the Scrolls. We hope, however, that it will be of service in the uncertain interval until a more systematic treatment is available. In contrast to Ringgren, we speak of the religion of the Scrolls rather than of their theology. The subject includes not only the beliefs of the sect about God and the world, but also their religious practice.

The topics treated in this volume may be grouped in four clusters. The articles of John Collins and Eileen Schuller deal with the understanding of divinity — Collins with the issue of monotheism and the plurality of heavenly beings, Schuller with determinism and the efficacy of prayer.[14] The articles of Rob Kugler and Hannah Harrington deal with halakic issues — Kugler with the interpretation of sacrifice in 4QMMT and Harrington with the continuity of halakic tendencies in the Scrolls.[15] Martin Hengel and Timothy Lim address the question of Hellenistic influence in the Scrolls. Hengel deals with all aspects of this issue, while Lim focuses on the influence of the Greek language. Finally, James VanderKam and Craig Evans deal with apocalypticism and messianism.[16] In all of these essays, issues of tradition and continuity figure prominently. Lim's essay addresses the novel way of interpreting the Bible that we find in the pesharim or biblical commentaries. Kugler discusses the interpretation of legal texts as a means of innovation. VanderKam approaches the subject of apocalypticism from the angle of the appropriation of apocalyptic traditions that had been formulated before the rise of the Dead Sea sect in the books of *Enoch*, Daniel, and *Jubilees*. The issue of continuity and innovation is at the heart of Hengel's discussion of Hellenistic influence in the Scrolls.

A comprehensive discussion of the religion of the Scrolls would need to encompass many other topics. These include:

14. S. Beyerle, "Der Gott der Qumraniten. Anmerkungen zum Gottesbild der Qumran-Texte aus der Sicht der Mischna, der Talmudim, frühen Midraschim und des Josephos," *Henoch* 20 (1998) 271-89, appeared after these essays were completed. On other aspects of Qumran prayer see B. Nitzan, *Qumran Prayer and Religious Poetry* (STDJ 12; Leiden: Brill, 1994); E. Chazon, "Hymns and Prayers in the Dead Sea Scrolls," in *The Dead Sea Scrolls after Fifty Years,* 1.244-70; and D. K. Falk, *Daily, Festival and Sabbath Prayers from Qumran* (STDJ 27; Leiden: Brill, 1997).

15. See also J. Kampen and M. Bernstein, eds., *Reading 4QMMT: New Perspectives on Qumran Law and History* (SBLSS 2; Atlanta: Scholars Press, 1996); M. Bernstein, F. García Martínez, and J. Kampen, eds., *Legal Texts and Legal Issues: Proceedings of the Second Meeting of the International Organization for Qumran Studies, Cambridge 1995, Published in Honour of Joseph M. Baumgarten* (STDJ 23; Leiden: Brill, 1997).

16. For a more comprehensive treatment see J. J. Collins, *Apocalypticism in the Dead Sea Scrolls* (London: Routledge, 1997).

- the cultic practice of the community, whether they offered sacrifice or not, and their relation to the Jerusalem temple and its leadership;[17]
- the evidence for mysticism in the Scrolls, especially in the *Songs of the Sabbath Sacrifice;*[18]
- the Bible at Qumran, both the form of the biblical text[19] and the ways in which it was interpreted (a subject touched on here by Timothy Lim);[20] also the question of the canon, or the extent of the writings regarded as authoritative, and the kind of authority attributed to them;[21]
- the nature of the community reflected in the Qumran rule books, and its relation to other forms of community organization in the Hellenistic world;[22]
- the wisdom teachings found at Qumran, and more generally the ethics of the Dead Sea sect;[23]
- the use of horoscopes[24] and texts that fall under the category of magic,[25] which reflect the popular practices current within the sect, rather than its formal theology; and
- the calendar of the Qumran community.[26]

---

17. F. Schmidt, *La pensée du Temple de Jérusalem à Qoumran* (Paris: Seuil, 1994).

18. C. A. Newsom, *Songs of the Sabbath Sacrifice: A Critical Edition* (Atlanta: Scholars Press, 1985); idem, "Shirot ʿOlat HaShabbat," in E. Eshel et al., *Qumran Cave 4, VI: Poetical and Liturgical Texts, Part 1* (DJD 11; Oxford: Clarendon, 1998) 173-401; J. R. Davila, "Heavenly Ascents in the Dead Sea Scrolls," in *The Dead Sea Scrolls after Fifty Years,* 2.461-85.

19. E. Ulrich, *The Dead Sea Scrolls and the Origins of the Bible* (Grand Rapids: Eerdmans, 1999); idem, "The Dead Sea Scrolls and the Biblical Text," in *The Dead Sea Scrolls after Fifty Years,* 1.79-100.

20. T. H. Lim, *Holy Scripture in the Qumran Commentaries and Pauline Letters* (Oxford: Clarendon, 1997).

21. J. A. Sanders, "The Scrolls and the Canonical Process," in *The Dead Sea Scrolls after Fifty Years,* 2.1-23.

22. M. Weinfeld, *The Organizational Pattern and the Penal Code of the Qumran Sect* (Göttingen: Vandenhoeck & Ruprecht, 1986); S. Metso, "Constitutional Rules at Qumran," in *The Dead Sea Scrolls after Fifty Years,* 1.186-210; C. Hempel, "Community Structures in the Dead Sea Scrolls: Admission, Organization, Disciplinary Procedures," in *The Dead Sea Scolls after Fifty Years,* 2.67-97

23. D. J. Harrington, *Wisdom Texts from Qumran* (London: Routledge, 1996).

24. M. Albani, "Horoscopes in the Qumran Scrolls," in *The Dead Sea Scrolls after Fifty Years,* 2.279-330.

25. P. S. Alexander, "'Wrestling against Wickedness in High Places': Magic in the Worldview of the Qumran Community," in *The Scrolls and the Scriptures: Qumran Fifty Years After,* ed. C. A. Porter and C. A. Evans (JSPSup 26; Sheffield: Sheffield Academic Press, 1997) 318-37; A. Lange, "The Essene Position on Magic and Divination," in *Legal Texts and Legal Issues,* 377-435.

Great advances have been made in scholarship on the Dead Sea Scrolls in the 1990s, especially in the publication of the primary texts. The next phase of scholarship will need to integrate this material into the study of Judaism in the Second Temple period.

26. James VanderKam, *Calendars in the Dead Sea Scrolls: Measuring Time* (London: Routledge, 1998).

Powers in Heaven: God, Gods, and Angels in the Dead Sea Scrolls

JOHN J. COLLINS

Hear O Israel: The Lord is our God, the Lord alone.

Deut 6:4

No principle is more central or sacred in Judaism than this declaration from Deuteronomy. Many people regard it as the essential, constitutive principle that distinguished ancient Israel from the pagan world.[1] So, for example, the distinguished Egyptologist Jan Assmann has recently written of "the Mosaic distinction" between true and false religion, which pitted monotheism against polytheism.[2] The question of monotheism is especially important for the separation of Christianity from Judaism. For most Jews, the scandal of Christianity was the worship of the man Jesus. Yet Christianity began as a Jewish sect, and we should expect that it was in some way continuous with its Jewish matrix.

Whether we can really speak of monotheism in connection with Moses is debatable.[3] Even the Decalogue says only that "you shall not have strange

---

1. This idea was given classical expression by Yehezkel Kaufmann, *The History of Israelite Religion* (Hebrew; Jerusalem: Bialik, 1960); abridged and translated by Moshe Greenberg as *The Religion of Israel* (Chicago: The University of Chicago Press, 1960).

2. Jan Assmann, *Moses the Egyptian: The Memory of Egypt in Western Monotheism* (Cambridge: Harvard University Press, 1997) 1-6.

3. See the discussion by Jon D. Levenson, *Sinai and Zion: An Entry into the Jewish Bible* (Minneapolis: Winston, 1985) 56-70.

9

gods before me," not that you shall deny that other gods exist. There is now considerable evidence that the religion of Israel evolved gradually, and indeed the reform of King Josiah and the promulgation of Deuteronomy toward the end of the seventh century BCE were major steps in this process.[4] Even Deuteronomy, however, still includes a celebrated passage in chapter 32 that describes the division of the nations:

> When the Most High apportioned the nations, when he divided human-kind, he fixed the boundaries of the peoples according to the number of the sons of the God.[5]

Israel was reserved for the Lord, but the existence of other deities was not denied.

Monotheism strictly defined — the view that only one God exists, as opposed to henotheism or monolatry, the view that only one God should be worshiped — may owe more to the systematic reasoning of Greek philosophy than to "the Mosaic distinction." Antisthenes, a pupil of Socrates and teacher of Diogenes, had declared that there are many gods by convention but only one god in nature.[6] The natural theology of the Stoics was conducive to monotheism, as can be seen in Cleanthes' famous "Hymn to Zeus," which hailed the deity as sovereign of nature, ruling all by law.[7] Jewish apologists naturally found such reasoning congenial to the demand for monolatry in the biblical tradition. In the Hellenistic age, the unity and singularity of God was regarded as one of the most fundamental, non-negotiable, pillars of Judaism.[8] The philosopher Philo wrote that "He that is truly God is one, but those that are so called by analogy are more than one."[9] Yet he could unabashedly refer to the Logos, or Word, the principle by which God governs the world, as

---

4. For recent overviews of the development of Israelite religion see Mark S. Smith, *The Early History of God: Yahweh and the Other Deities in Ancient Israel* (San Francisco: Harper & Row, 1990); Rainer Albertz, *A History of Israelite Religion in the Old Testament Period* (Louisville: Westminster, 1994) vol. 1.

5. Deut 32:8, following 4QDeut[j] (Julie Ann Duncan, ed., *Qumran Cave 4, IX: Deuteronomy to Kings* [DJD 14; Oxford: Clarendon, 1995]) 90, and LXX. The MT reads "sons of Israel."

6. Cicero, *De natura deorum* 1.32.

7. For the text, see A. A. Long and D. N. Sedley, *The Hellenistic Philosophers* (Cambridge: Cambridge University Press, 1987) 2.326-27. For Stoic theology see the texts collected in Long and Sedley, *The Hellenistic Philosophers*, 321-32.

8. G. Delling, "Monos Theos," in idem, *Studien zum Neuen Testament und zum hellenistischen Judentum* (Göttingen: Vandenhoeck & Ruprecht, 1970) 391-400.

9. *De somniis* 1.227-29.

"the second God."[10] Even in the most sophisticated philosophical exponent of Judaism, then, divinity was an analogous concept, and while the uniqueness of the creator was affirmed, it remained possible to speak of other divine beings in a qualified sense.[11]

The world of the Dead Sea Scrolls was far removed from the philosophical niceties of Philo. In theological matters, its mode of discourse was predominantly mythological rather than philosophical. The immediate context for this discourse was provided by the Jewish apocalyptic writings in the names of Daniel and Enoch, which were preserved in multiple copies at Qumran.[12] Apocalypticism, contrary to popular stereotypes, was not only concerned with an imminent final judgment but also imagined a heavenly world, peopled by watchers, angels, and holy ones.[13] When God appears in a vision to Daniel, he does not appear alone; rather "a thousand thousands served him and ten thousand times ten thousand stood attending him" (Dan 7:10). Similarly in *1 Enoch*, "ten thousand times ten thousand stood before him . . . and the Holy Ones who were near to him did not leave by night or day" (*1 Enoch* 14:22). This entourage of heavenly beings is conceived after the model of the divine council in ancient Near Eastern mythology.[14] The council was often conceived on the analogy of a royal court.

The Heavenly Host in the Scrolls

In the Dead Sea Scrolls, the most elaborate document dealing with the heavenly host views it primarily as a cultic or liturgical assembly. This is the *Songs of the Sabbath Sacrifice*, which consists of compositions designed for each of thirteen Sabbaths, one-quarter of the year.[15] Each song calls on the angels to

10. *Quaest in Gen* 2.62; *De somniis* 1.230-33.

11. See further Alan F. Segal, *Two Powers in Heaven: Early Rabbinic Reports about Christianity and Gnosticism* (Leiden: Brill, 1977) 159-81.

12. J. J. Collins, *Apocalypticism in the Dead Sea Scrolls* (London: Routledge, 1997) 12-29.

13. See especially Michael Mach, "From Apocalypticism to Early Jewish Mysticism?" in *The Encyclopedia of Apocalypticism*, vol. 1: *The Origins of Apocalypticism in Judaism and Christianity*, ed. J. J. Collins (New York: Continuum, 1998) 229-64, and idem, *Entwicklungsstadien des jüdischen Engelglaubens in vorrabbinischer Zeit* (Tübingen: Mohr-Siebeck, 1992).

14. Theodore E. Mullen, *The Assembly of the Gods: The Divine Council in Canaanite and Early Hebrew Literature* (HSM 24; Chico, Calif.: Scholars Press, 1980).

15. Carol A. Newsom, *Songs of the Sabbath Sacrifice. A Critical Edition* (Atlanta: Scholars Press, 1985). See now C. A. Newsom, "Shirot 'Olat Hashabbat (4Q400-407)," in

give praise to God, but the actual words of the angels are not cited. The first five songs are concerned with the establishment of the angelic priesthood: God "has established for himself priests of the inner sanctum, the holiest of the holy ones" (4Q400 i 19). They are "ministers of the Presence in His glorious *debîr*" (the inner sanctuary of the temple, presumably the heavenly temple; 4Q400 i 4). These holy ones are also called "gods" (*'ēlîm*), angels, spirits, and princes. There are seven angelic priesthoods in seven heavenly sanctuaries, presided over by seven chief angels, each with a deputy. The extant fragments do not contain the full name of any individual angel, but the name Melchizedek can be restored plausibly in two places, one of which describes him as a

> "priest in the assemb[ly of God]."[16] The songs go on to give a description of the heavenly temple, based in part on Ezekiel 40-48, and of the throne-chariot or *merkavah*. The chariot differs from that of Ezekiel insofar as references to angels and spirits are woven into the description: "when the wheels move, the holy angels return. They go out from between its glorious [h]ubs. Like the appearance of fire (are) the most holy spirits round about, the appearance of streams of fire like *hashmal*. And there is a radiant substance with glorious colors, wondrously hued, purely blended, the spirits of living godlike beings which move continuously with the glory of the wondrous chariot(s)."[17]

The editor of this text, Carol Newsom, described it as

> a quasi-mystical liturgy designed to evoke a sense of being present in the heavenly temple. . . . Although no claim is made that the audience which recited or heard the Songs were actually transported to the heavenly realms, the hypnotic quality of the language and the vividness of the description of the celestial temple cause even the modern reader of these fragments to feel the power of the language to create a sense of the presence of the heavenly temple.[18]

The focus on the heavenly temple is readily intelligible in the context of the Qumran sect. It is well known that the sect was alienated from the Jerusalem temple, which it regarded as defiled. The community in the wilderness was

---

E. Eshel et al., *Qumran Cave 4, VI: Poetical and Liturgical Texts, Part 1* (DJD 11; Oxford: Clarendon, 1998) 173-401.

16. Newsom, *Songs,* 37. The references are 4Q401 11:3 and 4Q401 22:3.

17. 4Q405 20-22; Newsom, *Songs,* 306.

18. Newsom, *Songs,* 59, 72.

supposed to be "a house of holiness for Israel, an assembly of holiness for Aaron . . . they shall be an agreeable offering, atoning for the Land and determining the judgment of wickedness" (1QS 8:4-10). The community in effect was a substitute temple. It was connected, however, to the highest form of cult, that of the angels in the heavenly temple. The members could join with the angels in their praises. They might be barred from the Jerusalem temple, but the heavenly temple was open to anyone capable of imagining it. Since a fragment of this text was also found at Masada,[19] there has been some doubt as to whether it should be considered a sectarian work.[20] The whole atmosphere of the work, however, and especially its putative function, would seem to fit the context of the Qumran sect more closely than any other. The view of the angelic world, however, is not especially distinctive. The number of archangels in this period is usually four. (The *War Scroll* lists Michael, Gabriel, Sariel, and Raphael; 1QM 9:14-16.) However, a list of seven is found in the Greek text of *1 Enoch* 20, so the seven chief angels of the *Songs* are not without parallel. Neither is the cultic function of the angels unusual, although they are often cast in other roles in other texts.[21]

The *Songs of the Sabbath Sacrifice* is an important text for the history of Jewish mysticism and for the development of conceptions of the heavenly world. It throws little light, however, on two of the more distinctive and important developments of the Hellenistic period that will concern us in the remainder of this essay: the notion of a single, preeminent, principal angel and the belief that human beings could be elevated to join the angelic host. These developments have been central to recent debates associated with the so-called "new *religionsgeschichtliche Schule*," which examines the origins of New Testament Christology against the background of Jewish precedents.[22] It may be that these ideas are presupposed in the *Songs*. We shall see that Melchize-

---

19. See Eshel, *Qumran Cave 4*, DJD 11, 239-52.

20. C. A. Newsom, "'Sectually Explicit' Literature from Qumran," in *The Hebrew Bible and Its Interpreters*, ed. W. H. Propp et al. (Winona Lake, Ind.: Eisenbrauns, 1990) 179-85.

21. For a systematic review of angelic functions see Mach, *Entwicklungsstadien*, 114-278.

22. L. W. Hurtado, *One God, One Lord: Early Christian Devotion and Ancient Jewish Monotheism* (Philadelphia: Fortress, 1988). Recent contributions to this debate include Loren T. Stuckenbruck, *Angel Veneration and Christology: A Study in Early Judaism and in the Christology of the Apocalypse of John* (Tübingen: Mohr-Siebeck, 1995); Peter R. Carrell, *Jesus and the Angels* (SNTSMS 95; Cambridge: Cambridge University Press, 1997); Crispin H. T. Fletcher-Louis, *Luke-Acts: Angels, Christology and Soteriology* (Tübingen: Mohr-Siebeck, 1997); and Carey C. Newman, James R. Davila, and Gladys S. Kewis, eds., *The Jewish Roots of Christological Monotheism: Papers from the St. Andrews Conference on the Historical Origins of the Worship of Jesus* (Leiden: Brill, 1999).

dek elsewhere appears as a principal angel, and human fellowship with the angels in their worship is most probably implied. For explicit discussion of these ideas, however, we must turn to other texts.

Principal Angels

One of the most influential visions in all apocalyptic literature is found in Daniel 7, where Daniel sees an Ancient of Days, seated on a throne and surrounded by a cast of thousands. Then he sees a second figure, described as "one like a son of man," or like a human being, coming with the clouds of heaven. He is presented before the Ancient One and receives kingship and dominion. As has often been pointed out, the oddity of this passage in a Jewish context is that it seems to involve two divine beings. Elsewhere in the Hebrew Bible, the figure who rides on the clouds is always YHWH; yet he is clearly subordinated to the Ancient of Days here.[23] There is good reason to think that in the context of Daniel the "one like a son of man" is the archangel Michael, who is later identified, in Daniel 10, as the "prince" of Israel, who does battle with the angelic "princes" of Persia and Greece.[24] The idea of an angelic prince of Israel was itself an innovation over against the dominant theology of the Hebrew Bible. According to Deuteronomy 32, the Most High divided the boundaries of the peoples according to the number of the sons of God, but he kept Israel as his own portion. In Daniel, however, Michael is the prince of Israel, and he is a being of comparable rank to the princes or gods of the other nations.

Daniel's "one like a son of man" was developed in various ways, both in Judaism and in early Christianity, especially in the Synoptic Gospels.[25] Especially noteworthy is the *Similitudes of Enoch,* a work of uncertain provenance, which is most plausibly dated to the first half of the first century CE. There Enoch sees "one who had a head of days, and his head was white like wool; and with him there was another, whose face had the appearance of a man, and his face was full of grace, like one of the holy angels" (*1 Enoch* 46:1). The latter figure is subsequently referred to as "that Son of Man." In this case, he is dis-

23. J. A. Emerton, "The Origin of the Son of Man Imagery," *JTS* 9 (1958) 225-42. The background of the imagery is to be found in the Canaanite myths that distinguish between the venerable god El and Baal, the rider of the clouds.

24. See John J. Collins, *Daniel* (Hermeneia; Minneapolis: Fortress, 1993) 304-10.

25. Adela Yarbro Collins, "The Influence of Daniel on the New Testament," in Collins, *Daniel,* 90-105; John J. Collins, "The Son of Man in First Century Judaism," *NTS* 38 (1992) 448-66.

tinguished from Michael, who is merely "one of the holy angels." His exaltation is shown especially by two things: first, all who dwell on earth fall down and worship before him (*1 Enoch* 48:5), and, second, he is enthroned on a glorious throne that is similar to, if not identical with, that of the Lord of Spirits, or the Most High (*1 Enoch* 61:8; 62:5). Yet in an epilogue to the *Similitudes* we are told that Enoch was lifted up to heaven and greeted: "You are the Son of Man who was born to righteousness" (71:14). Whether this greeting implies that the figure earlier called "that Son of Man" is really Enoch, is disputed. (Alternatively, Enoch may be a "son of man," or human being, who is righteous like the heavenly Son of Man.[26]) The two figures seem to be clearly distinguished in another passage (*1 Enoch* 70:1), where Enoch is lifted up "to the presence of that Son of Man." Since chapter 71, where the greeting is found, is a duplicate account of the exaltation of Enoch, there is reasonable suspicion that it is a secondary addition to the *Similitudes*. In any case, the assumption of Enoch to heaven, and his greeting as "Son of Man," raises the question whether a human being can be exalted to a divine, or semidivine, state, in a Jewish context.

The "Son of Man" figure in Daniel and the *Similitudes of Enoch* may be taken as representative examples of "principal angels" in Jewish literature from the general period of the Dead Sea Scrolls.[27] The *Similitudes of Enoch* are absent from the collection and may have been the product of a different sect. Daniel, however, was preserved in multiple copies at Qumran and was cited as scripture in other scrolls.[28] Remarkably, however, there is no clear interpretation of, or allusion to, the "one like a son of man" in the other scrolls. I have suggested elsewhere that there is a possible implicit interpretation in 4Q246, the *Son of God Text*, to which I shall return below.[29] Yet this is admittedly uncertain, and in any

26. Collins, "The Son of Man," 457. The identification is defended by P. M. Casey, *Son of Man: The Interpretation and Influence of Daniel 7* (London: SPCK, 1979) 99-112, and J. C. VanderKam, "Righteous One, Messiah, Chosen One, and Son of Man in *1 Enoch* 37–71," in *The Messiah,* ed. J. H. Charlesworth (Minneapolis: Fortress, 1992) 169-91.

27. For further discussions of principal angels, including notably the figure Jaoel in the *Apocalypse of Abraham* from the end of the first century CE, see Christopher Rowland, *The Open Heaven: A Study of Apocalyptic in Judaism and Early Christianity* (New York: Crossroad, 1982) 94-113; Carrell, *Jesus and the Angels,* 53-76.

28. See Peter W. Flint, "The Daniel Tradition at Qumran," in *Eschatology, Messianism and the Dead Sea Scrolls,* ed. Craig A. Evans and Peter W. Flint (Grand Rapids: Eerdmans, 1997) 41-60.

29. John J. Collins, *The Scepter and the Star: The Messiahs of the Dead Sea Scrolls and Other Ancient Literature* (New York: Doubleday, 1995) 167. The possibility is rejected by J. D. G. Dunn, "'Son of God' as 'Son of Man' in the Dead Sea Scrolls? A Response to John Collins on 4Q246," in *The Scrolls and the Scriptures: Qumran Fifty Years After,* ed. Stanley E.

case the figure in question is not understood as angelic.[30] It appears then that one prominent scriptural source for formulating a concept of a principal angel was passed over by the authors of the Scrolls.

Principal Angels in the Dead Sea Scrolls

At this point it may be well to comment on the coherence of the corpus of the Scrolls as I see it. I share the majority view of scholars that the Scrolls are the library of a particular sect, not a random collection of Jewish writings from the turn of the era. This library includes books that were not composed by members of the community, including, for example, the Hebrew scriptures and early apocalyptic works in the name of Enoch. The provenance of some works, including the *Songs of the Sabbath Sacrifice,* is debated. Whether the sect itself required any form of orthodoxy in matters of belief is debated; orthopraxy in matters of halakic observance was certainly a higher priority. I make no assumptions here about the consistency with which beliefs were held by different members, or settlements, of the sect, or whether beliefs changed over time, as we might expect but can not easily demonstrate. Ideas attested in the Scrolls did not necessarily have the status of official sectarian beliefs, and neither were they necessarily widely shared by other branches of Judaism. For the present, it will suffice to note that these ideas and beliefs are attested in the Scrolls, regardless of the status they enjoyed.

We may begin with a passage in the *Rule of the Community,* which is arguably the best known doctrinal statement in the whole corpus of the Scrolls, the "Treatise on the Two Spirits." There we read, in the translation of Geza Vermes:

> From the God of Knowledge comes all that is and shall be. Before ever they existed He established their whole design, and when, as ordained for them,

---

Porter and Craig A. Evans (JSPSup 26; Sheffield: Academic Press, 1997) 198-210, with a vehemence disproportionate to the tentative way it was proposed. See now Johannes Zimmermann, "Observations on 4Q246 — 'The Son of God,'" in *Qumran-Messianism,* ed. J. H. Charlesworth, H. Lichtenberger, and G. S. Oegema (Tübingen: Mohr-Siebeck, 1998) 185-88, who argues more strongly for dependence of 4Q246 on Daniel 7, but takes the "one like a son of man" as a human being. See also J. Zimmermann, *Messianische Texte aus Qumran* (Tübingen: Mohr-Siebeck, 1998) 128-70.

30. An angelic interpretation of the "Son of God Text" has been proposed, however, by Florentino García Martínez, "The Eschatological Figure of 4Q246," in idem, *Qumran and Apocalyptic* (STDJ 9; Leiden: Brill, 1992) 162-79.

they come into being, it is in accord with His glorious design that they accomplish their task without change. The laws of all things are in His hand and He provides for all their needs. (1QS 3:15-17)

This would appear to be as strong an affirmation of monotheism as one could ask for. The passage goes on, however, to say that God created for humanity two spirits in which to walk. These spirits not only are psychological dispositions but also are embodied in two angelic beings, called "the Prince of Light" or "Angel of Truth" on the one hand, and "the Angel of Darkness" on the other.[31] The powers of these spirits or angels are clearly limited by the creator, but they are supernatural powers nonetheless. What we have here is a qualified dualism, a division of the world between two evenly balanced forces subject to the ultimate authority of one God. While the "Treatise on the Two Spirits" in the *Rule of the Community* is the most systematic exposition of this dualism, it is expressed in different ways in several other texts from Qumran.

Perhaps the best known of these texts is the *War Scroll*, which gives instructions for an eschatological struggle between the Sons of Light and the Sons of Darkness.[32] In the opening column of the Scroll, the leaders of the opposing forces appear to be God and Belial, the Prince of Darkness. God, however, does not act alone. "Migh[ty men and] a host of angels are among those mustered with us, the Mighty One of War is in our congregation, and the host of his spirits is with our steps" (1QM 12:8). More significantly for this discussion, "Thou didst appoint from of old the Prince of Light to assist us . . . and all the spirits of truth in his dominion. And thou wast the one who made Belial to corrupt" (1QM 13:9b-12). Immediately after this passage we read, "Who is like unto Thee in strength, O God of Israel, and yet Thy mighty hand is with the poor. What angel or prince is like unto the help of [Thy face]." We may detect here some ambivalence about the status of the Prince of Light. The author or compiler of the *War Scroll* wanted to be sure that the uniqueness of God was not compromised. There is no reason, however, to regard the angelic Prince of Light as a secondary insertion here.[33] The role of the principal angel is again affirmed in column 17 of the *War Scroll:* "He has magnified the authority of Michael through eternal light . . . so as to raise amongst the angels the authority of Michael and the dominion of Israel amongst all flesh" (1QM 17:6-7). The identification with Michael is significant. It shows that the *War Scroll* is adapting the tradition of Daniel and at-

31. See Collins, *Apocalypticism in the Dead Sea Scrolls,* 38-43.
32. Collins, *Apocalypticism in the Dead Sea Scrolls,* 91-109.
33. *Pace* Jean Duhaime, "Dualistic Reworking in the Scrolls from Qumran," *CBQ* 49 (1987) 32-56, who rightly perceives the tension in the text.

tempting to correlate the dualism of the "Treatise on the Two Spirits" with established Jewish traditions. The main difference over against Daniel is that Michael is now paired with Belial, the Prince of Darkness, rather than with the angelic princes of specific nations. It is also apparent that these angelic figures can each be known by more than one name.

The multiplicity of the names of angelic figures is most clearly indicated in a fragmentary Aramaic text, the *Testament of Amram*.[34] This composition is the deathbed speech of the patriarch Amram, son of Qohath, son of Levi, in which he reports a vision in which two angelic figures were quarreling over him. One of them is called a "watcher," like the fallen angels in *1 Enoch*, and he is said to rule over darkness. He is named Melchiresha, king of wickedness. The other figure rules over all light and is said to have three names. Melchiresha is the only name preserved, but it is reasonable to infer that each figure has three names. The obvious counterpart to Melchiresha is Melchizedek ("king of righteousness"), whom we shall meet at some length momentarily. Other plausible matching pairs are "Prince of Light" and "Prince of Darkness," and Michael and Belial.[35] It is unfortunate that this text is so poorly preserved, especially since it seems to be one of the earliest dualistic texts. The extant fragments, however, are an important witness to the concept of opposing, dualistic, angels. Melchiresha also appears in another fragmentary text (4Q280), where he is cursed, just as Belial is cursed in the second column of the *Rule of the Community*.

Melchizedek, the presumed counterpart of Melchiresha, is featured at length in another scroll that is more extensively preserved than 4QAmram.[36] 11QMelchizedek is a midrashic composition that explains the law of the jubilee of Leviticus 25 by juxtaposing with it several other biblical texts, notably Isaiah 61. We are told that the jubilee refers to the end of days, and that the day of atonement is the end of the tenth jubilee, when expiation will be made for all the sons of light and for the men of the lot of Melchizedek. Melchizedek, then, appears to be equivalent to the Prince of Light in other texts. The end of the tenth jubilee is "the time for Melchizedek's year of favor." The text then applies to Melchizedek a passage from Psalm 82: "*Elohim* (God) stands in the assembly of El, in the midst of *Elohim* (gods) he judges." In interpretation, we are told that "Melchizedek will exact the vengeance of El's judgments. Several other texts from Isaiah and Daniel are brought into the discussion, including Isaiah

34. Paul J. Kobelski, *Melchizedek and Melchiresha* (CBQMS 10; Washington: Catholic Biblical Association, 1981) 24-36.

35. J. T. Milik, "4Q Visions d'Amram et une citation d'Origène," *RB* 79 (1972) 77-92.

36. Kobelski, *Melchizedek*, 3-23; Zimmermann, *Messianische Texte*, 389-412.

52:7, where a herald says to Zion "your God *(Elohim)* is king." The passage goes on to interpret Zion and king in the pesher-style, where one thing stands for another. Unfortunately the text is very fragmentary at this point. It has been restored to read "'your God' *('ĕlohēkā)* is Melchizedek."[37] This may seem to be a very bold restoration, but in fact Melchizedek had already been identified with the *Elohim*, or God, of Psalm 82. In the view of the midrash, the Most High God is El. *Elohim* is a lesser deity, an angel, if you prefer. But the striking thing about this passage is that the term *Elohim*, which is usually understood to refer to the Most High in the biblical psalm, now refers to a lesser heavenly being. There are, at least, two divine powers in heaven, even if one of them is clearly subordinate to the other.

The Divinity of the Messiah

The *Melchizedek Scroll* from Qumran presents Melchizedek as a heavenly being and gives no indication that he was ever a mortal man. A person with the same name, however, appears twice in the Hebrew Bible. In Genesis 14, he is king of Salem and priest of El Elyon, and Abraham gives him a tithe of all that he has. In Psalm 110, the king is told: "you are a priest forever according to the order of Melchizedek." We do not know whether the Dead Sea sect at all associated the priest of El Elyon with the heavenly Melchizedek. It is quite possible that they regarded the Melchizedek of Psalm 110, at least, as a heavenly being. In the *Melchizedek Scroll*, in any case, he is *Elohim*, god or divine being, and not *adam*, or human.[38]

There were precedents, however, for regarding certain exalted human beings as *elohim*. Psalm 110, which mentions Melchizedek, also invites the king to sit at the right hand of God. It has also been taken to say that God has begotten the king "from the womb of dawn, like the dew," but the text is unfortunately corrupt.[39] Two other passages in the psalms, however, are less

---

37. Kobelski, *Melchizedek*, 6.

38. Michael O. Wise, *The First Messiah: Investigating the Savior before Christ* (San Francisco: HarperSanFrancisco, 1999) 231, claims that the Melchizedek is identical with the messianic herald or prophet, and that both are identical with the Teacher of Righteousness, whom he names, arbitrarily, Judah. None of these identifications has a solid basis. Melchizedek is not the herald but the one whom the herald announces. In 11QMelch 2:16 the herald proclaims to Zion "your God is king," while 2:24-25 is restored, even by Wise, to read "your god is Melchizedek."

39. See H. J. Kraus, *Psalms 60–150* (Minneapolis: Augsburg-Fortress, 1989) 344. The LXX reads "from the womb before the Day-Star I have begotten you." See William

controversial. In Psalm 2, God tells the king: "you are my son; this day I have begotten you." This is often understood as an adoption formula, spoken when the king ascended the throne.[40] The language, however, indicated a very special bond between God and the king. Psalm 45 is even bolder: "Your throne, O God, endures forever and ever. Your royal scepter is a scepter of equity; you love righteousness and hate wickedness. Therefore God, your God has anointed you with the oil of gladness beyond your companions." "God, your God," 'ĕlōhîm 'ĕlohēkā, clearly reflects the need to distinguish between two 'ĕlōhîm. They are not on the same level, any more than Melchizedek was on the same level as El in the Qumran text, but they are both divine, in Semitic terminology. Implicit here is the Israelite variation of the royal ideology of the ancient Near East, whereby the king might be conceived in different ways but was always considered to be more than human, and in some places, notably Egypt, was thought to be fully divine.[41]

Against the background of these psalms we must consider the controversial "Son of God" text from Qumran.[42] This Aramaic text (4Q246) has attracted a lot of attention because it contains a remarkable parallel to the Gospel of Luke. It prophecies a figure of whom it says: "Son of God (El) he shall be called, and they will name him 'Son of the Most High (Elyon).'"[43] The text goes on to describe a period of conflict on earth "until the people of God arise," after which all will rest from the sword. Since the "Son of God" figure appears before the rise of the people of God, several scholars have reasoned that he must be a negative figure and identified him as a Syrian king.[44] This reasoning is not compelling. In Daniel 12 the rise of Michael, indisputably a positive figure, is followed by a period of anguish such as never occurred

Horbury, *Jewish Messianism and the Cult of Christ* (London: SCM, 1998) 97; J. Schaper, *Eschatology in the Greek Psalter* (Tübingen: Mohr-Siebeck, 1995) 101-7.

40. J. J. M. Roberts, "The Old Testament's Contribution to Messianic Expectations," in *The Messiah: Developments in Earliest Judaism and Christianity,* ed. James Charlesworth (Minneapolis: Fortress, 1992) 42-43.

41. The classic account of Israelite royal ideology in its Near Eastern context remains Sigmund Mowinckel, *He That Cometh* (Nashville: Abingdon, 1955). See also T. N. D. Mettinger, *King and Messiah: The Civil and Sacral Legitimation of the Israelite Kings* (Lund: Gleerup, 1976).

42. Émile Puech, "4Qapocryphe de Daniel ar," in George Brooke et al., *Qumran Cave 4, XVII: Parabiblical Texts, Part 3* (DJD 22; Oxford: Clarendon, 1996) 165-84. See Collins, *The Scepter and the Star,* 154-72.

43. Cf. Luke 1:32, 35.

44. So, for example, E. M. Cook, "4Q246," *Bulletin for Biblical Research* 5 (1995) 43-66. See my critique of this position in "The Background of the 'Son of God' Text," *Bulletin for Biblical Research* 7 (1997) 1-12.

since nations came into existence, before the people of God arise in the resurrection. The closest parallels by far to the terminology of the Qumran text are provided by the Gospel of Luke, in Greek: "He will be great, and will be called the Son of the Most High, and the Lord God will give to him the throne of his ancestor David . . . he will be called the son of God."[45] In Luke, these are clearly titles for a Jewish messiah, and we must assume that they were known to the evangelist from Jewish tradition.[46]

The title "Son of God" does not necessarily imply metaphysical divine status. It can be understood as an adoptive formula, as in Psalm 2, or simply as an honorific title. Regardless of the interpretation of the "Son of God" text, there is other evidence for the view that the Davidic messiah could be regarded as son of God at Qumran.[47] The clearest evidence is provided by the *Florilegium* (4Q174), which interprets 2 Samuel 7:14 as follows:

> The Lord declares to you that He will build you a House. I will raise up your seed after you. I will establish the throne of his kingdom [for ever]. I [will be] his father and he shall be my son. He is the Branch of David who shall arise with the interpreter of the Law [to rule] in Zion [at the end] of days.

The Branch of David is called "the Messiah of Righteousness" in 4Q252, the *Commentary on Genesis*. It is a messianic title based on Jeremiah 23 and 33.[48] This text provides unambiguous evidence for reference to the messiah as "Son of God," although the phrase may be understood in an honorific rather than a metaphysical sense.

A more problematic instance is provided by 1QSa. Geza Vermes translates the disputed passage "when God engenders" the messiah, reading the Hebrew verb *yōlîd*.[49] This reading was championed by most of the original team of editors, who saw the fragment in the mid-fifties. It was subsequently

---

45. To my knowledge, there is no exact parallel for these titles in Aramaic. Hellenistic rulers were often regarded as sons of specific deities — Zeus, Apollo, Ammon, etc. Beginning with Augustus the Roman emperor was known in Greek as *huios theou,* son of God, Latin *divi filius* (son of Jove or Jupiter). See W. von Martitz, "*Huios, huiothesia:* II. Hellenism," *TDNT* 8 (1972) 336-40.

46. See now Craig A. Evans, "Are the 'Son' Texts at Qumran Messianic? Reflections on 4Q369 and Related Scrolls," in *Qumran-Messianism,* 141-43; Zimmermann, "Observations on 4Q246," 175-90; Zimmermann, *Messianische Texte,* 128-70.

47. Evans, "Are the 'Son' Texts at Qumran Messianic?" 135-53.

48. Martin G. Abegg and Craig A. Evans, "Messianic Passages in the Dead Sea Scrolls," in *Qumran-Messianism,* 197-98.

49. Geza Vermes, *The Complete Dead Sea Scrolls in English* (London: Penguin, 1997) 159.

rejected by most scholars, including Vermes, in favor of other readings, such as *yōlîk,* "causes to come." Now Vermes claims that *yōlîd* is confirmed by computer enhancement, and this is the reading presupposed in all the current major translations of the Scrolls.[50] Nonetheless, the reading is still disputed by other competent paleographers, such as Émile Puech.[51] The reading must be considered uncertain. It should be emphasized, however, that it is by no means a matter of Christian eisegesis. (Vermes is Jewish.) In fact it would correspond rather nicely to what we have seen in the Psalms. The force of such a statement would be that God causes the messiah to be born, and that he enjoys the status of son of God. It does not entail birth from a virgin, and we need not infer that the spirit of the messiah is preexistent.[52] If the reading *yōlîd* is correct, however, it affirms the divine or quasi-divine status of the Davidic messiah.[53]

The Exaltation of Human Beings

There is good evidence that the Davidic messiah was regarded as divine in a qualified sense (which certainly did not imply equality with the Almighty) not only in the Dead Sea Scrolls but also in Jewish tradition more generally. The messiah was not the only human being who might take on divine attributes, however. According to the book of Exodus, God made Moses "a god to Pharaoh" (Exod 7:1). A Hellenistic Jewish author named Ezekiel wrote a tragedy on the Exodus, in which he had Moses recount a remarkable dream. First he saw a figure enthroned on Mt. Sinai, who was surely God. Then this figure arose, gave Moses the scepter, and told him to sit on the throne. This text was written no later than the second century BCE, most

50. Michael Wise translates the disputed term as "fa[th]ered (?)," in Michael O. Wise, Martin Abegg, and Edward Cook, *The Dead Sea Scrolls: A New Translation* (San Francisco: HarperSanFrancisco, 1996) 147. Florentino García Martínez, *The Dead Sea Scrolls Translated* (Leiden: Brill, 1994) 127, translates "begets." See also Evans, "Are the 'Son' Texts at Qumran Messianic?" 138-39.

51. Émile Puech, "Préséance sacerdotale et messie-roi dans la règle de la congrégation (1QSa ii 11-22)," *RevQ* 63 (1994) 351-65.

52. *Pace* Horbury, *Jewish Messianism,* 98.

53. Vermes, *The Complete Dead Sea Scrolls,* 159, implausibly applies the reference to the priestly messiah. Evans, "Are the 'Son' Texts at Qumran Messianic?" 145-53, and Zimmermann, *Messianische Texte,* 211-22, also argue for a messianic interpretation of the "firstborn son" of 4Q369 *(Prayer of Enosh),* but see James Kugel, "4Q369 'Prayer of Enosh' and Ancient Biblical Interpretation," *DSD* 5 (1998) 119-48, who identifies the firstborn son as Israel.

probably in Alexandria.[54] While the dream is interpreted to mean that Moses would judge and lead all humankind, it evidently reflects traditions about the exaltation of Moses to divine status.[55] Philo, the great Jewish Alexandrian philosopher from the early first century CE, also noted that "Moses was named god and king of the whole nation."[56] Yet this tradition of reflection on Exodus 7:1 was not peculiar to the Greek-speaking Diaspora. We also find it in a fragmentary text from Qumran, 4Q374, which says that "he made him as God to the mighty ones and a cause of reeli[ng] to Pharaoh." This passage goes on to say that "they melted and their hearts trembled and th[ei]r inward parts dissolved. [But] he had compassion upon. . . . And when he caused his face to shine upon them for healing they strengthened [their] hearts again." Melting and trembling is how human beings are typically said to react to a theophany, or a manifestation of the divine. It has been suggested, however, that the shining face here is that of Moses (cf. Exod 34:29-35) and that he has a theophany-like effect on the Israelites.[57] In view of the fragmentary nature of the text the interpretation is uncertain.[58] If indeed it is Moses who causes people to melt and then makes his face to shine on them, then he is being assimilated to the Most High in a remarkable way. There are some parallels for such assimilation. In Sirach 24, wisdom is said to dwell in the highest heaven and have its throne in a pillar of cloud. It is presumably the medium through which God acts in the world. Similarly, in the Qumran text Moses is the agent of God, but in the process he becomes an *'ĕlōhîm* in the eyes of other human beings.

Communal Exaltation

One of the most distinctive features of the Qumran sect was the belief that the members of the community were *ipso facto* companions to the hosts of

---

54. For the text see Carl R. Holladay, *Fragments from Hellenistic Jewish Authors,* vol. 3: *Poets* (Atlanta: Scholars Press, 1989) 301-529.

55. See Pieter W. van der Horst, "Moses' Throne Vision in Ezekiel the Dramatist," in idem, *Essays on the Jewish World of Early Christianity* (Göttingen: Vandenhoeck & Ruprecht, 1990) 63-71.

56. *Life of Moses* 1.55-58.

57. Crispin Fletcher-Louis, "4Q374: A Discourse on the Sinai Tradition: The Deification of Moses and Early Christology," *DSD* 3 (1996) 236-52.

58. For a more cautious interpretation see Carol A. Newsom, "4Q374: A Discourse on the Exodus/Conquest Tradition," in *The Dead Sea Scrolls: Forty Years of Research,* ed. D. Dimant and U. Rappaport (STDJ 10; Leiden: Brill, 1992) 40-52.

heaven and so living an angelic life, even on earth.[59] The hymn appended to the *Rule of the Community* (1QS 11:5-8) says:

> My eyes have gazed on that which is eternal, on wisdom concealed from men, on knowledge and wise design (hidden) from the sons of men; on a fountain of righteousness and on a storehouse of power, on a spring of glory (hidden) from the assembly of flesh. God has given them to His chosen ones as an everlasting possession, and has caused them to inherit the lot of the holy ones. He has joined their assembly to the Sons of Heaven to be a Council of the Community, a foundation of the Building of Holiness, an eternal Plantation throughout all ages to come.

Again in the *Hodayot* the hymnist thanks God

> because you have saved my life from the pit, and from Sheol and Abaddon you have lifted me up to an everlasting height, so that I can walk on a boundless plain. . . . The corrupt spirit you have purified from great sin so that he can take his place with the host of the holy ones, and can enter into communion with the congregation of the sons of heaven. (1QH 11:19-23; trans. García Martínez)

The belief expressed in these passages has rightly been described as a kind of realized eschatology. In the book of Daniel, the wise are elevated after the resurrection to shine like the stars of heaven. In the *Epistle of Enoch,* another early apocalyptic work, the righteous are told, "You will shine like the lights of heaven and will be seen and the gate of heaven will be opened to you . . . you will have great joy like the angels of heaven . . . for you shall be associates of the host of heaven" (*1 Enoch* 104:2, 4, 6). The stars are the host of heaven. The hope of sharing their heavenly life is promised to the righteous after death in the apocalypses of Daniel and Enoch. The community at Qumran claimed to enjoy, in effect, heaven on earth (in the improbable setting of the Judean desert) by becoming companions to the angels already in this life. This claim, incidentally, is immediately relevant to the much disputed issue of celibacy at Qumran. While no text states explicitly that the sectarians were celibate, sexual activity would be difficult to reconcile with the angelic life.[60]

---

59. See Collins, *Apocalypticism in the Dead Sea Scrolls,* 117-20.

60. Fletcher-Louis, *Luke-Acts,* 193-95. He notes 4Q511 35 (from the *Songs of the Maskil*), which seems to indicate that God will appoint certain elite, holy human beings as heavenly priests, angels of his glory.

A Throne in Heaven

Among the hymnic texts that speak of exaltation to the heavenly rank, one fragmentary text stands out. This text, originally published as a fragment of the *War Scroll,* is now recognized as a variant form of a hymn in the *Hodayot.*[61] It speaks of "a mighty throne in the congregation of the gods," on which none of the kings of the east shall sit. The author boasts "I have taken my seat . . . in the heavens . . . I shall be reckoned with gods *('ēlîm).*" It goes on to speak of enduring contempt and evils, and of the figure's prowess as a teacher or legal expert ("Who will restrain the utterance of my lips and who will arraign me and equal my judgment?"). The end of the passage affirms: "I shall be reckoned with gods, and my glory with (that of) the king's sons."[62]

Unlike other passages in the *Hodayot* that speak of a representative member of the community, this hymn seems to envision an exceptional individual. If we may assume that the mighty throne is where the speaker takes his seat, then this is the only passage in the Dead Sea Scrolls that speaks of an individual other than God being enthroned in heaven. (Another text, 4Q521, says that God "will glorify the pious on the throne of an eternal kingdom.") The original editor, Maurice Baillet, thought that the speaker must be an angel and dubbed the text "The Canticle of Michael."[63] Morton Smith, however, argued persuasively that the figure was an exalted human being.[64] Smith spoke here of deification, which is not unreasonable, since the speaker claims

61. 4Q491 11. Variants of this hymn are found in 4Q427 7 and 4Q471b. See Devorah Dimant, "A Synoptic Comparison of Parallel Sections in 4Q427 7, 4Q491 11 and 4Q471b," *JQR* 85 (1994) 157-61, and John J. Collins and Devorah Dimant, "A Thrice-Told Hymn," *JQR* 85 (1994) 151-55. Yet another variant is found in 1QH^a cols. 25-26. See Esther Eshel, "4Q471b: A Self-Glorification Hymn," *RevQ* 17 (1996) 177-203, and idem, "The Identification of the 'Speaker' of the Self-Glorification Hymn," in *The Provo International Conference on the Dead Sea Scrolls,* ed. Donald W. Parry and Eugene Ulrich (Leiden: Brill, 1999) 619-35. In the latter publication she accepts the suggestion of Hartmut Stegemann that 4Q471b is identical with 4Q431. See now also Zimmermann, *Messianische Texte,* 285-310.

62. So 4Q491 11. This is the only fragment that mentions a throne, but both 4Q471b and 4Q427 use the verb *yašabtî,* I sit or dwell. 4Q471b parallels the claim to be reckoned with the gods, and both 4Q471b and 4Q427 claim companionship with the holy ones.

63. M. Baillet, *Qumrân Grotte 4, III (4Q482-4Q520)* (DJD 7; Oxford: Clarendon, 1982) 12-68.

64. Morton Smith, "Ascent to the Heavens and Deification in 4QM^a," in *Archaeology and History in the Dead Sea Scrolls: The New York University Conference in Memory of Yigael Yadin,* ed. L. H. Schiffman (JSPSup 8/ASOR Monographs 2; Sheffield: JSOT, 1990) 181-99.

to be reckoned with gods. What human being would make such an audacious claim?

There are several examples in the literature of Second Temple Judaism where figures other than God are said to be enthroned in heaven, usually in the context of eschatological judgment. (The *Similitudes of Enoch,* where the Son of Man sits on his throne of glory, is a case in point.[65]) A noneschatological parallel is the enthronement of Moses in *Ezekiel the Tragedian,* which I have cited above. This parallel is of particular interest since the speaker in the Qumran text appears to be a teacher or legal expert. Martin Abegg has suggested that the figure was none other than the Teacher of Righteousness, the most prominent teacher in the history of the Dead Sea sect and putative author of the core corpus of *Hodayot.*[66] Michael Wise assumes that the figure enthroned is the Teacher after his death.[67] That this figure is related to, or modeled on, the Teacher, to some degree, seems undeniable; yet, as even Wise admits, this is a hymn unlike any other. There is a striking difference in tone between this hymn and the other Teacher hymns of the *Hodayot.* While the speaker in this hymn boasts of his ability to bear evils, he does not complain of persecution. Neither does this hymn show the sense of human sinfulness that is typical of the *Hodayot.* I have suggested then that the figure in question is "the teacher at the end of days," or eschatological high priest, a figure who is admittedly modeled to some extent on the historical Teacher.[68] In the *Rule of Blessings* (1QSb 4:22-28) the blessing for the high priest is that he be "as an Angel of the Presence in the Abode of Holiness." Such a blessing was only likely to be realized in the eschatological age.[69] It must be acknowledged, however, that the speaker is never identified in the Scrolls, and uncertainty as to his identification is inevitable. What is important for our present purpose is the clear attestation of the idea that some human being can be reckoned with the gods and enthroned in heaven.

---

65. See Collins, *The Scepter and the Star,* 141-46.

66. Martin G. Abegg, "Who Ascended to Heaven? 4Q491, 4Q427, and the Teacher of Righteousness," in *Eschatology, Messianism and the Dead Sea Scrolls,* 61-73. On the Teacher as author of the core group of Teacher hymns see now Michael C. Douglas, "Power and Praise in the Hodayot: A Literary-Critical Study of 1QH 9:1–18:4," (Ph.D. diss., University of Chicago, 1998).

67. Wise, *The First Messiah,* 223-24.

68. Collins, *The Scepter and the Star,* 148-49. Similarly, the eschatological high priest in 4Q541 bears some resemblance to the historical Teacher but should not be identified with him. See now also, tentatively, Zimmermann, *Messianische Texte,* 307-8.

69. See Eshel, "4Q471b," 198-201; idem, "The Identification of the 'Speaker,'" 632-33.

Conclusion

In view of the material surveyed rapidly here, monotheism hardly seems the right word to describe the religion of the Dead Sea Scrolls. To be sure, the supremacy of the Most High is never in doubt. But this is not a God who dwells alone. He is surrounded by 'ēlîm and 'ĕlōhîm, holy ones and angels. Some of these angels (Michael, Melchizedek, the Prince of Light) are exalted above their fellows. Yet we do not find any figure in the Scrolls who exercises judgment on a throne of glory like the Son of Man in the *Similitudes of Enoch*, still less any one exalted above the angels as Christ is in the New Testament.[70] Even a text that is thoroughly peopled with 'ĕlōhîm and 'ēlîm, like the *War Scroll*, can still insist that no angel is like to God in might.

The exalted angels of the Scrolls are relevant to the background of the divination of Christ in the New Testament, although no sectarian passage can be said to have influenced that development in the way that Daniel 7 obviously did. The idea that the messiah could be called Son of God bears more directly on the New Testament, although the implications of that title remain debatable. Finally the belief that a human being could be lifted up and enthroned in heaven, whether before or after death, is obviously relevant to the exaltation of Jesus. This belief was not without basis in the Hebrew Bible. It was grounded in the royal ideology of the Psalms, where "the Lord said to my Lord, sit on my right hand."[71] Both the Scrolls and the New Testament, however, interpreted and developed the idea in novel ways, in accordance with the new cosmology of the Hellenistic period that is reflected in the apocalyptic literature.

Moreover, the idea that a human being could be exalted and enthroned in heaven lived on in Judaism in the common era, even if it was controversial.[72] The Jewish culmination of this tradition is found in the late mystical

---

70. E.g. Heb 1. See further John J. Collins, "Jewish Monotheism and Christian Theology," in *Aspects of Monotheism: How God Is One*, ed. Hershel Shanks and Jack Meinhardt (Washington: Biblical Archaeology Society, 1997) 81-105.

71. Martin Hengel, "'Setze dich zu meiner Rechten!' Die Inthronisation Christi zur Rechten Gottes und Psalm 110,1," in *Le Trône de Dieu*, ed. Marc Philonenko (Tübingen: Mohr-Siebeck, 1993) 108-94.

72. See Martha Himmelfarb, "Revelation and Rapture: The Transformation of the Visionary in the Ascent Apocalypses," in *Mysteries and Revelations: Apocalyptic Studies since the Uppsala Colloquium*, ed. J. J. Collins and J. H. Charlesworth (JSPSup 9; Sheffield: Sheffield Academic Press, 1991) 79-90. See also J. H. Charlesworth, "The Portrayal of the Righteous as an Angel," in *Ideal Figures in Ancient Judaism*, ed. J. J. Collins and G. W. Nickelsburg (Chico, Calif.: Scholars Press, 1980) 135-51.

text known as *3 Enoch* or *Sēpēr Hēkhālōt*.[73] There Enoch is transformed in heaven into the figure of Metatron, Prince of the Divine Presence. He is given a throne like the throne of glory and is appointed prince and ruler over all the heavenly beings (ch. 10). A crown is placed on his head, and even the most exalted angels tremble before him. His flesh is transformed into fire. Yet there were misgivings in Jewish tradition about such exaltation of a human being. These misgivings are expressed in chapter 16 of *3 Enoch,* which is probably a secondary addition to the work since it runs counter to the previous fifteen chapters. There we read that, when the heretical mystic Elisha ben Abuya, known as *Aḥēr* ("the other" or "strange one") saw Metatron enthroned, he exclaimed, "There are indeed two powers in heaven."[74] Consequently Metatron was dethroned and given sixty lashes of fire! This insertion reflects the controversy in rabbinic circles as to whether there were two powers in heaven.[75] Ultimately such ideas were marginalized in Judaism, perhaps in reaction to the central place of such speculation in Christianity. The evidence of the Scrolls, however, reminds us that both Jewish and Christian traditions had common roots in the rich and varied world of Second Temple Judaism.

73. Philip Alexander, "3 (Hebrew Apocalypse of) Enoch," in *The Old Testament Pseudepigrapha,* ed. J. H. Charlesworth (New York: Doubleday, 1983) 1.223-315.

74. *Aḥēr* was one of the four who entered Paradise, according to the Talmudic tractate *b. Ḥagiga* 14b.

75. For the history of this controversy see Segal, *Two Powers in Heaven.*

Petitionary Prayer and
the Religion of Qumran

EILEEN SCHULLER

The category of texts from the Dead Sea Scrolls that are brought together under the rather amorphous heading of "prayers, hymns, psalms, and liturgies" both makes its own contribution and presents its own challenges in the overall study of the Scrolls. Esther Chazon, in her recent comprehensive survey of this material, finds in the Scrolls some "two hundred hymns and prayers,"[1] in addition to copies of at least some portion of 126 of the 150 psalms in the Psalter of the Hebrew Bible.[2] The exact number could be disputed — it depends to some extent on what is included and how certain texts are classified — but this is undoubtedly a significant corpus of material.

These texts can be organized into general categories:[3] (1) prayers for fixed times: short prose prayers for morning and evening of each day of the month; another collection of prose prayers for each day of the week; prayers for various festivals; songs for the Sabbath; (2) poetic, psalmic-type compositions: the *Thanksgiving Hymns, Hodayot,* many of which begin "I thank you, Lord" (אודכה, *ʾôděkâ*); another collection of psalms of praise that begin "Bless the Lord, my soul" (ברכי נפשי, *barkhî nafshî*); pseudepigraphic psalms

---

1. Esther Chazon, "Hymns and Prayers in the Dead Sea Scrolls," in *The Dead Sea Scrolls after Fifty Years: A Comprehensive Assessment,* ed. Peter W. Flint and James C. VanderKam (2 vols.; Leiden: Brill, 1998, 1999) 1.245.

2. For this total, see Peter W. Flint, *The Dead Sea Psalms Scrolls and the Book of Psalms* (STDJ 17; Leiden: Brill, 1997) 48.

3. This list is illustrative rather than exhaustive, and the material could be organized in different ways. For a fuller discussion, see Chazon, "Hymns and Prayers," 258-68.

attributed to biblical figures (David, Manasseh, Obadiah); (3) hymnlike compositions for the expulsion of demons; (4) the liturgy for the annual covenant renewal ceremony; (5) collections of blessings to be recited at times of ritual purification and for special occasions; (6) prayers and psalms for the final eschatological war and blessings to be pronounced in the last days when the Prince of the Congregation appears; and (7) prayers that are inserted into a narrative. Most of these are "new" compositions in that they were not known to scholars before the finding of the Scrolls, although a few poetic compositions had been preserved in other forms (Ps 151 in the Greek Psalter; the wisdom poem in Sir 51:14-25; Pss 154 and 155 in the Syriac Psalter). Apart from the Scrolls, few actual texts of public prayers have been preserved from the Second Temple period, in part because of the pharisaic-rabbinic strictures against committing prayer to writing. There are some literary prayers in the books of the Apocrypha/Pseudepigrapha (Tobit, 1 Maccabees, and *1 Enoch* being our richest resources), but much more study is required to determine precisely how these relate to more liturgical materials.[4]

In the last five years there have been a number of articles that have surveyed the prayer and psalmic manuscripts of the Scrolls and provided a brief introduction to the key texts, and so I need not duplicate that comprehensive type of overview here.[5] Of all the different categories of Scrolls material — legal regulations, apocalypses, biblical interpretation, narrative retellings, rules of life — it seems a truism to say that prayers and hymns have a particular import for the topic of this book "Religion in the Dead Sea Scrolls." Words addressed to God or spoken in praise of God, specifically devotional in intent and expressing fundamental sentiments of thanksgiving, praise, petition, and

4. For general surveys, see James H. Charlesworth, "Jewish Hymns, Odes, and Prayers (ca. 167 BCE–135 CE)," in *Early Judaism and Its Modern Interpreters*, ed. Robert A. Kraft and George W. E. Nickelsburg (Philadelphia: Fortress, 1986) 411-36; David Flusser, "Psalms, Hymns, and Prayers," in *Jewish Writings of the Second Temple Period: Apocrypha, Pseudepigrapha, Qumran Sectarian Writings, Philo Josephus*, ed. Michael E. Stone (CRINT; Assen: Van Gorcum, 1984) 551-77.

5. Chazon, "Hymns and Prayers," 244-70; Eileen Schuller, "Prayer, Hymnic, and Liturgical Texts from Qumran," in *The Community of the Renewed Covenant*, ed. E. Ulrich and J. C. VanderKam (CJA 10; Notre Dame: University of Notre Dame Press, 1993) 153-71; Daniel K. Falk, "Prayer in the Qumran Texts," in *The Cambridge History of Judaism*, vol. 3, ed. W. D. Davies and Louis Finkelstein (Cambridge: Cambridge University Press, forthcoming). The first book-length study of at least a substantial portion of these texts was by B. Nitzan, *Qumran Prayer and Religious Poetry* (STDJ 12; Leiden: Brill, 1994). For a more specialized study of a specific body of texts, see Daniel K. Falk, *Daily, Sabbath, and Festival Prayers in the Dead Sea Scrolls* (STDJ 27; Leiden: Brill, 1998).

confession of sin, should give us a particular insight into the religion of the authors of these texts.

Yet there are problems specific to the study of this material, and it may be helpful to articulate some of these explicitly as we begin our discussion:

(1) The history and delays surrounding the publication of the Scrolls are well known and do not need another rehearsal here. Particularly in the category of texts under discussion, manuscripts were allotted to different scholars and redivided and subdivided over the years with the result that sometimes parts of the same composition have been edited by different people over a span of twenty, thirty, even forty years. For example, two copies of the *Thanksgiving Hymns (Hodayot)* from Cave 1 were published in 1954-55. One substantial, though badly damaged, scroll had been purchased from an antiquities dealer by Eleazar L. Sukenik and was edited at Hebrew University in West Jerusalem.[6] A few pieces containing similar content had been gathered up from the debris of Cave 1 in the excavations carried out by the Jordanian Department of Antiquities and were edited by Józef T. Milik at the Scrollery in East Jerusalem.[7] Only after the material had been published could it be established for certain that there was overlapping text and that both scholars had been working independently on different copies of the same collection, now designated as 1QH[a] (Sukenik's manuscript) and 1QH[b] (= 1Q35).[8] In addition, by 1955, from the mass of fragments found in Cave 4, six more scrolls had been identified as containing overlapping text;[9] these manuscripts (4Q427-432) were published in 1999.[10] Thus, certain fundamental questions about these psalms that one might have expected to have been discussed at length and settled over the last forty years are only now being asked, as all the manuscripts become available for study. Similarly, the multiple copies of the biblical Psalter are soon to be published, and fundamental questions about the nature and formation of the Psalter need to be re-

---

6. Eleazar L. Sukenik, *The Dead Sea Scrolls of the Hebrew University* (Jerusalem: Magnes Press, 1954 [Hebrew edition]; 1955 [English edition]).

7. J. T. Milik, "1Q35. Recueil de cantiques d'action grâces (1QH)," in *Qumran Cave 1*, ed. D. Barthélemy and J. T. Milik (DJD 1; Oxford: Clarendon, 1955) 136-38, pl. xxxi.

8. The correct relationship was recognized early on by a number of scholars, including John Strugnell and Hartmut Stegemann; for a published discussion, see É. Puech, "Quelques aspects de la restauration du Rouleau des Hymnes (1QH)," *JJS* 39 (1988) 38-55.

9. John Strugnell, "Le travail d'édition des manuscrits de Qumrân," *RB* 63 (1956) 64-66.

10. Eileen Schuller, "The Hodayot Manuscripts 4Q427-432," in *Qumran Cave 4, XX: Poetical and Liturgical Texts, Part 2,* ed. Esther Chazon et al., in conjunction with J. VanderKam and M. Brady (DJD 29; Oxford: Clarendon, 1999) 69-232.

examined as all of the relevant scrolls in Cave 4, in Cave 11, at Masada, and at Naḥal Ḥever can now be brought to bear upon the discussion.[11]

(2) Many of the manuscripts containing prayers are, unfortunately, very fragmentary. (One could, of course, make the same lament about other types of material.) To get a sense of the reality of the situation and the limitations on what is recoverable, it is instructive to read Maurice Baillet's introductory comments to the *editio princeps* of the material given to him to edit. He describes poignantly his frustration after working for so many years with the 313 little pieces of the *Festival Prayers* (4Q509) or the 215 small fragments of the *Song of the Sage* (4Q511).[12] Although a cursory glance through the complete "List of Texts from the Judaean Desert" identifies a number of manuscripts still not published as "hymnic" or "prayers," many of these are only identified as such on the basis of some second person address to what seems to be God, or some isolated words and phrases that seem vaguely psalmlike.[13] Scholars will probably glean very little from such material.

(3) Yet the problems go deeper than this. It is surprisingly difficult to study prayers, hymns, and psalms. Prayers are "prayerful"; hymns are "beautiful" or "pious." What else can be said? For those who have a personal devotional life and spirituality and participate in a lived experience of worship (whether within the Jewish or Christian tradition), it is difficult to stand back from one's own vocabulary and experience. In analyzing a prayer text with students in class, it is often fascinating to discover how terminology and liturgical preferences are influencing us, even though we may hardly be conscious of their influence; such factors are less likely to be operative when we study a pesher interpretation or a wisdom reflection. However, for those whose experience with this genre is only textual and "from a book," it can be difficult to reconstruct or even imagine an experiential dimension. There is an academic

---

11. For the publication of the Psalms scrolls, see *Qumran Cave 4, XI: The Writings* (DJD 16; Oxford: Clarendon, forthcoming). For a preliminary presentation of the content and variants from all the Psalms scrolls, see Flint, *The Dead Sea Psalms Scrolls.*

12. "Introduction," *Qumrân Grotte 4, III (4Q482-4Q520)* (DJD 7; Oxford: Clarendon, 1982) xi-xiv. I might note that this is a "censored" version of his lament; when I was at the École Biblique in the early 1980s, one day Père Benoit happened to show me the original introduction that M. Baillet had written, a piece that Benoit felt was far too pessimistic and defeatist to be printed as submitted!

13. For the most recent listing and updated names for many of these small manuscripts, see Emanuel Tov, "Appendix III: A List of the Texts from the Judaean Desert," in *The Dead Sea Scrolls after Fifty Years*, 2.669-717. An attempt is made to categorize many of these very fragmentary scrolls by J. Strugnell and E. Schuller in "Further *Hodayot* Manuscripts from Qumran?" in *Antikes Judentum und Frühes Christentum*, ed. B. Kollmann, W. Reinbold, and A. Steudel (Berlin: Walter de Gruyter, 1999) 51-72.

discipline of liturgical studies, ritual studies, and liturgical phenomenology, but few specialists of the Scrolls have ventured into these fields in any depth, and students of liturgy per se often only know the material from the Scrolls superficially or secondhand. As scholars finish with the more technical tasks of preparing primary editions, one of the first challenges will be to reach out and incorporate insights from these other disciplines in the next stage of study.

But enough of the problems. The editors of this volume have challenged us to turn from the minutiae of editorial work to the broader, more comprehensive questions of the "Religion of the Dead Sea Scrolls." This paper takes those organizers at their word that our efforts at this stage are exploratory and preliminary; we are still learning how to formulate questions that will be both true to the material before us and productive of new insights.

In Christian liturgical studies, there is an oft-quoted dictum: *lex credendi est lex orandi* — the norm/rule of faith is the norm/rule of prayer. The monk Prosper of Aquitane, a fifth-century disciple of Augustine, coined the adage in its original, slightly longer form, *legem credendi lex statuat supplicandi* (the rule of supplicating establishes the rule of believing).[14] According to Prosper, the Church's practice of petitionary, intercessory prayer in public liturgy proves, against the semi-Pelagians, that everyone is in need of grace. Augustine had likewise related the prayers of the Church and its faith. In the first Council of Nicea, the proclamation of the dogma of Christ's full divinity and his role as definitive mediator between God and humankind was based, in part, on the Church's prayer.[15] Throughout the centuries, in certain times and places, the axiom has been reversed so that *lex credendi* — what is believed — determines and fixes *lex orandi* — what is prayed.[16] Many contemporary liturgical theologians would claim that the ideal is a parity in which prayer and belief mutually influence each other — but that is a discussion in its own right.[17]

The dialectic of belief and prayer is never simple or univalent; usually

14. See Paul de Clerck, "*Lex Orandi, Lex Credendi:* The Original Sense and Historical Avatars of an Equivocal Adage," *Studia Liturgica* 24 (1994) 178-200.

15. Peter E. Fink, ed., *The New Dictionary of Sacramental Worship* (Collegeville, Minn.: Liturgical Press, 1990) 210-12.

16. Pope Pius XII exemplifies this reversal in the encyclical letter Mediator Dei, "Let the law of belief determine the law of prayer," *Acta Apostolica Sedis* 39 (1947) 540.

17. For a discussion from the perspective of liturgical theology, see Mary M. Schaefer, "*Lex Orandi, Lex Credendi:* Faith, Doctrine, and Theology in Dialogue," *SR* 26 (1997) 467-79.

there are multiple interrelating factors.[18] Although the *lex credendi, lex orandi* adage was developed in a specifically Christian theological context, the same fundamental principle has been applied in the study of the daily Jewish liturgy. For example, Reuven Kimmelman, in his analysis of the *Shema* and the *Amidah,* the central texts of the daily prayer book, describes what he is doing as an attempt "to show how the liturgy functions as an expression of the ideology of the composers as well as an expression of worship."[19]

Let us move now to apply these more general observations to the Dead Sea Scrolls. If there is at least some sense in which we can talk of a particular shape to the "religion of the Scrolls," or, to use other terminology, the religion of this particular "Judaism," we can ask about the relationship between the specific theological emphasis of "this religion/this Judaism" and its prayer texts and practice. What do people with the theological perspective and worldview of this community actually say when they address God in prayer?

In theory, there are a number of different ways in which we might demonstrate a relationship between belief and a specific formulation of prayer texts. We could begin on the basic level of God-language, looking at distinctive terminology, epithets, attributes of God that appear in more discursive, abstract theological statements, and comparing them with the actual language used to address God in prayer. It is surely not without theological significance, for example, that in the *Hodayot* we find repeatedly the epithet אל הדעות "God of knowledge" (1QH^a 9:28 [1:26]; 20:13 [12:10]; 22:34 [frg. 4:15]; 25:32-33 [frg. 8:8-9][20]), but never the designation אל ישראל "God of Israel." Or, to take another quite different example, given the strong sense of the reality and presence of the angelic world, does the fact that a member of the *yaḥad* is able, even already in this earthly life, "to take his place with the host of the holy ones and enter into community with the congregation of the sons of heaven" (1QH^a 11:22-23 [3:21-22]) affect how praise is expressed? From the possible ways of approaching the issue, this paper will limit itself to one specific question: What is

---

18. A brief aside: it was when I served on the editorial committee of a modern hymnbook and worked my way through huge stacks of unsolicited new compositions that I became convinced that there is another axiom that is equally influential in modern church practice, namely, that "people will sing any heresy as long as it rhymes."

19. Reuven Kimmelman, "The Literary Structure of the Amidah and the Rhetoric of Redemption," in *The Echoes of Many Texts,* ed. William G. Dever and J. Edward Wright (BJS 313; Atlanta: Scholars Press, 1997) 173.

20. The first set of column and line numbers are according to the way the scroll of 1QH^a has been reconstructed by H. Stegemann and É. Puech; the numbers in brackets are according to E. L. Sukenik's *editio princeps.* There may be some differences in line numbering in certain English translations that follow the reconstructed column order.

the interplay between a strongly deterministic theology such as is generally recognized in the Scrolls and specifically petitionary prayer? That is, does "the religion" of the Scrolls allow for petition, supplication, or intercession, and how is this expressed in actual petitions?

When the major Cave 1 manuscripts (the *Rule of the Community,* the *Thanksgiving Hymns,* the *War Scroll*) were studied for the first time, one of the most striking features observed was the strongly deterministic element in the theology. To recall briefly some key passages (by way of example, rather than completeness or full analysis):[21]

> From the God of Knowledge comes all that is and shall be.
> Before ever they existed he established their whole design,
> and when, as ordained for them, they come into being,
> it is in accord with his glorious design
> that they accomplish their task without change.
> (1QS 3:15-16 ["Treatise on the Two Spirits"])

> By your wisdom [all things exists from] eternity,
> and before creating them you knew their works for ever and ever.
> [Nothing] is done [without you] and nothing is known unless you
>   desire it. . . .
> In the wisdom of your knowledge
> you established their destiny (תעודתם) before ever they were.
> All things [exist] according to your will,
> and without you nothing is done. (1QH^a 9:9-10, 20-22; 1:7-8, 18-20)

The *Damascus Document* takes up this concept in a passage that draws upon and perhaps quotes the "Treatise on the Two Spirits":

> he knew their deeds before ever they were created . . .
> for he knew the years of their coming and the length and exact duration
> of their times for all ages to come and throughout eternity. (CD 2:6-10)

The *Ages of Creation* (4Q180 1 2) states the same succinctly, "before he created them he knew their plans." It is within the framework of this type of worldview that the *War Scroll* can give the outline of a final eschatological battle: the end result is assured; it has been determined from the beginning.

---

21. Translations are usually taken from G. Vermes, *The Complete Dead Sea Scrolls in English* (London: Penguin, 1997), with minor adaptations to contemporary English usage. However, in some places in the *Hodayot* I base my translation on a different reading and restoration of the Hebrew text.

There is, as many scholars have observed, a "striking harmony"[22] between statements such as these and Josephus's presentation, albeit in more abstract, philosophical terminology, of a basic tenet of the Essenes: "The sect of the Essenes declares that Fate is the mistress of all things, that nothing befalls humankind unless it be in accordance with her decrees" (*Ant* 13.172). Josephus contrasts this position both with the Sadducean disavowal of Fate, "so that all things lie without our own power," and with the more nuanced stance of the Pharisees, who tried to hold together both providence/Fate and human freedom since "certain events are the work of Fate, but not all; for some events, it depends upon ourselves whether they shall take place or not." To quote the words attributed to Rabbi Akiba, "Everything is foreseen, yet freedom of choice is given." Thus James C. VanderKam can list "Determinism" as the first in his arguments for identifying the authors of the Scrolls with the Essenes.[23]

This predeterministic element in the religion of the Dead Sea Scrolls is considerably more nuanced and complex than a series of quotations can indicate.[24] It cannot totally be separated from — indeed, it is rooted in — certain impulses that are to be found already in the Hebrew Bible: for example, Psalm 139:4, 16, "even before a word is on my tongue, O Lord, you know it completely; in your book were written all the days that were formed for me when none of them as yet existed." Yet almost all commentators on the Scrolls would agree that the Scrolls go beyond what are considered "standard" biblical statements of divine foreknowledge and power. In his recent book, Armin Lange has reexamined in some detail both the key texts from Cave 1 and other compositions more recently published, and emphasized the wisdom/sapiential matrix for this complex of ideas.[25] Lange suggests that certain of the Scrolls that speak of a preexistent order of creation and history — such as *Sapiential Work* A, the *Book of Mysteries,* the fifth song of the *Songs of the Sabbath Sacrifice* (4Q402 4) and even the "Treatise of the Two Spirits" (1QS 3:15-18) — may be pre-Essene in origin. There are clear parallels with ideas in *Jubilees,* and indeed this is a fundamental supposition in an apocalyptic worldview.

Over the years when this question of predestination has been discussed,

---

22. The expression is from James C. VanderKam, *The Dead Sea Scrolls Today* (Grand Rapids: Eerdmans, 1994) 76.

23. VanderKam, *The Dead Sea Scrolls Today,* 76.

24. For early specific studies of the issue, see A. Marx, "Y a-t-il une prédestination à Qumrân?" *RevQ* 6 (1967) 163-81; Eugene H. Merrill, *Qumran and Predestination: A Theological Study of the Thanksgiving Hymns* (STDJ 8; Leiden: Brill, 1975).

25. Armin Lange, *Weisheit und Prädestination: Weisheitliche Urordnung und Prädestination in den Textfunden von Qumran* (STDJ 18; Leiden: Brill, 1995); "Wisdom and Predestination in the Dead Sea Scrolls," *DSD* 2 (1995) 340-54.

most studies have focused on the classic dilemma of predestination versus human freedom. Passages claiming both can be brought forth, often from the same document. There are statements that God has determined, from the beginning, the lot of each individual under the dominion of one of the two spirits, so that God has caused his elect "to inherit the lot of the Holy Ones" (1QS 11:7), even as others "he caused to go astray" (CD 2:13), that is, a double predestination. Yet other passages speak unabashedly of human choice, of "those who have chosen the way" (1QS 9:17-18) of righteousness or evil. We can find paradoxical combinations such as the reference in the *Pesher on Micah* to "those who volunteer to join the chosen of God" (1QpMic 10 7). Considerable ink has been spilt on this incongruity. It is often stated that the authors of the Scrolls were not systematic theologians, and therefore contradictory positions are to be expected; some commentators have postulated an unintegrated strain of Zoroastrian influence or emphasized differences in literary genre. E. P. Sanders has refocused the question in terms grace and works, distinguishing "the intimate and necessary connection between God's grace in putting one in the covenant and the requirement to obey once in the covenant."[26]

Whatever the reconciliation of the general issue of predestination and free will, there is still our specific question how a predestinarian thrust affects not just "works" in general but worship in particular. The question is not just can an individual choose to act freely, but, more specifically, can or should an individual act to make petition to God? What is the point of petitioning the God of knowledge who has determined all things from the beginning? What might be the proper object of petition? This is, of course, a classic question in all theological systems that admit of an all-knowing, all-powerful God, a question taken up by Calvin in the *Institutes* and Thomas Aquinas in his *Summa Theologiae*.[27] The Scrolls contain very little of this type of second-level theological reflection (the "Treatise on the Two Spirits" in 1QS 3:13–4:26 is perhaps the most systematic and sustained discourse), but they do contain prayers that were uttered by people who espoused a theology with a strong predestinarian emphasis.

When the issue is formulated in this way, the significance of certain ele-

---

26. E. P. Sanders, *Paul and Palestinian Judaism: A Comparison of Patterns of Religion* (Philadelphia: Fortress, 1977) 296.

27. For example, John Calvin, *Institutes of the Christian Religion*, III 20 section 3; Thomas Aquinas, *Summa Theologiae* 222ae.83.2. Helmer Ringgren, in *The Faith of Qumran: Theology of the Dead Sea Scrolls* (Philadelphia: Fortress, 1963) 110-11, remarks that systematic theologians — Muslim, Christian, or Jewish — have not been particularly successful in coming up with neat formulations that logically reconcile divine sovereignty and human freedom.

ments that have long been accepted as commonplace becomes more focused. It is a matter of interest theologically that so much of the material involves praise: the *Hodayot*, the *Barkhi Nafshi* psalms (4Q434-438), and the *Songs of the Sabbath Sacrifice* (4Q400-407, 11Q17). The liturgical calendar in the *Ordo* (4Q334) lists multiple "songs" (שירות) and "words of praise" (דברי תשבוחות) for morning and night, through no actual texts are given. The *Hodayot*, the most extensive collection of poetic texts, at least some of which have often been attributed to the revered founder figure, the Teacher of Righteousness, are written in the form of thanksgiving psalms and blessings (we need not make too much distinction for our purposes here between those psalms that begin with the אודכה formula "I thank you, O Lord," and those that begin with the ברוך אתה formula "blessed are you, O Lord"). These psalms are full of repeated expressions of gratitude for what God has done, wonder at being chosen, and acknowledgment of divine graciousness and righteousness. Even in those passages where the psalmist graphically describes the weak and sinful condition of all humankind, including himself, this too is an acknowledgment of what God has determined; it is God who created the psalmist as "a shape of clay, kneaded in water, a ground of shame, and a source of pollution, a melting-pot of wickedness and an edifice of sin" (1QH^a 9:23-24 [1:21-22]).[28] In the terminology coined by Heinz-Wolfgang Kuhn, such statements are given the designation *Niedrigkeitsdoxologie*.[29] Paradoxically, they function to introduce praise of God's justice and mercy to such a wretched creation, and never as a petition for a change in the human condition.

It might seem tautological to emphasize that these thanksgiving psalms do not contain petition, because if they are modeled on the biblical psalms of thanksgiving, this is a genre that did not traditionally mix thanksgiving and petition.[30] Yet this only reiterates our starting premise that the very choice of the thanksgiving genre is an expression of a certain theological stance. Moreover, since the author/s of these psalms — for this does not seem to be a unified collection — did not seem to feel compelled to reduplicate the classical biblical genre in a rigid way (note the extended didactic reflections, the omis-

---

28. For example, 1QH^a 5:31-35 [13:14-18], 9:23-29 [1:21-27], 11:24-26 [3:23-25], 19:22-25 [11:19-22].

29. Heinz-Wolfgang Kuhn, *Enderwartung und gegenwärtiges Heil: Untersuchungen zu den Gemeindeliedern von Qumran mit einem Anhang über Eschatologie und Gegenwart in der Verkündigung Jesu* (SUNT 4; Göttingen: Vanderhoeck and Ruprecht, 1965) 27.

30. For the classic delineation of psalm genres, see Hermann Gunkel, *Introduction to Psalms: The Genres of the Religious Lyric of Israel*, completed by Joachim Begrich, trans. James D. Nogalski (Macon, Ga.: Mercer, 1998). Gunkel (p. 207, n. 115) notes only three examples where petitions are part of individual thanksgiving psalms.

sion of any reference to a thanksgiving vow or sacrifice), the emphasis on blessing and praise instead of petition is based on something more than form-critical constraints.

However, the *Hodayot* does not wholly eschew petition. This is not the place to do a detailed linguistic analysis of specific passages, and there are a few places where there is some ambiguity about how certain verbal forms are to be interpreted or reconstructed. The clearest passage with imperatives is 1QH^a 19:32-34 (11:29-31):

> Blessed are you, O God of mercy and compassion,
> for the might of your [power] and the greatness of your truth,
> and for the multitude of your favors in all your works.
> Rejoice the soul of your servant with your truth,
> and cleanse me by your righteousness.

A similar imperative petition is probably to be found in 1QH^a 4:35 (17:23), "make strong (חזק) his loins," but here the reading of the Hebrew is disputed. (Eleazar L. Sukenik and others read the problematic middle letter as a *waw*, and thus the noun as חוק, "decree," eliminating any imperative.)[31] The combination of a blessing statement followed by an imperative is also found in 1QS 11:15-16:

> Blessed are you, my God,
> who opens the heart of your servant to knowledge.
> Establish all his deeds in righteousness,
> and grant that the son of your handmaid may stand before you
> for ever.[32]

There is one passage, the bottom section of column 8 in the reconstructed scroll (col. 16 in Sukenik), that is quite distinctive. In his commentary, Jacob Licht already gave this passage the title בקשה "a request."[33] The psalmist describes himself as petitioning God: "I implore you" ואחלה פניך

---

31. The reading חזק is adopted, for example, by M. Delcor, *Les Hymnes de Qumrân (Hodayot)* (Paris: Letouzey et Ané, 1962) 285; Theodor Gaster, *The Scripture of the Dead Sea Sect* (London: Secker and Warburg, 1957) 194; and H. Stegemann in his unpublished edition of 1QH^a. J. Licht, *The Thanksgiving Scroll* (Jerusalem: Bialik, 1957 [Hebrew]), and Svend Holm-Nielsen, *Hodayot: Psalms from Qumran* (Acta Theologica Danica II; Aarhus: Universitetsforlaget, 1960), follow the edition of Sukenik in reading חוק.

32. At one stage, the blessing may have ended one composition, while the petition began another, but in the form that the psalm comes to us in 1QS, these lines form a single composition.

33. Licht, *The Thanksgiving Scroll*, 200.

(cf. Exod 32:11 where the same verb is used when Moses implores God after the Golden Calf incident):

> I implore you . . . to perfect your [favors] to your servant [for ever];
> purifying me by your holy spirit;
> and drawing me near to you by your grace. (1QH^a 8:29-30 [16:11-12])

This is followed by two negative petitions: "Let no scourge [come] near him" (1QH^a 8:33 [16:15]) and "reject not the face of your servant" (1QH^a 8:36 [16:18]). There may be other instances of negative petitions in the reconstructed psalm in 1QH^a 22:37 (frg. 4 18) ואל תעזובני בקצי "do not forsake me in times [of distress]," and in the next column in 1QH^a 23:10 (18:9) אל תשב ידכה, "withdraw not your hand"; however, this section is fragmentary, and it is possible that these are to be taken as purpose clauses rather than as petitions.[34]

There is yet another type of passage to be brought into the discussion: statements about the prayer of the psalmist. In these texts it is difficult to judge whether various terms for different types of prayer were always distinguished from one another in the Second Temple period and used in a technical sense.[35] For example, 1QH^a 19:36-37 (11:33-34) gives a list, "you set in the mouth of your servant thanksgivings, [prai]s[e], and entreaty and answer of the tongue," ותשם בפי עבדכה הודות ת[ה]ל[ה ותחנה ומענה לשון 1QH^a;[36] 17:10-11 (9:10-11) says "you put a supplication (תחנה) in the mouth of your servant"; and the rubrical heading in 1QH^a 20:7 (12:4) begins "[for the Ma]sk[il, tha]nksgivings (הודות) and a prayer (ותפלה), to fall down (להתנפל) and to entreat (והתחנן) always."[37] The verbal root used in all these examples (חנן) has some sense of entreaty or supplication.[38]

---

34. As translated by É. Puech, *La croyance des Esséniens en la vie future: Immortalité, Résurrection, Vie Eternelle?* (Paris: Gabalda, 1993) 2.402: "Car/Et je sais qu'il y a]de espérance pour ton servieur et (que) tu ne m'abandonneras pas aux temps [de la colère."

35. See Eileen Schuller, "The Use of Biblical Terms as Designations for Non-Biblical Hymnic and Prayer Compositions," in *Biblical Perspectives: Early Use and Interpretation of the Bible in Light of the Dead Sea Scrolls,* ed. Michael E. Stone and Esther G. Chazon (STDJ 28; Leiden: Brill, 1998) 207-22.

36. Following the reading and reconstruction proposed by H. Stegemann, unpublished edition.

37. É. Puech reconstructs a very similar rubric in 1QH^a 5:12 (frg. 15 Ia 3), though the traces are very minimal: [מזמור למש]כיל להתנפל לפנ]י אל ולהתחנן תמיד], "[A psalm for the *Mas]kil* to bow down befo[re God and to make supplication always]"; see "Un hymne essénien en partie retrouvé et les Béatitudes. 1QH V 12-VI 18 (= col XIII-XIV 7) et 4QBéat," *RevQ* 13 (1988) 59-88.

38. See discussion of חנן in *The Theological Dictionary of the Old Testament,* ed. G. J. Botterweck and H. Ringgren (Grand Rapids: Eerdmans, 1986) 5.29-32.

It is difficult to know what conclusion to draw from all this. Both the imperative verbs and the statements quoted above are all from psalms of the category of "Hymns of the Community," and not from the "Hymns of the Teacher," except for the reference to God putting תחנה, "supplication or entreaty," in the mouth of the Teacher in the final "Hymn of the Teacher" (1QH[a] 17:10-11 [9:10-11]). Israel Knohl has observed that what is asked for in these petitions — cleansing, purification, to be drawn near to God — are the very things for which the psalmist customarily gives thanks.[39] These examples do not negate the first and primary observation that praise and thanksgiving are the fundamental response to a God who has determined all from the beginning. Yet the *Hodayot* give evidence that petitions can also be directed toward this God.

To turn to a different body of material, there is the question of whether petition played any part in the covenant initiation or renewal ceremony. The situation is not as straightforward as might appear at first glance. The liturgy of entrance into the covenant, held annually on the Feast of Weeks and described in 1QS 1:18–2:18, drew upon three traditional elements: the "covenant formulary" (the recounting of God's saving acts, the blessings, and the curses);[40] postexilic penitential prayers (such as in Neh 9, Ezra 9, 1 Kings 8) with their communal confession of sin and explicit acknowledgment of God's righteousness;[41] and the priestly blessing of Numbers 6. It is the specific combination of these elements, rather than the components per se, that makes this liturgy distinct.[42] What we do not find in this liturgy is any explicit petition, either for mercy or for God to bring the initiates into the covenant — an omission that is all the more striking because some element of petition is intrinsic to the postexilic penitential prayer structure that, at some level, lies be-

---

39. See the appendix, "Petitionary Prayer in the Qumran Writings," in his article "Between Voice and Silence: The Relationship between Prayer and Temple Cult," *JBL* 115 (1996) 29-30. In a very helpful response to my paper, Craig Broyles has pointed out the same phenomenon in a number of the biblical psalms; e.g., Ps 139 begins by affirming "Lord, you have searched me and know my heart," but closes with the petition, "Search me, O Lord, and know my heart"; Ps 33 closes with a petition for God's mercy (v. 22) even though it earlier affirmed that "the earth is full of his mercy" (v. 5).

40. For a discussion of both biblical and Qumran examples, see K. Baltzer, *The Covenant Formulary: In Old Testament, Jewish, and Early Christian Writings* (Philadelphia: Fortress, 1971) 167-70.

41. For a recent study of these prayers, see Rodney Alan Werline, *Penitential Prayer in Second Temple Judaism: The Development of a Religious Institution* (Atlanta: Scholars Press, 1998).

42. See the discussion by Falk, *Daily, Sabbath, and Festival Prayers,* esp. pp. 222-25.

hind this material.[43] According to the theological stance of this community, petition at this point is unnecessary; the initiate who is entering the covenant has been part of the lot of the chosen by divine determination from the beginning of time. Yet the confession of sin and acknowledgment of divine righteousness is followed immediately by an expanded form of blessings and curses. And the specific style of the priestly blessing of Numbers 6, which is maintained here albeit with expansion, is a formulation in the jussive. This is in contrast to the style of blessing of humans that is to be found, for example, in 1QM 13:3-4 "blessed be all those who [serve] him," משרתיו ברוכים כול, which in form is much closer to the declaratory blessing of God, "blessed are you, O Lord," ברוך אתה אדוני. By choosing the blessing of Numbers 6 as the base text, the formulators of this liturgy adopted a style of blessing that is close to petition — "May he bless you with all good and preserve you from all evil. May he enlighten your heart with life-giving wisdom and grant you eternal knowledge. May he raise his merciful face towards you for everlasting bliss" (1QS 2:2-4) — and to those cursed — "May he deliver you up for torture . . . may he visit you with destruction . . . may God not heed when you call on him . . ." (1QS 2:5-8). In this way a certain petitionary element finds a place in the covenant renewal liturgy.

Finally, surprisingly, there is a petitionary element in some of the eschatological scenarios that describe that future time which will bring "healing, bountiful peace in a long life . . . eternal enjoyment . . . and a crown of glory" to those of the lot of light, but "eternal damnation . . . bitter weeping and harsh evils in the abysses of darkness" to those in the domain of the spirit of iniquity (1QS 4:6-14). In such a context, there should be no need for petition, for the events of the end are fixed and in the hands of God. Yet when we look at the *Rule of Blessings* (1QSb) — and since this is a series of blessings, with no corresponding curses, and one of the blessings is for the Prince of the Congregation, most scholars have assumed this is a set of blessings for the future messianic era, even if it might have had some proleptic use when it was written[44] — we find the same anomaly as noted above with regard to the priestly blessing, namely, that the linguistic form, with the series of jussive verbs, introduces at least a sense of petition. This is not straightforward praise of the Prince of the Congregation (for example),

43. Werline, *Penitential Prayer,* 137, assumes that there is a petition — "The initiates' speech concludes in 2.1 with their request that God be gracious and merciful toward them forever" — but the line in question is better read as an affirmation rather than a petition.

44. Harmut Stegemann, *The Library of Qumran* (Grand Rapids: Eerdmans, 1998) 116.

nor of God who has appointed him, but there is some sense of request that would be appropriate even in the final day of fulfillment. Similarly, at the time of the final eschatological battle, the high priest is to say the "prayer in time of war," תפלת מועד המלחמה (1QM 15:5). The text of this prayer is found in the mysterious *Book of the Order of the Times,* בס[פר סרך עתו (1QM 15:5). Although the actual words to be said are not given, the designation תפלה, *tĕpillāh,* suggests that it is a prayer of petition. What need is there of petition in a war when victory is assured? Bilha Nitzan suggests that this prayer is inserted here simply by force of habit; the Sons of Light "are expected to behave in the same way as other human beings do in the time of war."[45] Whatever the reason, for the final redactors of the *War Scroll* a request for victory was not considered incompatible with an overarching confidence that victory was assured.

The compositions examined up to this point have a strong claim of being specifically sectarian, that is, Essene, in origin.[46] Yet the total picture is more varied and complex, particularly now that we can take into account the full corpus of the Scrolls. There is, in fact, a substantial number of texts preserved that are prayers of petition. Most significant of these are the two, perhaps three, copies of a series of prose prayers for each day of the week (*Words of the Luminaries,* 4Q504, 506)[47] and the *Festival Prayers* (4Q507-509). In the *Words of the Luminaries,* the material for Sabbath is distinctive in form and content. It is written in poetic parallel lines, is totally doxological, and contains no petitions.[48] For the other days of the week, the petitionary element is embedded in the very form. Rubrical titles, "Prayer for the second day," "Prayer for the sixth day," are usually reconstructed with תפלה on analogy with the preserved title for the "Prayer for the day of atonement" (1Q34^bis 2 6), תפלה ליום כפורים, though no instance of תפלה is actually preserved in the daily prayers. Although there is a concluding blessing (ברוך) formula, the

45. Nitzan, *Qumran Prayer,* 138, n. 64.

46. For the distinction of sectarian versus nonsectarian, see especially the carefully nuanced discussion of Carol Newsom, "'Sectually Explicit' Literature from Qumran," in *The Hebrew Bible and Its Interpreters,* ed. W. Propp et al. (Winona Lake, Ind.: Eisenbrauns, 1990) 167-87.

47. The identification of the very fragmentary manuscript 4Q505 is disputed. M. Baillet in *Qumrân Grotte 4, III (4Q482-4Q520)* (DJD 7; Oxford: Clarendon, 1982) judged that it was a copy of the *Words of the Luminaries,* but in a review of the volume F. García Martínez suggested that these fragments belong instead to *Festival Prayers* (4Q509); see *JSJ* 15 (1984) 161-62. This division of fragments is argued also by Falk, *Daily, Sabbath, and Festival Prayers,* 59-61.

48. Esther Chazon, "On The Special Character of Sabbath Prayer: New Data from Qumran," *Journal of Jewish Music and Liturgy* 15 (1992-93) 1-21.

prayer begins with a petition זכור, "remember," and each prayer contains a series of imperatives: "teach us law, circumcise the foreskin of our heart, strengthen our heart, . . . deliver from evil." The *Festival Prayers* are similar in form: they are designated as תפלה,[49] begin with the introductory petition "remember" (זכור), and are probably also petitionary, although due to their very fragmentary state, there are no absolutely clear imperative verbs preserved.[50] In addition to these larger collections, often preserved in multiple copies, there are also single copies of prayers for forgiveness and deliverance (e.g., *Communal Confession*, 4Q393; *Apocryphal Lamentations B*, 4Q501) and "apocryphal" psalms that contain petitions such as the "Plea for Deliverance" (11QPs[a] 19:1-18) and Psalm 155 (11QPs[a] 24:3-18).

All of these petitionary compositions are generally considered nonsectarian in their origin; that is, they were not authored by the Essenes, they predate the foundation of their distinct community, and they reflect a more widespread practice of prayer in Second Temple Judaism.[51] Yet the fact that multiple copies of many of these texts were found in the caves has suggested at least to most scholars that there was some ongoing use of these prayers and psalms in the liturgical life of the Essene community.

In reconstructing — however tentatively — the content of the daily, weekly, and festive prayer cycle, special attention must be paid to the presence of the very large number, perhaps as many as thirty-seven, of Psalter scrolls.[52] If this abundance of psalm manuscripts (more copies than of any other single book at Qumran) can be taken as an indication of some form of liturgical usage of psalmody (in addition to the studied exegesis that lay behind the various pesharim that were written on the psalms), the community's worship must have included many psalms of lament with their petitions for divine help and deliverance. Certainly there is no evidence to think that this major

49. In addition to the heading "Prayer for the day of atonement," see also 4Q509 10 ii + 11 8 [תפ]לה למועד] "Prayer for the festival of [."

50. Some words are most easily taken as imperatives, although there is not enough context for certainty; e.g., כפר ע]ל, "atone fo[r]," 4Q508 7 1; רחמהם על תעניתם["have mercy on them because of their affli[ction," 4Q509 16 3.

51. See the discussion of Esther Chazon, "Is *Divre Ha-me'orot* a Sectarian Prayer?" in *The Dead Sea Scrolls: Forty Years of Research,* ed. Devorah Dimant and Uriel Rappaport (Leiden: Brill, 1992) 3-17.

52. For a listing of the Psalm scrolls, see Flint, *The Dead Sea Psalms Scrolls,* esp. pp. 31-43, and add the 4QPs[v] (4Q98e), a fragment of Ps 112 recently identified (see Peter Flint, "The Contribution of the Cave 4 Psalms Scrolls to the Psalms Debate," *DSD* 5 [1998] 321). Flint counts thirty-seven Psalms scrolls from Qumran (in addition to the three from Masada and Naḥal Ḥever), but it is disputable whether or not two of these should really be counted as Psalms Scrolls (*Apocryphal Psalms,* 11Q11; and *Prophecy on Joshua,* 4Q522).

element of the Psalter was consistently excluded.[53] The specific compilation of the Psalter that is reflected in what Peter Flint has designated "11QPs^a-Psalter" (an edition of the Psalter reflected in 11QPs^a, 11QPs^b, and 4QPs^e, a Psalter that Flint argues was copied at Qumran though not composed there) included a significant number of psalms of supplication (Pss 109, 141, 144, 142, 143, the "Plea for Deliverance," and Ps 155).[54]

The move from written scrolls to liturgical practice involves considerable speculation, and thus the scenario that is reconstructed here can only be tentative and a starting point for further reflection. Our study has led us to suggest that the prayer texts used by the Essene community in their daily, weekly, and festival worship consisted, in part, of works composed by the Teacher of Righteousness and other members of the community. These were predominantly psalms and hymns of praise that confessed and acknowledged the sovereignty and power of the God who has determined all things in his wisdom. Such expressions of doxology and thanksgiving were a direct outgrowth of a strongly deterministic theology; that is, there was a basic congruity between *lex credendi* and *lex orandi*. Yet the community also continued to use some older, traditional compositions that had been fashioned by the pious in days past: the prayers for each day of the week and for festivals; confessions and lamentations; and the corpus of the much-beloved psalms of their ancestors, which included numerous lament psalms. In the praying of these texts, petition to God — with its implication that all is not absolutely fixed, that the human plea has a place in the divine economy and will be heard — became part of the religious experience of this praying community. Perhaps this *lex orandi* even exercised a certain restraining influence on the theological development of the *lex credendi* so that the theology of the Essenes never became absolutely deterministic. Both the *lex credendi* and the *lex orandi* must be considered as we seek to understand the religion of the Dead Sea Scrolls.

---

53. Over 60 of the 150 psalms are generally classified as psalms of lament; see the categorization of the psalms by genre in Bernhard W. Anderson, *Out of the Depths: The Psalms Speak to Us Today* (Philadelphia: Westminster, 1983) 239-42.

54. Flint, *The Dead Sea Psalms Scroll*, 198-200. The same conclusion is applicable even if 11QPs^a is considered a "prayer book" rather than a scriptural Psalter.

Qumran and Hellenism

MARTIN HENGEL

The community of Qumran has its roots in the Maccabean revolt and the failure of the "Hellenistic reform" between 175 and 164 BC. Without these events this radical eschatological reform party would never have come into being. It therefore can be understood, *inter alia,* as a movement of strict opposition against the expansion of Hellenistic civilization in Jewish Palestine. Because of this history, the link between Hellenism and the Essene community from its beginning around 150 BC to its sudden end in 68 CE has been rather neglected in Qumran studies. Greek thought and civilization has been seen as separated from the Qumran community by an unbridgeable gulf.

Twenty-three years ago in 1976, when I gave a lecture about the subject "Qumran und der Hellenismus"[1] in the *Journées bibliques de Louvain,* I therefore began with the following: "This theme sounds like 'fire and water' or in the language of Qumran like 'light and darkness.' For the Essenes the *da'at,* the divine knowledge, revealed to themselves, and the *ḥokmāh yĕwānit,* the Greek wisdom, were two absolutely opposite entities." Qumran's fundamental opposition to Hellenism seems even more visible when we compare the luxurious Herodian palaces in Jericho or Masada with the extremely modest, even poor buildings of Khirbet Qumran, which lie between them both. It is no coincidence that the Essenes called themselves "the poor."[2] We can also see opposition in Qumran's language. The Essenes from Qumran endeavored to

---

1. In *Qumrân: Sa piété, sa théologie, son milieu,* ed. M. Delcor (BETL 46; Paris: Duculot, 1978) 333-72 = M. Hengel, *Judaica et Hellenistica. Kleine Schriften I* (Tübingen: Mohr-Siebeck, 1996) 258-94.

2. Cf. 1QpHab 12:3, 6, 10; 1QM 11:9, 12; 13:14.

write a pure biblical Hebrew, with only a few Aramaisms and no Graecisms at all: It was a linguistic purism that could be compared with Greek Atticism. By contrast, the Hebrew of the Mishnah and Tosefta, the language of the rabbis and descendants of the Pharisees, is full of Greek loanwords. However, so also are the *Copper Scroll* of Qumran, with its spoken, nonliterary, mostly technical Hebrew, and the book of Daniel.[3]

Hellenistic Technology

In Jerusalem the ruling class with its manifold links to the Greek-speaking world wanted, as families or individuals, to remain or to become rich. As a whole community, the Essenes, like the abbeys in the Middle Ages, were also rather rich. Their catalogue of treasures hidden in the Jewish War contains about thirty tons of gold and silver and more than six hundred vases, along with other precious metals, incense, spices, and perfumes.[4] They also did not despise the technical achievements and inventions of the Hellenistic age. We see this in the elaborate artificial water supply system at Khirbet Qumran. The cultivation of the desert between Khirbet Qumran and Ein Feschkha could hardly have been possible without artificial irrigation. In the hymn that appears in 1QH[a] 16 (column 8 in Eleazar Sukenik's edition), the poet, possibly the Teacher of Righteousness, is well acquainted with the construction of an irrigated, flourishing orchard in the desert. Probably the whole region around Khirbet Qumran was a large estate cultivated by the members of the community. Large domains, often the possession of the king, the state, or a temple, were typical of the agriculture in the Hellenistic and Roman eras.

The imitation of the technical superiority of Hellenistic civilization is also visible in the imitation of the Greek art of warfare and weapons in the *War Scroll* and other texts describing the eschatological messianic war. Yigael Yadin thought that the author used a Roman military handbook, but because the original version of this text may already go back to the Maccabean period, we must suppose a Hellenistic source. The Roman arms and tactics developed

3. J. T. Milik, *Les 'Petites Grottes' de Qumrân* (DJD 3; Oxford: Clarendon Press, 1962) 222: "un long texte rédigé en hébreu populaire, parlé effectivement par les Juifs résidant en Judée." Cf. pp. 237, 246, *'ksdrn = exedra* , Nr. 84; p. 268, *hst'n = stoa*, Nr. 1000; *prstlyn = peristylion*, Nr. 104; p. 251, *l'h = aloē*, Nr. 128; p. 253, *str(yn) = statēr* Nr. 149. For the musical instruments in Daniel 3, see Martin Hengel, *Judaism and Hellenism: Studies in Their Encounter in Palestine During the Early Hellenistic Period*, trans. John Bowden (2 vols.; Philadelphia: Fortress Press, 1974) 1.60, n. 18.

4. See the newsletter, *International Friends of the École Biblique* (Winter 1998-99) 9.

in close connection with Greek military standards.[5] In my essay "Qumran und der Hellenismus" in 1978, I posited that a Maccabean military instruction manual from the second century using Greek and Roman models underlay the *War Scroll*.[6]

We even possess a text fragment that probably mentions a sea battle between the Davidic Prince of the Community and the enemy of God, an event that has no parallel in the Old Testament. Sea battles, however, play an important role in Hellenistic times.[7] Before Pompey, in the time of Alexander Jannaeus, the Jews from their seaport of Joppa participated in the piracy of the eastern Mediterranean. In the tomb of Jason of that time we find a wall drawing of a battleship pursuing a smaller boat.[8]

The *Yaḥad* as a Voluntary Association

A sign of the new Hellenistic era is also the juridical and sociological status of the community, the *yaḥad*, as a free religious-political association — religion and politics cannot be separated strictly in antiquity. This is reminiscent of a Greek *koinon*, which has the same meaning as *yaḥad*, *thiasos*, or *synodos* and is comparable to the synagogue communities in the Greek cities.[9] Entrance into the *yaḥad* was a personal decision based on an act of individual conversion. It is an indication of the progressing individualization of religious life in Jewish Palestine and became also a presupposition for the Jesus movement and the beginnings of Christianity. The inner circle of the Qumran Essenes,

5. Y. Yadin, *The Scroll of the War of the Sons of Light against the Sons of Darkness* (London: Oxford University Press, 1962). For references about the importance of war and warfare, see the index of J. Maier, *Die Qumran-Essener: Die Texte vom Toten Meer* (3 vols.; München: E. Reinhard, 1995) 3.273ff. About the messianic war, see "Krieg" in the index of J. Zimmermann, *Messianische Texte aus Qumran* (WUNT 104; Tübingen: Mohr-Siebeck, 1998) 536.

6. M. Hengel, *Judaica et Hellenistica*, 265ff.

7. 4Q285 4; see Zimmermann, *Messianische Texte aus Qumran*, 88-93, 471. Probably in this connection the enemy will be taken prisoner and killed. The Kittim, i.e., the Greeks and the Romans, came from the west over the sea.

8. See M. Hengel, *Judaica, Hellenistica, et Christiana. Kleine Schriften II* (WUNT 109; Tübingen: Mohr-Siebeck, 1999) 291ff. About Joppa as a place of piracy see Strabo 16.2.28; M. Stern, *Greek and Latin Authors on Jews and Judaism* (2 vols.; Jerusalem: The Israel Academy of Sciences and Humanities, 1974) 1.290, 292, nr. 114; cf. Josephus *Ant.* 14.43.

9. See M. Weinfeld, *The Organizational Pattern and the Penal Code of the Qumran Sect* (Göttingen: Vandenhoeck & Ruprecht, 1986).

living in celibacy and having community rather than personal property, impressed the Greeks, as we can see from the writings of Philo, Josephus, Pliny the Elder, and Dio Chrysostom.[10] In the Old Testament we find the remark "There will be no poor among you for the Lord will bless you generously" (Deut 15:4), but we never have a specific command concerning community property. This and the rejection of individual property was an old philosophical and utopian ideal in Hellenism according to the widespread proverb "common is the property of friends"[11] in Greek literature. Josephus can therefore call them a Jewish "group which follows a way of life taught to the Greeks by Pythagoras."[12] This typical Greek utopian ideal must have been introduced to the Essene movement from outside, but it served as a sign of fundamental protest against the antisocial attitude of the upper class and their "Hellenized" way of life. A possible — but only indirect — Old Testament basis could be found in the opinion of the Torah that the soil of Eretz Israel belonged to God and was God's heritage lent out to his people, and therefore the common property was distributed by drawing lots among the twelve tribes. Another possibility is that the priestly meals in the sanctuary knew no private property. However, the harsh rejection of "private property and profit"[13] is a new attitude and typical of a protest movement in Hellenistic times.

As I have already remarked, the Essenes had the ambition to write pure biblical Hebrew. The majority of the numerous Aramaic texts in the caves probably came from outside the community. A still unsolved and probably unsolvable problem is the differentiation between genuine Essene, older proto-Essene texts, and those that did not originate in the movement itself. However, I think that those which are preserved in several copies were important for the Qumran people. The library contained even a few Greek scrolls, from which only small fragments survived. From Cave 7 we have nineteen Greek fragments, most of them unidentifiable, although one belongs to Exodus and another to the apocryphal letter of Jeremiah. From Cave 4 we have six texts of a paraphrase of Exodus, two of the Septuagint of Leviticus, and one of Numbers and Deuteronomy. We find Greek letters in the cryptic script of the *Horoscope* and in the

---

10. See A. Adam, ed., *Antike Berichte über die Essener* (Berlin: de Gruyter, 1961).

11. *koina ta philōn;* Aristotle *Nic. Eth.* 115b, 116b; cf. Hengel, *Judaica et Hellenistica,* 267ff.

12. *Ant* 15.371; Philo *Quod Omn. Prob.* 2 speaks about the teaching of the "most sacred *thiasos* of the Pythagoreans." O. Betz, "Die jüdischen Qumran-Essener als Modell für das griechische Gemeinschaftsideal," in *Internationales Hellenismus-Kolloquium (1994: Berlin, Germany),* ed. B. Funck (Tubingen: Mohr-Siebeck, 1996) 319-27.

13. For the formula, see Hengel, *Judaica et Hellenistica,* 268 n. 45.

Copper Scroll and ostraca.[14] The "overseer *(měbaqqēr)* over all the camps" in the *Damascus Document*[15] should be "one that has acquired mastery . . . in every language *(lāšōn)* according to their families." Of all foreign languages, Greek was the most important. Greek-speaking Jews had probably entered the community, and there was a relation between the Essenes in Eretz Israel and the Therapeutai of Philo's *De vita contemplativa* in Egypt.

The form of a strictly organized, hierarchically established free community, where entrance was an individual decision and a sign of personal conversion, is without analogy in ancient Israel. The conversion of a single person to the truth of the Torah and to the *yaḥad* has its closest parallel in the Greek conversion to a philosophical school and to the community of that school stamped by the teaching and authority of its leading or founding philosopher.

These schools had the legal form of an association and could possess property common to all. They had their fixed statutes about entrance and exclusion, the purpose and the obligations of the association, penal provisions, and honors — elements we find in the *Rule of the Community* or the *Damascus Document.* An important part is played by the founder of such a philosophical or religious association: Here we can refer to the "Teacher of Righteousness." The rights and duties of the different authorities were precisely regulated in statutes. As a rule the highest authority of a community in Hellenistic times was the plenary assembly, but in the Roman *collegia* the responsibility of the officials was greater. We have a similar distinction in the *Rule of the Community,* which emphasizes the role of the assembly, and the *Damascus Document,* where the role of the *měbaqqēr* is stressed. The entrance into the community was legally a private contract between the novice and the *yaḥad.* The jurisdiction of the community extended to the obligations under private law: the highest punishment was expulsion for life. This is similar to the gymnasia in Jerusalem, founded in 175 BCE by the high priest Jason, and to the synagogue communities in Ptolemaic Egypt, which were associations under private law. During the Ptolemaic rule in the third century the legal institution of private associations had become common.

The examination of the members before their admission has its parallel in the Greek *dokimasia* of young men who wanted to become citizens of a Greek polis or members of an association. The yearly repetition of such an examination in Qumran as a test for the progress of the members corre-

14. Hengel, *Judaica et Hellenistica,* 264.
15. CD 14:9ff. On the occurrence of the Greek language in the Qumran texts see the contribution of T. H. Lim in this volume. He supposes that some members knew and used the LXX.

sponds to the Greek agonistic ideal of education with permanent contests to measure the progress of intellectual and ethical improvement. The Greeks, for instance the Stoics, spoke here of *prokoptein,* to make progress, and of *teleiotēs,* the aim of perfection.[16] The Essenes aimed at perfect obedience to the Torah and perfect knowledge. Their ideal included self-control, taciturnity, and liberation from emotions, virtues that were typical philosophical attitudes for the Greeks. No wonder that in the *interpretatio graeca* of Philo and Josephus the Essenes appear as Jewish philosophers who could awaken the interest of Greeks and Romans, like the older Pliny and Dio Chrysostom.

The Intellectualization of Piety

Here we meet the center of our problem, the relation of the religious-theological opinions of the Essenes to those of the Greco-Roman world. Of course, we can not prove any direct influence of Greek thought, literature, philosophy, and religion upon the Qumran people. The source of their wisdom was the Torah of Moses and the manifold scriptures of the prophets. But there are relations that are connected with the *Zeitgeist.* For the first time in Jewish history a group developed a system of universal wisdom with a theocratic character, a system that encompassed God and creation, heaven and earth, humankind and history. We find the first steps in this direction in Deutero-Isaiah, the priestly code with its history of creation, or in Job. Above all, we encounter in Qumran a compact picture of history. Much more than in Greek thought, creation and history formed together an inseparable unity *ad maiorem Dei gloriam,* to the greater glory of God. This means that the system was totally theocentric, its point of departure being the free decision of God and his revelation. We could therefore speak here of "apocalyptic wisdom" in the full sense of the word. I remind you only of the well-known teaching of "the Master to teach all the Sons of Light" from the *Rule of the Community:* "From the God of knowledge comes all that is and that shall be. Before they came into being he established all their designs, and when they come into existence in their fixed times, they perform their task according to his glorious design. Nothing can be changed."[17] It sounds like a strictly deterministic philosophical tract. If we replace the "God of knowledge" with the "Logos" or

---

16. Cf. the young ambitious talmid *ḥakham* Paul in Gal 1:14: "I advanced *(proekopton)* in Judaism beyond many of my people of the same age"; Phil 3:5-6: "as to the law, a Pharisee . . . as to righteousness under the law, blameless."

17. 1QS 3:13-16.

the "Heimarmene," it could be of Stoic origin. We do not find abstract formulations like *kol hôweh wěnihyeh* in the Old Testament, but it could easily be translated into Greek: *panta ta onta kai ta esomena*.[18]

In the great hymn at the end of the *Rule* the author confesses: "The light of my heart beheld the mystery of what shall occur and is occurring forever." The *'ôr lěbîbî* is his cognitive faculty, his *nous*, enlightened by revelation of the mystery of what is and will be forever. We find none of these formulas in the Old Testament except the Persian loanword *raz* in its latest book, Daniel. It already sounds a bit like the language of Greek mysticism: *to mystērion tōn ontōn kai tōn esomenōn tōn aiōniōn*. This new abstract universal language[19] refers to the unity of creation and history and God's unchangeable plan for the world and its destiny, which the Stoics define as the *pronoia, heimarmenē*, or *boulē* of Zeus, and which leads, as in Qumran, to a strict determinism. In this abstract theological system of world and history the old enigmatic question of the origin of evil is solved by the dualistic teaching of the two spirits, which may be deduced from Iranian dualism and texts like Deutero-Isaiah 45:6 and 7: "I am the Lord and no other. I form light and create darkness. I make weal and create woe." Possibly this theory of the two spirits and their activity in humanity itself was mediated by Hellenistic sources, because we find it in Greek texts, especially in Philo:[20] "In every soul at its very birth there enter two powers, the salutary and the destructive. If the salutary one is victorious and prevails, the opposite one is too weak to attack. And if the latter prevails, no profit at all or little is obtained from the salutary one. Through these powers the world too was created."[21] Further Jewish and later Christian parallels with teaching about the two ways are found in the *Testament of Asher*, the *Shepherd of Hermas*, the *Didache*, and *Barnabas*.

This universal and systematic construction of a theocentric worldview with a strong rational element is an indication of the "intellectualization of piety" that we meet later — on a more juridical basis — with pharisaism, but also in Greek mysticism, Middle and Neoplatonism and Gnosticism. Only the wise, the sage, who possesses "knowledge," can be really pious. May I quote here Hillel:[22] "A brutish man dreads not sin, and an ignorant man (an '*am*

---

18. 1QS 3:15; Hengel, *Judaica et Hellenistica*, 2; Hengel, *Judaism and Hellenism*, 1.218ff.

19. Cf. 11:11, 18; 1QH 9:7ff. (1:7ff in Sukenik's edition).

20. Philo, *Quaestiones et solutiones in Exodum* 1.23.

21. Cf. Plutarch, *Isis and Osiris* 47, 369F-370C; Hengel, *Judaica, Hellenistica, et Christiana*, 283.

22. Hillel, *Pirke Abot* 2:6(5); cf. 1:13: "He that learns not is worthy of death." See Hengel, *Judaica et Hellenistica*, 280ff.

hā'āreṣ) cannot be saintly." Knowledge, *da'at*, becomes identical with deliverance or salvation, but this delivering knowledge does not come from rational thinking alone; it is ultimately based on divine revelation. This insight occurs in Qumran, in Philo, where Middle Platonism and Jewish faith in the Law revealed by God concur, and later in platonizing Christian Gnosticism and Neoplatonism. Another tendency of the time is the reluctance to use anthropomorphisms in describing God. In the *Songs of the Sabbath Sacrifice*, which is attested in the fragments of seven scrolls, we possess an angelic liturgy for God in his most holy, celestial sanctuary, comparable with the Hekhalot texts nearly a thousand years later. But unlike the Hekhalot texts, Daniel 7, the *Apocalypse of John*, or the Merkabah Vision of Ezekiel, we have no description of the appearance of God himself. He remains not only unapproachable but also beyond all description. The language is also very abstract. Thus, we find there twice, for the first time, the Hebrew neologism *'elohût*, Greek *theiotēs*, divinity.[23]

Nowhere in a Jewish text before the New Testament do we so often have the abstract *malkût, basileia*, which appears in the *Songs of the Sabbath Sacrifice* about twenty-five times and is repeatedly combined with *kābôd*. It should better be translated by majesty than by kingship. The tetragrammaton appears nowhere, and the angels are often called *'elohîm*. This language underlines the absolute transcendence of God, as we find it in another form in Philo.

To this "rational" order in creation belongs a strictly hierarchic angelology. The lowest angels are nothing other than personified powers of nature, similar to those in later Middle and Neoplatonism, where angels and divine powers *(dynameis)* can be identified. Already Posidonius thought that the atmosphere was populated by innumerable *daimones*, which are particles of fiery divine Logos or Pneuma. In 11QMelchizedek Michael/Melchizedek becomes the divine heavenly eschatological savior. He is a key pre-Christian figure for the later development of high Christology in the New Testament. Angelology also forms the background of the Essene demonology and their exorcisms. The demons are related to the fallen angels, an idea that we already find in Hesiod.[24] Probably the Essene gift of healing stressed by Josephus has an exorcistic background.[25] Thus, we possess a Psalms scroll with four incantations against demonic obsession.[26]

23. 4Q400 1 i 2; 4Q403 1 i 33ff.
24. Hengel, *Judaica et Hellenistica*, 284.
25. Josephus, *J.W.* 2.136; Hengel, *Judaica et Hellenistica*, 285 n. 97.
26. For the whole complex, see A. Lange, "The Essene Position on Magic and Divination," in *Legal Texts and Legal Issues: Proceedings of the Second Meeting of the Interna-*

Last but not least is the community's special interest in the regular, "lawful" movements of the stars; in astrology; in an exact sun calendar with fixed dates for the Sabbath and the festivals and individual horoscopes; and in physiognomy and predictions based upon the stars and physical human attributes — a typical phenomenon of the rationalism of the Hellenistic age. Physiognomy together with the astrological nativity played an important role for the ranking of members within the community.[27] Since the third century BCE, astrology and related "sciences" conquered the whole eastern Mediterranean area, with Alexandria as its center, and became the most modern "progressive" and highly esteemed science. The predominance of Stoic determinism stimulated this development. The Essenes seemed to be up with the time in this interest, which fitted into their ideal of a fixed order of creation and history.

Already in the third century BCE astrological Greek books were ascribed to Abraham, and according to the Samaritan Anonymus (otherwise known as Pseudo-Eupolemus) it was he who brought astrology, which had been revealed to Enoch upon heavenly tablets, to the West.[28]

Another field, which I can only mention, is the dualistic anthropology of the Essenes, which prepares for the Pauline dialectic between "flesh" and spirit. According to Josephus the Essenes believed in the immortality of the soul but not in bodily resurrection.[29] By now a few fragments have been published that speak about resurrection. These texts, however, may not belong to the genuine texts of the Essene movement. Yet there need not be any contradiction between resurrection and immortality; both forms of expectation were closely related for the Palestinian Jew. That the Essenes had some interest in the resurrection may be deduced from their special appreciation for the

---

tional Organisation for Qumran Studies Cambridge 1995, ed. Moshe Bernstein, Florentino García Martínez and John Kampen (STDJ 23; Leiden: Brill, 1996) 377-435.

27. See the learned article of P. S. Alexander, "Physiognomy, Initiation and Rank in the Qumran Community," in Geschichte-Tradition-Reflexion: Festschrift für Martin Hengel zum 70: Geburtstag, vol. 1, Judentum, ed. P. Schäfer (Tübingen: Mohr-Siebeck, 1996) 385-94.

28. Hengel, Judaism and Hellenism, 1.89; Hengel, Judaica et Hellenistica, 293.

29. Josephus, J.W. 2.154; Hengel, Judaica et Hellenistica, 288. On the dualistic anthropology of Qumran see H. Lichtenberger, Studien zum Menschenbild in den Texten der Qumrangemeinde (SUNT 15; Göttingen: Vandenhoeck & Ruprecht, 1980); and now, in relation to Paul, J. Frey, "Die paulinische Antithese von 'Fleisch und Geist' und die palästinisch-jüdische Weisheitstradition," ZNW 90 (1999) 45-77 (53-67). Admittedly, I don't think we can separate Essene and non-Essene texts quite so neatly as Frey does. The "non-Essene" texts could also have had essential significance for the Qumran Essenes. The best examples of this are the Enoch tradition and the book of Daniel.

book of Daniel, and its fulminant end in chapter 12, the latest book of the Old Testament canon, written about 165-164. Surely they did not expect such a massive bodily form as we find later in pharisaic texts. Their expectation of the eschatological punishment of the wicked also has earlier Greek parallels. Martin P. Nilsson in his great *History of Greek Religion* emphasizes the fact that "hell is a Greek invention."[30] Probably already in Isaiah 66:24, the last sentence of the book, and in Daniel 12:2b, which is shaped according to this model, we have a hint at the changed eschatological expectation of the new Hellenistic era.

Conclusion

The Essenes were, as I said at the beginning, probably the sharpest enemies of the new Greek wisdom in Eretz Israel. But even they could not escape the penetrating *Zeitgeist* of the new era. It is a law of the history of thought that the enemy is often influenced by the opinions against which he is fighting. The Essene movement is thus — I almost dare to say — a typical product of the new age in its sociological structure and organization, its use of technical progress, and its ideological system from abstract language up to the holistic system of creation and history, including astrology and magic. All of these together gave impetus to a rational theocentric interpretation of heaven and earth, presence and history. It is not by accident that the Essenes, the most fervent enemies of the Greek way of life and thought in Eretz Israel, became the subject of a successful *interpretatio graeca* in the reports of Jewish philosophers such as Philo and Josephus, and even pagan writers, and that before the discovery of the Qumran texts leading scholars supposed the Essenes were Pythagoreans in Jewish Palestine.[31]

The whole rich and neglected subject "Qumran and Hellenism," or more precisely "Essenism and Hellenistic civilization," would deserve a monographic treatment, surely a worthwhile but difficult task, for the investigator would have to master quite a number of different fields, sources, and problems. Here I can give no more than a very imperfect sketch of a variety of

30. M. P. Nilsson, *Geschichte der griechischen Religion* (3rd ed.; München: Beck, 1967) 2.558; Hengel, *Judaica et Hellenistica*, 289. About Essene eschatology see É. Puech, *La croyance des esséniens en la vie future: Immortalité, resurrection, vie éternelle? Histoire d'une croyance dans le Judaisme ancien* (2 vols.; Paris: Gabalda, 1993); see also "Auferstehung" in the index of Zimmermann, *Messianische Texte aus Qumran*, 531.

31. I. Levy, *La légende de Pythagore de Grèce en Palestine* (Paris: École des Hautes Études, 1927).

aspects, and this more from the outside, for I am not a Qumran specialist. There are especially three interrelated fields: dualistic anthropology, the heavenly world and astronomy, and exorcism and magic. The Essene community found a violent end in the Jewish War of 66-70 CE. The recovering Jewish community in postwar Palestine under pharisaic leadership expelled the Essenes, just like they did the Jewish Christians, as *mînîm*, that is, as heretics. But they "survived" in a threefold way:

1. By the astonishing remnants of their unique library in Qumran, discovered more than fifty years ago, which demonstrated the abundant richness of Jewish-Palestinian religion and thought in the late Second Temple era;

2. By the quite unusual reports of ancient writers in Greek and Latin, Jews and non-Jews, which reshaped their way of life, manners, and teachings in a strange and sometimes enigmatic *interpretatio graeca;* and

3. Last but not least, by their influence upon another movement in Eretz Israel that was about 150-200 years younger, also eschatologically oriented but a universal missionary movement and not secluded: earliest Christianity. The early Christian missionaries brought parts of the Essene message in quite a new messianic form to the nations of the world, that is, early Christian language, to the "Greeks." It may be further noticed that before the discovery of the Qumran texts all traditions about the Essenes and their writings were handed down to us by Christian tradition. Rabbinic Judaism had nearly entirely lost the memory of the Qumran Essenes and related groups.

The Qumran Scrolls, Multilingualism, and Biblical Interpretation

TIMOTHY H. LIM

Since the publication of Helmer Ringgren's *The Faith of Qumran: Theology of the Dead Sea Scrolls* in 1963,[1] scholarship on the Scrolls has refined, and in many cases also clarified, various aspects of our understanding of the Qumran community's exegesis of Holy Scripture.[2] There is now greater recognition of the pluriformity of the precanonical "Bible" or "Old Testament" and a decided preference for more neutral descriptive tags like "authoritative writings." There is more sophistication in our thinking about the sectarians as

---

1. This book first appeared in Swedish as *Tro och liv enligt Döda-havsrullarna* (Stockholm: Diakonistyrelsens Bokförlag, 1961) and was translated and published by Fortress Press in 1963. The edition cited here is the 1995 reissue (New York: Crossroad, 1995).

2. The literature on the pesharim is vast. Two of the most insightful recent discussions in English are P. S. Alexander's "The Bible in Qumran and Early Judaism," in *Text in Context: Essays by Members of the Society for Old Testament Studies*, ed. A. D. H. Mayes (Oxford: Clarendon, forthcoming) and Michael Fishbane's "Use, Authority, and Interpretation of Mikra at Qumran," in *Mikra: Text, Translation, Reading, and Interpretation,* ed. M. J. Mulder (Assen: Van Gorcum, 1988) 339-78. Good discussions of various facets of the pesharim and other sectarian literature can be found in Maurya P. Horgan, *Pesharim: Qumran Interpretations of Biblical Books* (Washington: Catholic Biblical Association, 1979) and Devorah Dimant, "Pesharim, Qumran," in *Anchor Bible Dictionary*, ed. D. N. Freedman (6 vols.; New York: Doubleday, 1992) 5.244-51.

A very different version of this paper was read at the Hebrew and Old Testament Studies seminar at the University of Edinburgh and the Qumran seminar jointly held by the Universities of Manchester and Sheffield.

a group that existed for some 220 years. The former portrayal of a monolithic Qumran community and emphasis upon the formative stage of the Maccabean period are giving way to a more nuanced regard for a living and evolving community with its changing interpretation of the biblical texts.[3]

It seems timely, therefore, to survey some of these scholarly advances and their implications for the religion of the Dead Sea Scrolls. The title of this essay, "The Qumran Scrolls, Multilingualism, and Biblical Interpretation," broadly covers the areas to be discussed, the first and third components of which are self-evident. The second element, "multilingualism," needs a prior word of explanation. The recent publication of a sectarian text, 4Q464, attesting as it does to the earliest instance of the phrase "the holy tongue" (*lāšon haqodeš* [לשון הקודש]),[4] raises the issue of which language the Qumran community spoke. Was it Hebrew or Aramaic? Since they lived in the multilingual context of Greco-Roman Palestine, were they able to read, write, and/ or speak more than one language? Did they know Greek?

Old Problems, New Perspectives

In Ringgren's synthesis of the theological beliefs of the Dead Sea Scrolls, he devotes only five pages to the Qumran pesharim in his introductory chapter, even though he states that this literary genre "seems to have enjoyed great popularity at Qumran."[5] Elsewhere references to the particular form of sectarian biblical interpretation appear only here and there in his systematic treatment of the doctrine of the community. What he does discuss are the problems of the etymology of the term *pesher,* its literary genre, and the exegetical methods that the pesharim share with the rabbinic Midrashim and Targumim.

3. See, e.g., Annette Steudel's discussion of the different ways Qumran exegetes understood the end time and its inevitable delay ("4QMidrEschat: 'A Midrash on Eschatology' [4Q174 + 4Q177]," in *The Madrid Qumran Congress: Proceedings of the International Congress on the Dead Sea Scrolls, Madrid, 18-21 March 1991,* ed. Julio Trebolle Barrera and Louis Vegas Montaner [2 vols.; Leiden: Brill, 1992] 2.538-41). See also John J. Collins, *Apocalypticism in the Dead Sea Scrolls* (London: Routledge, 1997) 64-68, who calculates the sectarian's end time to be around 60 BCE.

4. Esther Eshel and Michael Stone, in *Qumran Cave 4, XIV: Parabiblical Texts, Part 2,* ed. M. Broshi et al. (DJD 19; Oxford: Clarendon, 1995) 215-30. The editors call this text 4QExposition on the Patriarchs. An earlier Hebrew article by them, "The Holy Tongue at the End of Days in Light of a Fragment from Qumran," *Tarbiz* 62 (1993) 169-78, focuses on the sectarian belief in the reunification of all human languages into one holy tongue, possibly Hebrew, at the end time.

5. Ringgren, *Faith of Qumran,* 7.

Etymology

Following the work of William H. Brownlee, Karl Elliger, and especially Geza Vermes, Ringgren discusses the technical term *pesher* as a noun based upon the Semitic root *pšr* (פשר), which is attested in Akkadian, Aramaic, Hebrew, and Arabic and means "to loosen, to release, to interpret." In the Hebrew Bible it occurs only in Hebrew at Ecclesiastes 8:1 ("Who is like the wise man? And who knows the interpretation [*pešer*] of a thing?"), but several times in the book of Daniel it appears as an Aramaic noun and verb. In chapters 2 and 4 it is used to describe the interpretation of dreams and visions, and in chapter 5, the meaning of the inscription "mene, mene, tekel, parsin" (v. 26).

> This is the interpretation (*pšr* פשר) of the matter: "mene," God has numbered the days of your kingdom and brought it to an end; "tekel," you have been weighed in the balances and found wanting; "peres," your kingdom is divided and given to the Medes and Persians. (vv. 26-28)

Although the more common root in the Hebrew Bible for expressing "to interpret" is *ptr* (פתר), the verbal and nominal forms of which occur in the oneirocritical context of Joseph's dream interpretations in Genesis 40 and 41, it is this passage in Daniel 5 that is particularly germane to the pesharim. Notwithstanding its numerous difficulties — the lexical variation between inscription and interpretation and the etymological derivation of the key terms[6] — this passage too interprets a written text, rather than visions or dreams, as it separates the inscription into its three elements, *mene, tekel,* and *peres* (for *parsin*). Moreover, it contemporizes the meaning of the mysterious writing on the wall by interpreting it as a prophecy about Belshazzar and his kingdom, the putative historical context of chapter 5.

In Qumran biblical exegesis, the technical term *pešer* means the interpretation or uncovering of the meaning of a biblical word, phrase, or verse. Typically, it is incorporated into a formula that introduces a comment (e.g., "the interpretation [*pešer*] of the verse concerns . . ." or "its interpretation [*pišro*] is . . .").[7] In many passages it shares with Daniel 5 the segmentation of key words and phrases of the biblical verse. Just as Daniel 5 atomizes "mene," "tekel," and "peres," and applies them to Belshazzar and his kingdom, so too the pesharim excises the name "Lebanon" from Habakkuk 2:16 and interprets

---

6. See John J. Collins, *Daniel* (Minneapolis: Fortress Press, 1993) 250-52.

7. For a list of the formulas, see Horgan, *Pesharim*, 239-44 and Moshe Bernstein's largely descriptive survey of the same, "Introductory Formulas for Citation and Re-Citation of Biblical Verses in the Qumran Pesharim," *DSD* 1 (1994) 30-70.

it as a reference to the sectarian community. This contemporizing move equates "Lebanon" with "the Council of the Community," another name for the Qumran sect (1QpHab 12:3-4), and is based upon a tradition that exegetically identifies Lebanon with the temple of Jerusalem — since wood from there was used to construct the building — and the temple with the Qumran community.

As a verb, the root is extant in 1QpHab 2:8 (so also in 1Q22), where it states that God has set understanding in the Teacher of Righteousness so that he might interpret (לפשור) all the words of his servants the prophets. The privilege that the Teacher *par excellence* enjoyed extended even beyond the biblical prophet's comprehension of his own oracles: "for God told Habakkuk to write down that which would come upon the final generation, but He did not make known to him the completion of the end-time" (1QpHab 7:1-3). But to the Teacher of Righteousness God had revealed "all the mysteries of the words of his servants the prophets" (1QpHab 7:4-5). While the prophet Habakkuk understood only in part, the chosen priest of the Qumran community did so fully. The Teacher of Righteousness, with divine sanction, inaugurated this sectarian form of biblical interpretation, and his followers carried it forward by composing exegetical works that modern scholarship now describes as pesharim.

Literary Genre

In the past fifty years there have been numerous studies that have compared the pesharim to other Jewish and Christian literature. Helmer Ringgren mentions the similarities to *Targum Jonathan*, *Midrash Shir Ha-shirim*, and the *Demotic Chronicle*. Many other literary genres, of course, could be added, and while some of the literary parallels are illuminating, it is the sum total of exegetical features — the line by line structure of the commentary, the atomization of key words, the contemporizing of biblical prophecy, the verbal plays, the vital role of the Teacher of Righteousness — that makes the pesher genre distinctive. It is fair, I believe, to characterize the pesher as *sui generis*, "of its own kind," or unique.

Let me, however, take up a specific point in more detail, namely, the suggestion that the Greek equivalent of pesher is *tout' estin* (τοῦτ' ἔστιν), the Greek phrase found several times in the Pauline letters and meaning simply "that is." Unfortunately, such a suggestion is imprecise and potentially misleading.

Charles K. Barrett, one of the most eminent British New Testament scholars of the past generation, transposes Paul's interpretation of Deuteronomy 30:12 in Romans 10:6-7 in order to bring out the pesher terminology that he finds latent in the expression "this is" or "that is."[8] Romans 10:6-7 says:

> Do not say in your heart, Who shall ascend into heaven? That is, to bring Christ down; or, Who shall descend into the deep? That is, to bring Christ up from the dead.

Barrett's modified version adds the term pesher to these verses in Romans 10.

> Do not say in your heart, Who shall ascend into heaven? The *pešer* of this is, Who shall bring Christ down? Do not say in your heart, Who shall descend into the deep? The *pešer* of this is, Who shall bring Christ up from the dead?

Similarly, E. Earle Ellis, in a recent contribution, states that *houtos (estin)* (οὗτος [ἔστιν]) is a variant of *tout' estin* and "is an equivalent of Qumran *pesher*."[9]

The Hebrew equivalent of *tout' estin* or *houtos (estin)* is not *pēšer* but the third person, feminine or masculine, independent pronoun *hy'* or *hw'* (היא or הוא), used with or without a demonstrative and substantive. So, for example, in 4QpIsa[b] 2:11, those who rejected the law of Yahweh in Isaiah 5:24c-25 are equated with the scoffers who reside in Jerusalem: "*This is* [*hy'*][10] the congregation of the scoffers who are in Jerusalem."

We are not told who these scoffers were, apart from the fact that they resided in Jerusalem, since the pesherist is writing for an insider audience. With the exception of the *Pesher on Nahum*, there is no explicitly historical reference in the Qumran Bible commentaries. What we are faced with typically is the situation of a biblical reference, say to "the Chaldeans" in Habakkuk, being identified in the commentary with "the Kittim." Who these Chaldeans were in the time of Habakkuk remains obscure, even though scholars often identify them with the Neo-Babylonians (between 612 BCE [the fall of Nineveh] and 605 BCE [the Battle of Carchemish]) in the period leading up the fall of Jerusalem in 587 BCE.

---

8. C. K. Barrett, "The Interpretation of the Old Testament in the New," in *Cambridge History of the Bible*, vol. 1, *From the Beginnings to Jerome*, ed. P. R. Ackroyd (Cambridge: Cambridge University Press, 1970) 392.

9. E. Earle Ellis, "Biblical Interpretation in the New Testament Church," in *Mikra*, 696-97.

10. Note that in Qumran Hebrew the independent pronoun agrees with the predicate that follows it.

A step removed and in the sectarian commentary, the Chaldeans, whoever they were, are now identified with "the Kittim." We have to deduce that "the Kittim" is most likely a coded reference to the Romans, but the pesherist himself does not tell us this. The Kittim who sacrifice to their standards resemble the Roman soldiers who used to worship their signa and weapons of war. The Qumran pesharim (with the sole exception of 4QpNah) have been described as an interpretation from "code to code," that is, from biblical code to sectarian code. It is a form of commentary that is directed toward those who are in the know.

The Greek equivalent of Hebrew *pešer* is *lusis*, "loosening, releasing, unraveling," as the LXX of Ecclesiastes 8:1 translates. Paul uses *lusis* only once in his letters, but not in the exegetical sense of interpreting an enigmatic word or saying. In 1 Corinthians 7:27 *lusis* has the legal sense of separation or divorce ("Are you bound to a wife? Do not seek separation [*lusis*]").

The linguistic fudge that blurs the exegetical markers *tout' estin* or *houtos (estin)* with *pešer* is symptomatic of a greater malaise. It is based upon the theory that there apparently exists a hybrid genre called "midrash pesher," which Paul also uses in his letters, the terminological equation being one important cog in the theory. Some twenty years ago, Matthew Black had dismissed this genre "as a modern invention probably best forgotten,"[11] but it continues to be discussed in New Testament scholarship as though midrash pesher actually exists. I have criticized this view recently by questioning one of its main assumptions that the term "midrash" is used in a titular sense in the Qumran scrolls and refers to the exegetical precursor of the rabbinic Midrashim.[12] My conclusion is that "midrash" in 4Q174 is best translated as "a study of" or "an instruction deriving from" Psalm 1:1, rather than as the title of an exegetical work.

Second, there is much greater variety in the literary genre of pesher than was once recognized. In *The Faith of Qumran*, Ringgren confines himself to what are now known as the *pesharim continus*, sectarian commentaries that follow larger and smaller passages from the biblical text. There are fifteen or sixteen texts of the continuous pesharim type (depending upon whether one counts 3QpIsa), with interpretations of the books of Isaiah, Psalms, and five of the twelve minor prophets. Since 1969, however, most scholars have adopted a more nuanced view of the pesharim, following Jean Carmignac in

11. Matthew Black, "The Christological Use of the Old Testament in the New Testament," *NTS* 18 (1971) 1.

12. Timothy H. Lim, "Midrash Pesher in the Pauline Letters," in *The Scrolls and the Scriptures: Qumran Fifty Years After,* ed. Stanley E. Porter and Craig A. Evans (Sheffield: Sheffield Academic Press, 1997) 280-92.

distinguishing between the *pesher continu* and *pesher thematique*.[13] Unlike the continuous running commentary of the former, based as it is upon the structure of the biblical passage, the thematic pesher draws its biblical proof texts from several scriptural sources in order to support a topic. Thus, for example, 11Q13 cites Isaiah 52:7; 61:1, 2-3; Leviticus 25:9, 13; Deuteronomy 15:2; Psalm 7:7-8, 82:1; and Daniel 9:25 to bolster its depiction of the mysterious biblical figure of Melchizedek as the eschatological redeemer.

Further refinements of Carmignac's classification have led to the recognition that pesher can be seen as both a literary genre and a method of biblical exegesis.[14] As an exegetical method, it can be used to interpret not simply texts, but a concept (e.g., the ages of creation in 4Q180; Abraham's promise in 4Q464) or a biblical law (e.g., interpretation of Lev 5 in 4Q159).

In 1991 I took this analysis several steps further.[15] I showed that even within the continuous pesharim there is variety, a conclusion that has now been independently corroborated by Moshe Bernstein.[16] The sixteen continuous pesharim should not be seen as attesting to a monolithic literary genre, but to a range of slightly different types of exegesis. So, for example, of the five pesharim on Isaiah, the commentaries of the second, third, and fifth (4Q162-163, 165) pesharim are little more than short glosses on the biblical text, as our above example of 4QIsa[b] shows. By comparison, 4QIsa[d] (4Q164) is more akin to what is considered as typical pesherite exegesis as it reads into the description of the postexilic restoration of Jerusalem in Isaiah 54 the establishment of the council of the community (frg. 1, ll. 1-5).

> *I shall establish you in sapphi[res]* (54:11) [The interpretation of the verse is tha]t they established the council of the community [among] the priests

13. Jean Carmignac, "Le document de Qumrân sur Melkisédeq," *RevQ* 7 (1969-71) 342-78.

14. Both George J. Brooke, "Qumran Pesher: Towards a Redefinition of a Genre," *RevQ* 10 (1979) 483-503 and Dimant, "Pesharim," 249-50, helpfully dissect the pesherite method into several exegetical steps of identification of subjects, correlation of details, and the use of various exegetical techniques. See also, Menahem Kister's discussion of allusions in "Biblical Phrases and Hidden Biblical Interpretations and Pesharim," in *The Dead Sea Scrolls: Forty Years of Research*, ed. Devorah Dimant and Uriel Rappaport (STDJ 10; Leiden: Brill, 1992) 27-39.

15. Timothy H. Lim, "Attitudes to Holy Scripture in the Qumran Pesharim and Pauline Letters," D.Phil. thesis, Oxford University, 1991. See now idem, *Holy Scripture in the Qumran Commentaries and Pauline Letters* (Oxford: Clarendon, 1997), ch. 8.

16. Bernstein, "Introductory Formulas," 69-70. Bernstein's 1994 analysis of the pesharim as falling along a continuum seems to echo my own 1991 conclusion that "between the thematic and continuous categories is 4QpIsa[c]" (Lim, "Attitudes to Holy Scripture," 105).

and peop[le]. [mutilated end of line] the congregation of his chosen ones as a stone of sapphire among the stones. [*And I shall set*] *all your battlements of agate* (54:12). Its interpretation concerns (*pišro 'l* [פשרו על]) the twelve men in their council of the community who will enlighten by the decision of Urim and Thumim [ ].

Next, I noted that there is also a range of exegeses within one pesher. Not every passage of a continuous pesher can be characterized as a fulfillment interpretation. For example, in 4QpPs[a] (4Q171) the commentary varies from the contemporizing exegetical turns of identifying the biblical figures of the wicked, righteous, Manasseh, and Ephraim with the wicked priest, Teacher of Righteousness, Sadducees, and Pharisees, to a mere paraphrase of Psalm 37:39. Likewise, the last columns of the *Pesher on Habakkuk* are no more than glosses on the woes against idolatry of Habakkuk 2:18-20.

Finally, I suggested that pesherite exegesis shares a number of features in common with other forms of biblical interpretation that do not contain the technical term pesher.[17] This can be illustrated by comparing columns 4 and 5 of 4Q252. In column 4, the Qumran exegete interprets the blessings of Jacob by using pesher in its customary manner, in the introductory formula of the commentary.

> The blessings of Jacob: Reuben, you are my firstborn and the first fruit of my strength, exceeding in destruction and exceeding in power. Unstable as water, you shall no longer exceed, (because) you went up to your father's bed. Then you defiled it. On his couch you went up (Gen 49:3-4) [vacat] Its interpretation is that (*pišro 'šr* [פשרו אשר]) he reproved him (i.e., Reuben) for having lain with Bilhah his concubine.

In column 5, the style of exegesis is identical, but the term *pesher* is not used.

> *A ruler shall not depart from the tribe of Judah.* (Gen 49:10) When Israel will have the dominion, one sitting in it (i.e., the throne) for David will not be cut off. For the *staff* is the covenant of the kingdom, the clans of Israel are *the standards,* until the coming of the messiah of righteousness, the scion of David. For to him and his seed has been given the covenant of the kingdom to his people for eternal generations which he kept.[18]

17. Brooke, "Qumran Pesher," 492, has argued that the technical term is not vital to the identification of the pesher genre. I would prefer a stricter use of "pesher" for exegeses that explicitly include this term, recognizing all the while the similarity of some of its techniques with other types of biblical interpretations.

18. Translation by George J. Brooke, *Qumran Cave 4, XVII: Parabiblical Texts, Part 3* (Oxford: Clarendon, 1996) 205.

Previously known as 4QPatriarchal Blessing, this messianic interpretation of Genesis 49:10 typifies pesherite exegesis without ever mentioning the term *pesher.*

I have suggested that should we wish to privilege the Qumran sectarian form of exegesis, then the term *pesheresque,* "like a pesher," can be used to describe other ancient interpretations that do not contain the technical term *pesher.*

Pesherite Biblical Quotations: Textual or Exegetical Variants?

In the past fifty years, one of the persistent problems of research is the evaluation of biblical quotations found in the pesharim.[19] Unnecessarily complicating what is essentially a textual and exegetical analysis is the occasional association of the topic with more theological issues of authority and canon. To be sure, the subjects are related, but they are also distinct and can be usefully discussed separately. Judging whether variants found in the citations are textual or exegetical does have implications for scriptural authority, but such ramifications are not necessary at the primary analytical level. The foremost issue is not which of the books of the Hebrew Bible the sectarians considered canonical or authoritative, but what the pesherite variants mean.

Another difficulty is the prominence of the pesharim in Qumran and biblical scholarship, *quod nimia familiaritas parit contemptum* ("for overfamiliarity breeds contempt"). The pesharim, especially the virtually completely preserved scroll of the *Pesher on Habakkuk,* are some of the best-known Dead Sea Scrolls by virtue of their inherent historical value and early publication. While I would not want to overplay what Bernstein calls "the significance of firstness,"[20] the familiarity, whether real or imagined, with the pesharim that is sometimes felt detracts from the issues at hand. Often the conclusion is drawn that the biblical text lying before the pesherists is a Masoretic Text (MT). But this is often based upon casual observation while reading the pesher rather than by following a rigorously controlled method. The common assumption that the pesherists had proto-MT texts that they then altered for their exegetical purposes becomes more difficult to sustain with our increasing recognition of the plurality of text types in this period.[21]

19. See Lim, *Holy Scripture,* ch. 5.
20. Bernstein, "Introductory Formulas," 65-70.
21. See Lim, *Holy Scripture,* ch. 5. Emanuel Tov, "The Significance of the Texts from the Judaean Desert for the History of the Text of the Hebrew Bible: A New Synthesis," in *Qumran Between the Old and New Testaments,* ed. Frederick Cryer and Thomas L. Thomp-

The study of the pesherite biblical quotations raises fundamental questions about how one classifies any biblical text. Within the context of the textual diversity of this period, can one speak sensibly about "a variant," exgetical or otherwise? From which standard is this reading seen to be diverging? Was the proto-MT the standard text and all others "vulgar" or sectarian copies?[22]

Qumran scholarship has clarified a number of these textual issues. First, it is no longer possible to posit the proto-MT as the standard from which all others varied. In the context of textual diversity, the proto-MT text is one text type, albeit an important and well-attested witness, among many. However, the description of a reading as "a variant" is for heuristic purposes only. It is meant to describe formally the relationship of one reading to an arbitrary textual standard, which by convention is the MT, Septuagint, or Samaritan Pentateuch. There is no good reason why a reading from the Isaiah pesharim should not be characterized as a variant vis-à-vis the Great Isaiah Scroll, but this is not done by convention.

Second, one has to distinguish the tasks of classifying the pesherite biblical texts and identifying an exegetical variant. Even if, for the sake of argument, the pesherite biblical texts are thought to be proto-MT, it will have to be admitted that this text type includes numerous divergent readings from the medieval MT, say as represented in the Leningrad Codex.[23] Each variant will have to be evaluated individually to determine whether it originated from the exegete or his source.

The pesherists did alter the very words of their scriptural texts, but these exegetical modifications have to be demonstrated by detecting internal incongruences rather than by simply comparing the quotations to the MT.[24] ·

---

son (JSOTSup 290; Sheffield: Sheffield Academic Press, 1998) 282-83, has helpfully outlined the maximalist and minimalist positions. I shall be addressing this topic in the Scriptorium Conference entitled "The Text of the Hebrew Bible in Light of the Discoveries in the Judaean Desert," 19-22 June 2000.

22. Lim, *Holy Scripture*, ch. 2.

23. There never existed a single text of the MT (see Harry Orlinsky, "Prolegomenon," in Christian D. Ginsburg's *Introduction to the Massoretico-Critical Edition of the Hebrew Bible* [New York: KTAV, 1966]). The Leningrad Codex, which forms the basis of the standard critical edition *Biblia Hebraica Stuttgartensia*, is now available in a superb facsimile edition (*The Leningrad Codex: A Facsimile Edition* [Grand Rapids/Leiden: Eerdmans/Brill, 1998]).

24. For a clear instance of exegetical modification, see my discussion of Hab 2:17 in 1QpHab 12 in *Holy Scripture*, 97-98.

The Languages of the Qumran Scrolls

The Qumran scrolls are written in three languages, Hebrew, Aramaic, and Greek. Of the 822 texts listed in the official catalogue, 61 (or 7 percent) are written in Aramaic, 25 (or 3 percent) in Greek, and the remaining 736 (or 90 percent) in Hebrew.[25] It is difficult to say what these proportions represent, since the Qumran library is a heterogeneous collection, containing as it did books that reflect the religious beliefs of the sectarian community as well as others that belong to Second Temple Judaism generally or those that circulated among like-minded groups. So, for instance, the biblical scrolls were not sectarian, despite what some would have us believe, but were the authoritative writings of all Jews who lived in the period dating to the turning of the era.

One of the recently edited and published texts, 4Q464, raises for me the entire question of the language of the Qumran community, for it contains the earliest instance of the phrase "the holy tongue" *(lašon ha-qodeš)*. According to Michael Stone and Esther Eshel, the official editors of the text, this concept of "the holy tongue" should be connected with the "pure speech" of Zephaniah 3:9 and "the tongue of creation" of *Jubilees* 12:26-27. Accordingly, the pesherite exegesis reflects the Qumran community's belief that the curse of Babel has been reversed and that now all nations will again speak a pure, single tongue, perhaps Hebrew, forever.[26]

The tradition embedded in *Jubilees* 12 is particularly appropriate for this interpretation, given the authoritative status of this book in the community:

> And I opened his (i.e., Abraham's) mouth and his ears and his lips and I began to speak with him in Hebrew, in the tongue of creation. And he took his father's books — and they were written in Hebrew — and he copied them.

Did the Qumran community consider Hebrew to be "the holy tongue"? This is certainly how later rabbinic tradition understood *lašon ha-qodeš*. If so, what does this imply about the language of the Qumran community?

I believe that Stone and Eshel have advanced a possible interpretation of 4Q464. However, I would advise caution in this matter, as the text is very

---

25. The official list of Qumran texts continues to change as editors sift, rearrange, and study the fragments. Comprehensive catalogues of documents and photographs can be found in Stephen A. Reed et al., *The Dead Sea Scrolls Catalogue: Documents, Photographs, and Museum Inventory Numbers* (SBLRBS 32; Atlanta: Scholars Press, 1994); E. Tov, *The Dead Sea Scrolls on Microfiche: Companion Volume* (Leiden: Brill, 1993; rev. ed. 1995), and Timothy Lim, *The Dead Sea Scrolls Electronic Reference Library,* vol. 1 (Oxford/Leiden: Oxford University Press/Brill, 1997).

26. Broshi, *Qumran Cave 4, XIV* (DJD 19), 215-30.

fragmentary. What we are reading in column 2 of fragment 3 are isolated phrases and not even sentences. Moreover, the reversal of the curse of Babel and the fragmentation of human language need not take on the form of speaking one holy language, Hebrew. In Acts 2, the eschatological reversal of the curse of Babel at Pentecost is not the speaking of one tongue, but the ability of the God-fearing Jerusalem Jews to understand and utter all languages.

The evidence of 4Q464 is suggestive, but not decisive. The view that the language of the Qumran community was Hebrew can be further supported by two other considerations, the cumulative force of which would tip the balance in favor of Hebrew. First, the undisputed "sectarian" documents are written in Hebrew. The *Rule of the Community*, the *Damascus Document*, and biblical interpretations have no counterparts in any Aramaic or Greek text. These reflect the sectarian orientation of the community or communities. Second, there is linguistic evidence from the *Copper Scroll* and more recently from 4QMMT that Hebrew remained a viable alternative. The use of several forms of the relative pronoun, *'šr* (אשר), *š'* (אש) or *š* (ש) in 4QMMT, for example, is explained as evidence that Hebrew was a living, spoken language.[27]

The multilingual context of Palestine between 200 BCE and 100 CE, however, does raise the question of whether the Qumran community knew any other language. Did they compose the *Genesis Apocryphon* in Aramaic? Could they read the Aramaic versions of Tobit (4Q196-199) as well as the Hebrew one (4Q200)? Did they in fact translate Job into Aramaic (11QTgJob) because of the difficulties of the original Hebrew?

What I have begun to do is investigate the multilingual context of the Qumran community by examining the other language attested among the Qumran scrolls, namely, Greek. Did the Qumran community know Greek? If so, how much Greek did they know? Were they able to converse fluently in it? Could they write a literary composition, or is their written language largely functional — writing short missives and notes? Were they fluent enough in both languages to be able to translate a text from Hebrew into Greek?[28]

27. E. Qimron (*Qumran Cave 4, V: Miqṣat Maʿaseh ha-Torah* [Oxford: Clarendon, 1994] 104) states: "It would thus appear that the language of MMT reflects, more than that of any other Qumran scroll, the Hebrew actually spoken at Qumran. This spoken language was distinct from the later MH, and it contained elements not known to us from other phases of the Hebrew language." Recently, William M. Schniedewind ("Qumran Hebrew as an Antilanguage," *JBL* 118 [1999] 235-52) suggests that Qumran Hebrew was intentionally created to set the speakers apart from others, but the linguistic features that he adduces may be due to the liturgical and religious nature of most of the Qumran scrolls or the archaizing tendencies of those who drew their inspiration from the past.

28. The languages of Palestine in the Greco-Roman period is a much debated sub-

Of the twenty-five Greek texts found at Qumran, nineteen of them were found in Cave 7 and the others in Cave 4.[29] The nineteen texts of Cave 7 are all very fragmentary. Two of these have been identified by the principal editors as LXX Exodus (7Q1) and the *Epistle of Jeremiah* (7Q2). The remaining seventeen are Greek but too badly preserved for any secure identification, despite the strenuous efforts of some to argue that 7Q5 is a fragment of Mark 6:52-53, that 7Q4 is 1 Timothy 3:16–4:1, or that 7Q10 is 2 Peter 1:15.[30]

The remaining six Greek texts all come from Cave 4. Two are of Leviticus (4Q119 and 4Q120) and there is one each of Numbers (4Q121) and Deuteronomy (4Q122). 4Q127 is taken to be a paraphrase of Exodus, and 4Q126 is written in Greek but remains unidentified.

Features of Greek language are also found in a handful of other documents. The *Copper Scroll* (3Q15) contains seven ciphers of Greek letters, which some have argued are measurements of weight, abbreviations of numerical values,[31] or the beginning of names.[32] Moreover, there are five or six

---

ject. A useful summary of the positions can be found in Greg Horsley's doctoral dissertation, now published in *New Documents Illustrating Early Christianity* (North Ryde: Macquarie University, 1989), especially ch. 1. It is not possible at this point to say to what degree and in what sense members of the Qumran community were multilingual.

29. The official list also includes a text written in Greek called *Account of Cereal gr* (4Q350) (Tov, *Companion*, 41). It will be edited by Hannah Cotton in DJD 36. I thank Emanuel Tov for his helpful answer to my query.

30. Carsten Thiede, *The Earliest Gospel Manuscript? The Qumran Fragment 7Q5 and Its Significance for New Testament Studies* (London: Paternoster, 1992), has vigorously defended Jose O'Callaghan's identification of New Testament passages in the Cave 7 fragments. Recent studies have identified these as fragments of the book of *Enoch* (G. W. Nebe, "7Q4: Möglichkeit und Grenze einer Identifikation," *RevQ* 13 [1988] 629-33; É. Puech, "Notes sur les fragments grecs du manuscrit 7Q4 = 1Hénoch 103 et 105," *RB* [1996] 596-60; idem, "Sept Fragments Grecs de la *Lettre d'Hénoch* [1 Hén 100, 103 et 105] dans la grotte 7 de Qumrân [= 7QHén gr]," *RevQ* 18 [1997] 312-23; and E. A. Muro, "The Greek Fragments of Enoch from Qumran Cave 7 [7Q4, 7Q8 & 7Q12 = 7QEngr = Enoch 103:3-4, 7-8]," *RevQ* 70 [1997] 307-12). While the latter identification is less sensational, it is no less difficult than the former as column widths are not preserved but assumed and identifications are open to challenge. See recently Victoria Spottorno, "Can Methodological Limits Be Set in the Debate on the Identification of 7Q5?" *DSD* 6 (1999) 66-77.

31. E. Ullendorf, "The Greek Letters of the Copper Scroll," *VT* 11 (1961) 227-28. However, É. Puech, "Quelque résultats d'un nouvel examen du Rouleau du Cuivre," *RevQ* 18 (1997) 183, on the basis of the Electricité de France facsimile copy, argues that the reading Θε, and not Ξε, is certain.

32. So Bargil Pixner, "Unravelling the Copper Scroll Code (3Q15): A Study of the Topography of 3Q15," *RevQ* 11 (1982-84) 335-45, followed by Puech, "Quelque résultats," 183.

loanwords occurring in the document, mostly architectural terms, from the Greek — for example, *peristyle, stoa, exhedra.*[33]

In 4Q186, two Greek letters, alpha (A) and beta (B), are used in the Cryptic script. Philip Alexander has plausibly argued that this document, a physiognomic and horoscope text, is not only sectarian, but a central document for the Qumran community and its vetting of novices. According to CD 13:12, the Guardian examines a novice and inscribes him in his place according to "his rank in the lot of light," and this physiognomic test may well have been applied to such volunteers.[34] Martin Hengel has also argued that 4Q186 is one of the direct points of contact between the Qumran community and Hellenism.[35]

Finally, there are a few Greek names that have been transliterated into Hebrew, namely, Demetrius (דמי[טרוס]) and Antiochus (אנתיכוס) in 4QpNah 3-4 i 2-3, and (פותלאיס]) Potlais or Ptolas in 4Q468g.[36] John M. Allegro's suggestion that 4QTherapeia is a medical document written in transliterated Greek, Aramaic, and Hebrew was debunked by Joseph Naveh, who argued that it is a writing exercise by a fairly skilled person practicing his scribal skills.[37]

I believe that at least some members of the Qumran community must have been able to read Greek. The Greek biblical texts in Caves 4 and 7 were not just library copies that no one was able to consult. The alternative scenario, that the Qumran community that existed for some 220 years (roughly between 150 BCE and 70 CE) never admitted a member who knew any Greek, seems improbable to me.

Once we admit this multilingual context as a possibility, avenues of investigation are opened up. Let me give you just one example of how we can think anew.

In the *Pesher on Habakkuk,* it is evident that the Qumran commentator had more than one text of Habakkuk in front of him. The prime example of

33. See J. T. Milik, *Les 'Petites Grottes' de Qumrân* (DJD 3; Oxford: Clarendon, 1961) 230.

34. P. S. Alexander, "Physiognomy, Initiation and Rank in the Qumran Community," in *Geschichte-Tradition-Reflexion: Festschrift für Martin Hengel zum 70: Geburtstag,* vol. 1, *Judentum,* ed. P. Schäfer (Tübingen: Mohr-Siebeck, 1996) 387-88.

35. Martin Hengel, "Qumrân und der Hellenismus," in *Qumrân: Sa piété, sa théologie et son milieu,* ed. M. Delcor (Paris-Gembloux: Leuven, 1978) 333-72.

36. See Magen Broshi, "Ptolas and the Archelaus Massacres (4Q468g = 4QHistorical Text B)," *JJS* 49 (1998) 345.

37. Joseph Naveh, "A Medical Document or a Writing Exercise? The So-Called 4Q Therapeia," *IEJ* 36 (1986) 52-55 + plate 1. Thanks to George Brooke for reminding me of this text.

this is the citation of two versions of Habakkuk 2:16. In the MT it reads "you will be sated with dishonor instead of glory, drink also *and be uncircumcised* (הערל)." This reading of "be uncircumcised" has puzzled many commentators. By comparison, in the pesherite quotation of Habakkuk 2:16, the verse reads "and you will be sated with dishonor instead of glory, drink also and *stagger* (הרעל)." In the context, the notion of a drunkard staggering is more understandable than the notion of being uncircumcised.

This variant is found in the double translation of the LXX of "staggering and tottering" (διασαλεύθητι καὶ σείσθητι). The pesherist, however, must also have known the MT, since the reading "to be uncircumcised" also appears in the comment when the pesherist charges the priest of more dishonor than glory "because he did not circumcise the foreskin of (עורלת) his heart" (1QpHab 11:13).

The pesherist was evidently aware of variant readings of Habakkuk in 2:16, and this is also borne out elsewhere. In Habakkuk 1:17, the MT reads "Is he then to keep on emptying *his net* (חרמו), and mercilessly slaying nations for ever?" Here the rhetorical question mixes the metaphor of fishing with that of a vengeful sword. In the quotation of the verse in column 6, however, the text is smoother and the metaphor is unmixed: "Therefore he will empty *his sword* (חרבו), slaying nations continually and he will not be merciful." The main difference between the two is the reading of "his sword" as the instrument that the Kittim, or Romans, used to slaughter many, the young and old, men and women, and even pregnant mothers.

So far as I am aware, the reading "his sword" is not preserved in any extant Hebrew manuscript but is found in the scroll of the Minor Prophets from Naḥal Ḥever (8HevXIIgr): μαχαιραν αυτου.[38] This scroll is dated to the first century BCE,[39] contemporaneous with the time of the composition of the *Pesher on Habakkuk,* and was found in the "Cave of Horrors" only a few miles south of Qumran. Given the multilingual context of first-century Palestine, it remains possible that the Habakkuk pesherist not only was able to read Greek, but did so on this occasion from a manuscript that was known to have circulated in his neighborhood.

Let me be explicit: I am not saying that the reading "his sword" is the more original reading. I am not claiming that the Hebrew variant of the

38. See Emanuel Tov, with R. A. Kraft and P. J. Parsons, *The Greek Minor Prophets Scrolls from Nahal Ḥever (8HevXIIgr) (The Seiyal Collection I)* (Oxford: Clarendon, 1990) 53, 152, and plate XI. Also attested in a marginal note of the OG mss 86 and the Bohairic. LXX agrees with the MT (τὸ ἀμφίβληστρον αὐτοῦ).

39. Parsons (Tov, *Greek Minor Prophets,* 26) dates this document to the later first century BCE.

pesher and the Greek reading of the scroll could not be ultimately traced to a single Hebrew source. What I am suggesting is that the sectarian commentator may have, on this occasion, used a Greek text of Habakkuk that was known to have circulated along the same western shore of the Dead Sea, not very far south of Qumran, at the time when he composed his commentary to the prophecy of Habakkuk.

Religious Significance of Biblical Interpretation

In Helmer Ringgren's 1963 synthesis of the theology of the Dead Sea Scrolls, he includes three sections on doctrines, organization and cult, and place within the history of religion. An obvious omission here is a section on the Qumran community's attitude toward Holy Scripture.

Biblical Authors and Exegetes

The Qumran pesherists are often described as postbiblical exegetes. By this is often meant that the sectarians were conscious that what they were composing was not "bible," but commentaries on texts that had an altogether different and higher status. Such a distinction seems to be overdrawn. To be sure the pesherists saw themselves as standing apart from the biblical texts when they separated their own comments with the introductory markers, but they also believed that God continues to reveal his mysteries beyond biblical prophecies through, above all, the Teacher of Righteousness, but also through them. These teachings appear to have ethical implications as the Teacher of Righteousness sent laws and precepts to the Wicked Priest, inciting the murderous ire of his adversary. Some scholars believe that 4QMMT is this very document that was sent. If so, then, the ethics of the revealed teachings included various matters of the legal observance of ritual and practice.

There are other good reasons for holding that the pesherist did not think of themselves only as postbiblical exegetes. The biblical texts are cited verbatim, but they were also modified and adapted to fit in with sectarian interpretation. Scripture, for them, was not the inviolable word of God, immutable and forbidden from change. Rather it was malleable in the hands of authorized interpreters. Why they resorted to scriptural modification in order to bring the biblical quotation closer to their interpretation remains puzzling, given that elsewhere they used literary techniques that could easily make the exegetical connection between source text and comment. One is drawn to the view that for them the distinction between biblical and nonbiblical was not hard and fast. There is a continuity between biblical writing and their own revealed interpretation. They were conscious of the special status of what they cited, but they also believed that what was being revealed to them in their time was also divine in origin. Like the later biblical authors who added, changed, and rewrote earlier texts, the Qumran pesherists also in some sense stood within the biblical tradition.

Prophecy, Revelation, and Fulfillment

It is often said that pesherite interpretation contemporizes the biblical texts by applying them to their first century BCE situation. This actualizing move is for the most part opaque, since a coded biblical figure or event is explained by another coded sectarian sobriquet or episode. On occasion, however, the code is deciphered and the names of the Greek kings Demetrius and Antiochus are given to assure us of the historical interests of the pesherists.

The pesherists regarded biblical texts, including the Psalms, as predictive prophecies more than admonitions. They believed themselves to be living in the end time when the events foretold by the ancients would now be fulfilled in their time. As with all such millenarian interpretations, the end time was inevitably delayed, and attention was turned instead toward the assurance of a faithful God — though the vision tarries, it will not lie.

The Halakah and Religion of Qumran

HANNAH K. HARRINGTON

With the discovery of many new fragments at Qumran, the legal material has become increasingly important. It is well understood that an analysis of a community's laws can often reveal its self-identity. Early Judaism of all types had to deal first and foremost with biblical law. Pharisees, Sadducees, Essenes, and others were all guided and distinguished by some interpretation of it. Early Jewish-Christian writers often allegorized the law, but nevertheless they too felt compelled to interpret it. In this essay I would like to try to uncover the primary goal of the Scrolls' writers through an analysis of their halakah, that is, their interpretation of biblical law.[1]

Scholars are now debating the number of communities behind the Scrolls and their dates and places of origin. However, with regard to their biblical legal interpretations, the material shows much more consonance than dissonance. In fact, while the organizational laws of the community do show fluctuation with reference to audience and date, the biblical laws remain relatively unaffected by these changes and repeatedly reflect a common bias in in-

---

1. P. Davies, "Halakhah at Qumran," in *A Tribute to Geza Vermes: Essays on Jewish and Christian Literature and History,* ed. Philip R. Davies and Richard T. White (JSOTSup 100; Sheffield: JSOT Press, 1990) 37-50, offers a good definition of halakah: "a body of law governing Jewish behaviour which in practice or in theory derives from Scripture and acquires its authoritative status thereby" (38). The halakic documents found at Qumran are primarily: 4Q266-73, 5Q512, 6Q15 (fragments of the *Damascus Document*); 4Q159, 4Q513, 4Q514 (4QOrdinances); 4Q394-99 (4QSome Works of the Law); 4Q251 (4QHalakha); 4Q274, 276-78 (4QTohorot); 4Q284a (4QHarvesting). Also halakah is found in parts of 1QS (the *Rule of the Community*); 1QM (the *War Scroll*); and 4Q174 (4QFlorilegium).

terpretation.[2] It is this undergirding ideology that I wish to bring into relief in this essay.

There are differences in opinion among scholars concerning the central ideological components of the Qumran community. Some suggest that purity is the matter of central importance to the Qumran sect.[3] If so, what is the goal behind the purity laws? Why is there so much emphasis on purity? Others find a certain brand of apocalypticism to be responsible for the shape of the sect's worldview. Does this apocalypticism impact the sect's halakah?[4] Jacob Licht, Frank M. Cross, and Martin Hengel may be right that the Dead Sea community represents a "merger between two different streams, an apocalyptic stream and a priestly one."[5] Does this merger have a unified goal?

Let us examine the halakic material anew to establish the biases behind it. I will divide it into two categories: (1) laws derived from Scripture; and (2) laws in excess of Scripture. Biblical law is ambiguous enough in many cases to be pulled toward one interpretive direction or another. Rabbinic interpretations are a case in point. They often steer the law in the direction of leniency in order to make it more tolerable for the Jewish community.[6] They

2. Some sectarian texts refer to all Israel, and others are directed only to the community of Qumran, but the biblical interpretations are by and large complementary. J. M. Baumgarten, *Qumrân Cave 4, XIII: The Damascus Document (4Q266-273)* (DJD 18; Oxford: Clarendon, 1996); C. Hempel, *The Laws of the Damascus Document: Sources, Traditions, and Redaction* (Leiden: Brill, 1998) 15-23; L. H. Schiffman, *Sectarian Law in the Dead Sea Scrolls: Courts, Testimony, and the Penal Code* (Chico, Calif.: Scholars Press, 1983) 213; J. Milgrom focuses on the consonance of the purity laws at Qumran in "The Scriptural Foundations and Deviations in the Laws of Purity of the Temple Scroll," in *Archaeology and History in the Dead Sea Scrolls*, ed. Lawrence Schiffman (JSPSup 8; JSOT/ASOR Monographs 2; Sheffield: JSOT Press, 1990) 95.

3. Cf. Florentino García Martínez, "Les limites de la communauté: Pureté et impureté à Qumrân et dans le Nouveau Testament," in *Text and Testimony: Essays in Honor of A. F. J. Klijn*, ed. T. Baarda et al. (Kampen: Kok Pharos, 1988) 111-12; Florentino García Martínez and Julio Trebolle Barrera, *The People of the Dead Sea Scrolls* (Leiden: Brill, 1995) 140; Ben Zion Wacholder, "Rules of Testimony in Qumran Jurisprudence: CD 9 and 11QTorah 64," *JJS* 40 (1989) 174.

4. J. J. Collins, "Apocalypticism and Literary Genre in the Dead Sea Scrolls," in *The Dead Sea Scrolls after Fifty Years: A Comprehensive Assessment,* ed. Peter Flint and James VanderKam (2 vols.; Leiden: Brill, 1998, 1999) 2.428.

5. Torleif Elgvin, "The Mystery to Come: Early Essene Theology of Revelation," in *Qumran between the Old and New Testaments*, ed. Frederick Cryer and Thomas L. Thompson (JSOTSup 290; Copenhagen International Seminar 6; Sheffield: Sheffield Academic Press, 1998) 150.

6. Y. Sussmann, "The History of the Halakha and the Dead Sea Scrolls: Preliminary Talmudic Observations on Miqṣat Maʿase Ha-Torah (4QMMT)," in *Qumran Cave 4, V: Miqṣat Maʿase Ha-Torah* (DJD 10; Oxford: Clarendon, 1994) 196; H. K. Harrington, *The*

also increase the authority of the legal exegete. The question here is, What is the agenda undergirding the law found in the Scrolls? What is the weave in the fabric of these laws that align them together?

I would like to present a few examples of Qumran halakic interpretation alongside their rabbinic counterparts. I present the latter, even though our data is from a later period, because rabbinic opinions emerge from another ancient Jewish, Torah-based community offering alternative interpretations of the same laws. This contrast will bring into relief more clearly the Qumran point of view.

Let us look at some examples. The Pentateuch regards food to be susceptible to impurity if water is put on it (Lev 11:38): "If water is put on the seed and any part of a carcass falls upon it, it shall be unclean for you." Does this verse mean that even rain, which is needed for the crop and comes from God himself, will cause a crop to become susceptible to impurity? The sect insists that it does (4Q274 3 i 4). The rabbis, however, capitalize on the word *yutan*, "be put," and claim that there must be intentional and desired putting of the water on the seed by permission of the owner in order for it to become susceptible to impurity; rain will not make a crop susceptible to impurity (*m. Mak.* 1:1; 3:6; *b. Qidd.* 59b). For the Qumran sectarians, the rabbinic exegesis would have appeared contrived.

Another ambiguity in the biblical text is found in Sabbath law. There is ambiguity in Scripture on exactly what is forbidden on the Sabbath. The Bible forbids work on the Sabbath (Exod 20:10), but what constitutes work? The rabbis ask a similar question and come up with forty kinds of work, including writing two letters and tying two threads together. The Qumran authors are even more restrictive. Perhaps following Jeremiah 17:24, which forbids burden bearing on the Sabbath, the *Damascus Document* forbids picking up a child, a stone, and even a piece of dust on this holy day (CD 11:7-11).[7]

Impurity Systems of Qumran and the Rabbis: Biblical Foundations (SBLDS 143; Atlanta: Scholars Press, 1993) 58-62; I. Knohl, "Post-Biblical Sectarianism and the Priestly Schools of the Pentateuch: The Issue of Popular Participation in the Temple Cult on Festivals," in *The Madrid Qumran Congress: Proceedings of the International Congress on the Dead Sea Scrolls, Madrid, 18-21 March 1991*, ed. Julio Trebolle Barrera and Luis Vegas Montaner (2 vols.; STDJ 11; Leiden: Brill, 1992) 2.602.

7. Michael Fishbane, "Use, Authority and Interpretation of Mikra at Qumran," in *Mikra: Text, Translation, Reading, and Interpretation of the Hebrew Bible in Ancient Judaism and Early Christianity*, ed. M. J. Mulder (CRINT; Philadelphia: Fortress, 1988) 368-71, claims that the *Damascus Document* uses several exegetical methods, similar to those of the rabbis, in order to derive its laws from Scripture. This has been contested by others; however, cf. Steven Fraade, "Looking for Legal Midrash at Qumran," in *Biblical Perspectives: Early Use and Interpretation of the Bible in Light of the Dead Sea Scrolls*, ed. M. Stone and

One might argue that this seems unnecessarily harsh, or that the law was based on Jeremiah, a nonlegal text. But indeed the Pentateuch informs that a man was stoned to death by divine decree for merely picking up sticks on the Sabbath (Num 15:32-36).

The law of the corpse gives another opportunity to observe the Qumran sect's stringent way of dealing with biblical ambiguity. Numbers 19:14 states, "This is the law: When a person dies in a tent, all who enter the tent and everything that is in the tent will be unclean seven days." The sectarians understand this law to mean that *kol*, not "everyone" (JPS), but "everything," including a nail and a peg within the tent, becomes unclean (11Q19 49:6). This seems also to be the thinking of Philo, who says that after sexual intercourse, bathing is mandatory before touching *anything* (*Laws* 3.63, 205). The rabbis, however, delimit the force of the law by using other verses from the Torah. Leviticus 11:32 discusses the impurity of swarming creatures: "And anything on which one of them falls when dead shall be unclean: be it any article of wood, or a cloth, or a skin, or a sack." Numbers 31:22 adds a list of metals. The rabbis take these listed substances to be definitive of the objects susceptible to impurity. Thus, in any context of impurity, even in the house of a dead person, these are the only items, in addition to human beings, that will be subject to impurity. The objects must form usable, complete vessels (*m. Kelim* 2:1; 11:2; *Ohal.* 5:5; *Sif. Num.* 126 [ed. Horowitz 162]).

A final example of ambiguity is Qumran's insistence that a man cannot marry his niece since Leviticus 18:12 forbids a man from marrying his aunt. The point is that the same relationship applies whether a man marries his aunt or a woman marries her uncle. However, it is curious that the law does not state the latter case. The rabbis, who are tied only to the letter of the law, permit a man to marry his niece. The Qumran stance, however, appears most consonant with the reality behind the text.[8]

It should be understandable, even from these few examples, how the sect could have accused other Jewish groups in antiquity of seeking easy ways out of the law's difficulties. The interpretations of biblical law found in the Scrolls are invariably more difficult to observe, but they are logical, straightforward interpretations of Scripture. Their stringency was championed at Qumran as part of the group's self-identity.[9] The sect accused its opponents

E. Chazon (STDJ 28; Leiden: Brill, 1998) 76-77. The methods of the Scroll writers are not so clear.

8. D. R. Schwartz, "Law and Truth: On Qumran-Sadducean and Rabbinic Views of Law," in *The Dead Sea Scrolls: Forty Years of Research,* ed. D. Dimant and U. Rappaport (STDJ 10; Leiden: Brill, 1992) 230-35.

9. Sussmann, "History of the Halakha," 196.

of violating the law (CD 1:20; 2:18-21) and looking for easy ways out of its requirements *(kî' baḥrû běkalût* 4Q171 1-2 i 19). Only the sect fulfilled the Torah according to its "correct interpretation" (CD 6:18-19). The sectarians regarded themselves as true scholars of the law (1QM 10:10; cf. 1QH 2:17), while others, in the sect's view, were satisfied with superficial conclusions (CD 1:18), and "falsehood was in their study" (4QpNah 2:8).[10]

Daniel Schwartz explains the strict legal interpretation at Qumran by pointing to its priestly constituency. These ex-priests had nothing to gain by looking for easier-to-observe interpretations. As priests, their authority was secured by genealogy. Rather, they were interested in the law's reality. In other words, if the law seems to imply a more stringent code of behavior than what is actually stated, the Qumran priests will adopt that strict behavior; they will not construct ways around it. The Qumran authors were interested in what they considered to be the perfect will of God, whether clearly stated in the law or not.[11] They were interested in settling ambiguity not simply in a manner compliant with the law, but in whatever way would, in fact, most please God.

However, if the rabbis can be accused of reducing the force of the law at every opportunity, the sectarians can be accused of intensifying it. Much of the law at Qumran legislates beyond even the strictest view of Scripture. Some rulings are in excess of the biblical commands. They are not required in Scripture even by the most paranoic interpretation. Aside from the organizational laws of the sect, in what category do we usually find extrabiblical supplements to the law? The answer is, in the areas of purity and the cult.

A quick survey of the legal texts found at Qumran yields a preponderance of laws centered around purity issues. In the *Damascus Document* Józef T. Milik has listed twenty-three legal passages. Fifteen deal with ritual purity and matters of the priesthood. In MMT, all of the laws deal in some way with matters of ritual purity. The six fragments of *Tohorot* are a group of texts totally devoted to rules of purification. *Ordinances A* (4Q159) centers around the purity of agriculture offered to the temple. *Ordinances B* (4Q513) deals with the marital purity of priests, the protection of holy food, and the depth of an immersion pool. The *Temple Scroll* deals with purity, holy festivals, and sacrifices. In short, the majority of this material is concerned with a broad range of purity matters.

10. Fishbane, "Use, Authority and Interpretation," 366-67.

11. As Schwartz explains, the rabbis depend on the law for their authority. The priestly community of Qumran did not have to defend their authority, since they were born with it as priests. It was more important that the law be defended, from the rabbis' point of view, than that one seek to uncover the fine points of the divine will (cf. *b. B. Meṣ.* 59); Schwartz, "Law and Truth."

What is purity? Purity is the state of cleanness effected by physical purification rituals required for lay participation in the cult. Purity can be better understood by defining its antonym, impurity. Jacob Milgrom defines impurity as an "active, malevolent force that grows in strength unless checked and reduced through ablutions."[12] Thus, an individual's pure status is never fixed but is constantly threatened by negative forces.

Purity laws at Qumran are known to be strict. In addition to the above examples, note the following: a purifying person may not touch even herbs, since they could be made susceptible to impurity (4Q274).[13] According to the *Damascus Document*, even such small organisms as bee larvae and small sea creatures cause impurity (CD 12:13-14). Physical purification rituals had to accompany atonement rituals at Qumran (1QS 3:4-6). Like Jacob, who ordered his household to purify themselves and change their clothes when they repented of idolatry (Gen 35:2), so for the Qumran sectarians, ablutions accompanied repentance. In terms of legal issues, the writers at Qumran are more interested in purity than in any other legal category.

However, purity laws are also excessive. The sect performed ritual bathing before meals (1QS 5:13). The Bible requires priests to wash before performing and eating sacrifices (Lev 7:20-21). In addition, Leviticus 11 is addressed to all Israel and requires purification after contact with anything impure. Apparently, the sect has combined the priestly purification instructions with the command to all Israel to wash after contact with impurity. The result is that all members must wash before eating lest impurity be transmitted to the community's pure food.[14] In another excess, again in the area of purity, ritual slaughter was considered necessary even for fish (CD 12:13-14). Pure food is so important at Qumran that if an individual is accused of a crime by even one witness, that is enough to exclude him from eating the pure food of the community. This is actually contrary to Deuteronomy 19:15, which requires at least two witnesses for legal claims.[15]

---

12. J. Milgrom, "First Day Ablutions in Qumran," in *The Madrid Qumran Congress*, 2.570.

13. J. Baumgarten, "Liquids and Susceptibility to Defilement in New 4Q Texts," in *The Community of the Renewed Covenant*, ed. E. Ulrich and J. VanderKam (CJA 10; Notre Dame, Ind.: University of Notre Dame Press, 1994) 98.

14. According to Milgrom's interpretation of the Purities texts (4Q274), even hopelessly impure persons must wash before eating their food; see J. Milgrom, "The Purification Rule (4Q514 = 4QOrd^c)," in *The Dead Sea Scrolls: Hebrew, Aramaic and Greek Texts with English Translations*, vol. 1, *Rule of the Community and Related Documents*, ed. J. Charlesworth (Tübingen/Louisville: Mohr-Siebeck/Westminster/John Knox, 1994) 177.

15. Wacholder, "Rules of Testimony in Qumran Jurisprudence," 174.

The Scrolls themselves present the idea that they are expecting a higher purity code than the simple intent of the law. The Bible requires all Israelites to avoid food that has been in an open pot in a house where someone has just died (Num 19:15). However, the *Temple Scroll* says that the איש טהור, the truly pure individual, will even avoid food that had been in sealed vessels in the house of the dead (11Q19 49:8). The *Purification Rules* too advocate being טהור יותר, more pure (4Q274 3.1.4). Sect members should strive to be the pure man as opposed to the אדם מישראל, the average Israelite. In other words, those truly seeking to please God will be more scrupulous.

The temple and its city are of special importance to the Qumran authors. According to the *Temple Scroll,* the *War Scroll,* and *Some Works of the Law,* physically impaired persons are not allowed within the entire temple city or war camp (11Q19 45:12-14; 1QM 7:3-5; 4QMMT B 42-57). However, the Bible mandates physical perfection only for the officiating priest (Lev 21:23). Sexual intercourse is prohibited within the entire city of Jerusalem according to both the *Temple Scroll* and the *Damascus Document* (11Q19 45:11-12; CD 12:1-2). The group at Qumran seems to have discouraged sexual relations altogether.[16] However, the holiest person in biblical Israel, the high priest, was a married man, and indeed the succession of the priesthood depended upon his marital relations. Thus, purity is demanded at the level of the priest and the sanctuary and sometimes even beyond that. There is clearly an effort to go beyond Scripture's requirements.

The *Temple Scroll* contains many other examples of extrabiblical requirements in the areas of purity and cult.[17] One obvious example is the nonbiblical harvest festivals. Separate festivals are ordained for wine, oil, and wood in addition to offering the firstfruits of grain. The author clearly regarded these extrabiblical assemblies as required by God although they cannot be directly gleaned from the biblical text.[18] These festivals are also alluded to in 4Q251 2:1-5. While these festivals may have been traditions inherited by the sect and not their creation, the author of the *Temple Scroll* for some reason felt it necessary to give them the authority of divine revelation.[19]

If we consider the most striking things about the biblical law at Qumran, that is, the strictness of the laws and their extra requirements espe-

16. See E. Qimron, "Celibacy in the Dead Sea Scrolls and the Two Kinds of Sectarians," in *The Madrid Qumran Congress,* 1.291-94.

17. Cf., for example, Milgrom, "Scriptural Foundations and Deviations," 89-95.

18. Baumgarten, *Qumrân Cave 4, XIII: The Damascus Document,* 16.

19. Milgrom, "Scriptural Foundations and Deviations," 95; L. H. Schiffman, "The Temple Scroll and the Nature of Its Law," in *The Community of the Renewed Covenant,* 51-52.

cially in the areas of purity and the cult, what do we find out about the agenda of these authors? Why do the Scrolls insist on such a high degree of purity in the community? Why legislate beyond the requirements of the law, especially in matters of cult?

It appears to me that the goal of the Qumran legal material is the achievement of maximum holiness. The community refers to itself as a "temple of men" (4QFlor 1-3 i 2-7) and a group *set apart* for Torah study in the desert (1QS 8:13-15).[20] It has been pointed out that the sect considered itself a congregation of priests elevating its members to the status of priests serving in the temple.[21] However, the ideology was even more dynamic. The group was trying to achieve as much holiness as possible, their motto being more like the levitical command "Be holy even as the LORD your God is holy" (Lev 11:45).

The Qumran writers themselves identify their community using the following terms: "a house of holiness for Israel and an assembly of holy of holies for Aaron (1QS 8:5); "holy house for Aaron" (1QS 9:6); "holy among all the peoples" (1Q34 3 ii 6); "assembly of holiness" or "holy community" (1QS 5:20; 9:2; 1Q28a 1:9, 13; 4Q181 1 ii 4); "holy council" (1QH 15:10 [7:10]; 1QM 3:4; CD 20:25; 1QS 2:25; 8:21; 1QSa 2:9); "temple of men" (4QFlor l. 6); "the holy ones" (1QM 6:6); "God's holy people" (1QM 14:12); "men of holiness" (1QS 8:17); "congregation of the men of perfect holiness" (CD 20:2-7; 1QS 9:20); "most holy dwelling for Aaron" (1QS 8:8). Each member is considered an איש הקודש, "a holy man" (1QS 5:13, 18; 8:17, 23, 9:8). Thus the Qumran community regarded itself as, first of all, holy. The *Rule of the Blessings* offers a sort of mission statement: "[May you] dedicate yourself for the holy of holies, for [you are made] holy for him, and shall glorify his name and his holiness" (1QSb 4:28). The author envisions the sect as an ongoing worship community at the highest level of holiness, the holy of holies.

The *Rule of the Community* gives a rationale for its rules and connects them explicitly with holiness. Israel is exhorted to live

> in accordance with these rules in order to establish the spirit of holiness in truth eternal, in order to atone for the fault of the transgression and for the guilt of sin and for approval for the earth, without the flesh of burnt offerings and without the fats of sacrifice — the offering of the lips in compliance with the decree will be like the pleasant aroma of justice and the cor-

20. J. Naude, "Holiness in the Dead Sea Scrolls," in *The Dead Sea Scrolls after Fifty Years*, 2.184.

21. D. Dimant, "*4QFlorilegium* and the Idea of the Community as Temple," in *Hellenica et Judaica*, ed. A. Caquot et al. (Leuven-Paris: Peeters, 1986) 188.

rectness of behavior will be acceptable like a freewill offering — at this moment the men of the community shall set themselves apart (like) a holy house for Aaron, in order to enter the holy of holies, and (like) a house of the community for Israel, (for) those who walk in perfection. (1QS 9:3-6)

The *Rule of the Community* insists that to join the "assembly of holiness," a person's insights and deeds of the law must be tested (1QS 5:20-21). Anyone "who enters the council of holiness . . . who breaks one word of the law of Moses" is to be banished (1QS 8:21). Thus, in the *Rule of the Community* the rationale for the laws is explicitly connected to acquiring holiness.

Specific laws are connected to holiness in other scrolls. Israel is exhorted to eat only pure foods and to refrain from certain customs such as shaving between the eyes, gashing oneself, and tattooing the body, because they are a "holy people unto the LORD your God" (11QT^a 48:7, 10). The *Damascus Document* too reasons that the feeble-minded, insane, blind, lame, deaf, and others are not to be allowed in the community because of the presence of the holy angels. The presence of divine holiness requires a community that can keep the law. Those who because of some impairment might transgress the law and cause holiness to depart cannot enter (CD 15:15-17). 4QMMT states its rationale for not allowing dogs into Jerusalem; it is because they might eat of the sacred food. The writer explains: "For Jerusalem is the camp of holiness" (4QMMT B 60ff).

More than anything else, holiness requires purity in order to act (Exod 22:31 [MT 30]). *The War Scroll* warns that priests will become defiled with the blood of the slain (1QM 9:8). The *Damascus Document* insists that Jews "separate from all impurities according to their law and to let no man defile his holy spirit" (CD 7:3-4). Moral purity is, of course, essential to holiness. The *Rule of the Community* explains that stubbornness, lewdness, and deceit are contrary to "the fruit of holiness" (1QS 10:21-23; cf. 1QM13:2-4; 1QS 8:11). Even the holiness of contributions from Israel to the priests is made impossible if the items were obtained in a wicked manner (CD 16:14, 16, 17; 4Q271 2 ii 14, 15). Thus, the many laws regulating various types of purity are necessary for the acquisition of holiness.

Sexual intercourse is discouraged at Qumran because it is a deterrent to holiness. Although the biblical laws are clear that celibacy is not the divine mandate for Israel, they are also clear that sexual intercourse causes impurity.[22] Thus, according to the Qumran reasoning, greater holiness is obtained

---

22. The *Acts of Thomas* 8 refers to abandonment of "filthy intercourse" in order to become "holy temples." J. Baumgarten, "The Qumran-Essene Restraints on Marriage," in *Archaeology and History in the Dead Sea Scrolls*, 23, n. 23.

if sexual intercourse is simply avoided. Unsurprisingly, even in the larger sectarian community sexual intercourse was not allowed on the Sabbath, a period of holy time.[23]

The concern with marriage in the *Damascus Document* and in 4QMMT is not family peace or proper child rearing, but a desire to maintain the purity of marriage partners and hence maintain holiness in Israel. This is emphasized in 4QMMT: "And concerning the practice of illegal marriage that exists among the people: (this practice exists) despite their being so[ns] of holy [seed], as is written, Israel is holy." The laws not to sow fields with mixed species, not to wear clothes of mixed fabrics, and not to crossbreed animals are all considered metaphors of the real issue — unholy, mixed marriages. 4QMMT continues: "Because they (Israel) are holy and the sons of Aaron are [most holy]. But you know that some of the priests and [the laity mingle with each other and they] unite with each other and pollute the [holy] seed [as well as] their own [seed] with women whom they are forbidden to marry" (4QMMT B 75-82).

The *Temple Scroll* too allots a great deal of space to marital purity. Proper choices for marriage are a matter of purity. An improper marriage is sometimes referred to as impurity (Lev 20:21; 11Q19 66:12-13). A captive woman must submit to various purification procedures including cutting her hair and nails before she can marry her fiancé (11Q19 63:10-15). Even then, she is considered impure for seven years and not allowed to eat pure food or sacrifices during that time. Polygamy is discouraged for everyone, especially for the king (cf. CD 4:20–5:9).[24] The reason given is not just the Deuteronomic one that foreign wives will turn the king's heart away from God (11Q19 56:18-19). The author expected the king to be on the same level of holiness as the high priest (11Q19 57:15-19). Again, the desire for maximal holiness emerges. Lawrence Schiffman concludes his study on women in the *Temple Scroll* with the following appropriate statements: "It is the potential for sanctification on the one hand, and for defilement on the other, which makes women the object of so much attention in the *Temple Scroll*. Yet to the *Temple Scroll* the power to live a life of sanctity lay not only in the hands of the priests, but in the hands of every man and woman in Israel."[25] The concern here is not just that the priests should be pure but that all of the commu-

23. M. Broshi, "Anti-Qumranic Polemics in the Talmud," in *The Madrid Qumran Congress*, 2.589-600.

24. L. H. Schiffman, "Laws Pertaining to Women," in *The Dead Sea Scrolls: Forty Years of Research*, 217.

25. Schiffman, "Laws Pertaining to Women," 228.

nity should adhere to a purity code that will bring about greater holiness in Israel.

The Qumran emphasis on the Sabbath and the festival calendar makes sense in light of maximal holiness. The Torah orders, "Remember the Sabbath day to keep it holy." Maximal holiness will be obtained if one carries nothing, not even a piece of dust, on the Sabbath. Similarly, the added festivals sanctify major crops in Israel, wine, and oil. Festivals increase holy contributions to the priests and holy times in Israel.

Seemingly miscellaneous laws often make more sense in light of the quest for holiness. The laws concerning oaths are a case in point (CD 15:1-4). The divine name is pronounced in these oaths, but because of the inherent holiness of the name, the authors discourage proclamation of it (CD 9:9). Oaths cannot be annulled at the price of death. The prohibitions to use the divine name in oaths, public readings, and benedictions (1QS 6:27–7:2) are due to its sanctity.[26]

What is holiness? How is it different than purity? Purity is a state of being. It refers to the absence of impurity. Holiness, קדושה, however, is an active force. Some Qumran texts appear to use purity and holiness interchangeably, and indeed there is some overlap since holiness requires purity, but the two terms are not identical.[27] Holiness can be defined loosely as divine energy. At its core, Holy is another way of saying God, and indeed the favorite rabbinic title for God is "the Holy [One], Blessed Be He." Qumran authors too use the word הקודש, the phrase קודש קודשים, and sometimes just קודש as a synonym for God (1QS 10:4; 1QSb 4:28; CD 6:1; 20:22).[28] Only God is inherently holy. Other persons and items can partake of God's inherent holiness only by extension and by divine designation. Although they can never be inherently holy, these holy items mirror the divine holiness in various ways. They imitate his otherness and separation from impurity, they strive for his perfection as far as possible, and they also exhibit the divine goodness, that is, true justice and mercy.[29]

Jacob Milgrom, in his work on Leviticus, defines holiness as "that which

26. Cf. Schiffman, *Sectarian Law,* 136-41, 144.

27. 11Q19 51:5-10 and CD 6:17-18; 12:20 connect holiness and purity synonymously. See also L. H. Schiffman, "The Theology of the Temple Scroll," *JQR* 85 (1994) 121, who claims that purity and holiness are equivalent in the *Temple Scroll,* both referring to the abstinence from impurity.

28. Naude, "Holiness in the Dead Sea Scrolls," 192, gives several references where קודש without the definite article still refers to God and is used to avoid using God's name directly.

29. Naude, "Holiness in the Dead Sea Scrolls," 176.

is unapproachable except through divinely imposed restrictions" or "that which is withdrawn from common use," in short, that which is "set apart for God."[30] Jacobus Naude, who has analyzed the root of קדוש in the Scrolls, defines the verbal inflections of holiness as denoting: "(a) a cultic/religious activity performed, (b) to accomplish the withdrawal of somebody (or oneself) who obeys the stipulations of the community/God, or of any object from profane use; (c) to submit to the distinctive rules of religion or to God's will."[31] An item that is קודש is on the side of or within the realm of God.[32] Those items that are designated holy are privileged. Only they partake of the divine energy and experience supernatural power (cf. Lev 5:15-16).

It seems to me that these definitions of holiness would have have been eagerly championed by more than one Jewish group in antiquity. The rabbis, for instance, would have had no problem with this description of holiness. What set the Qumran group apart from others was not its definition of holiness per se but the level of holiness it considered necessary for Israel. For Qumran, human holiness does not come simply by obedience to the law. That is a given, but holiness must increase by emulating God to the best of one's ability. Greater holiness is achieved by discovering and fulfilling God's perfect will. Keeping the revealed law is only the beginning. For the rabbis, by contrast, holiness is maintained solely by obedience to the law.

What is interesting is that both views of holiness are embedded in the Torah itself. The stringent, Qumranic view of holiness takes seriously the divine vision of Israel in Exodus as a "kingdom of priests, a holy nation" (Exod 19:6). To realize this ideal, the sect looks to the priestly laws of Leviticus for guidance. According to Leviticus, priests are divinely designated as holy (Lev 21:8). They must be physically perfect in order to officiate, and they must follow a stricter code of behavior than ordinary Israelites. In addition, Leviticus enjoins, "Be holy even as I the Lord your God am holy." Milgrom claims that in H, primarily the latter half of Leviticus, holiness is more dynamic than in P, most of chapters 1–16. This is especially true in Leviticus 19, where specific performative laws are given. Most of these exhortations are ethical laws that require more than simply keeping a cultic procedure such as avoiding an impurity or accepting the right portion of a sacrifice. Rather, laws such as "Show no partiality" (v. 15), "Do not hold a grudge," and "Love your neighbor as yourself" (v. 18) are more in the realm of the ideal. One can strive a lifetime

---

30. J. Milgrom, *Leviticus 17–27* (AB 3A; Garden City, N.Y.: Doubleday, forthcoming).

31. Naude, "Holiness in the Dead Sea Scrolls," 186.

32. Naude, "Holiness in the Dead Sea Scrolls," 193.

to fulfill them, and religious people will fulfill them to very different degrees. Holiness becomes a dynamic activity the boundaries of which can be expanded or diminished. It becomes a reciprocal process, whereby, in Milgrom's words, "God sanctifies Israel in proportion to Israel's self-sanctification."[33] In my view, this was exactly the goal of the Qumran community — members must sanctify themselves so that God will bestow greater holiness upon them. Holiness becomes an ideal for them to which they must always aspire. However, at least in the legal material, it is not the ethical component of holiness that they stress. Rather, they focus largely on diminishing the presence of ritual impurity as far as possible and on increasing cultic demands. In their view, God would be better served if all of the community adopted a stringent code of behavior, both in the temple and outside of it, and strove for the ideal holiness, even pushing beyond the explicit requirements of Scripture.

The rabbinic view is embedded in Deuteronomy. Here all the people of Israel are holy by divine designation, and they are obligated to maintain that holiness by observing the law (Deut 26:19; cf. also Deut 7:6; 14:2, 21). However, the level of holiness is only that which the law demands. Compare this statement from *Numbers Rabbah:* "Be holy, for as long as you fulfill my commandments you are sanctified, but if you neglect them you become profaned" (*Num. Rab.* 17:6). Holiness is linked directly to the explicit laws of the Torah. Even a minimal interpretation, if it can be supported, will suffice. The rabbis would stop with the laws as stated in the Pentateuch. The Qumran group, however, demands holiness as defined by the levitical priests and sometimes even beyond that. Some strains, nevertheless, of the maximalist position are present in rabbinic sources as well; for instance, the Talmud enjoins, "Sanctify yourselves even in what is permitted" (*b. Yebam.* 20a). If you just follow the Torah you could still be a glutton, a drunk, or full of animal lusts — restrain yourself. *Leviticus Rabbah* states that even an unchaste look is to be regarded as adultery (*Lev. Rab.* 23). Similar ideas are presented in the ethical instructions of the Gospels (Matt 5:27). However, the maximalist position is not the norm in rabbinic literature.

What was the underlying goal of all this effort at Qumran to be holy? What would be the result of greater holiness in the community? The answer is biblical. First of all, the divine energy fights wars. God can deliver because he is holy (Exod 15:11). The apocalyptic Qumran authors were expecting an eschatological finale soon in which they, the minority group, were going to face all outsiders in a battle between the Sons of Light and the Sons of Darkness. Holiness, which brings victory, is accessed by the divine name. According to

---

33. Milgrom, *Leviticus 17–27*.

the *War Scroll* David conquered the Philistines by means of the holy name (1QM 11:3). The *Damascus Document* claims that the *yaḥad* will be safe because it takes refuge in the holy name (CD 20:34).

Scripture is clear that maximum holiness must obtain in the war camp (Deut 23) in order for God's holiness to fight Israel's battles. "Because the LORD your God walks in the midst of your camp to save you and to give up your enemies before you, therefore your camp must be holy, that he may not see anything indecent among you, and turn away from you" (Deut 23:14). Like the holy war camp that the Israelite soldiers had to leave in order to relieve themselves, so the *yaḥad* had to keep impure bodily functions away from the community at Qumran. Like the priests performing the holy service, no blemished persons could participate in the community (Lev 21:17-21). In order to win this eschatological confrontation, the Qumran writers insist that the highest level of holiness possible will be necessary.[34]

The holy angels are believed to be present both in this final battle as warriors and among the community at present. They are the army of God (11Q13 2:9) — they are exalted as the triumphant host of God over Belial (1QM 12:1-8). At the same time, God's holy angels participate in the community meetings (11QBer 1:13-14; 11Q19 51:8, 10). Sometimes it is ambiguous whether the referent of קדושים is supernatural or human.[35] Humans and angels combine their worship together in the liturgies (1QŠirŠabb and 4QBerakhot). This statement expresses the level of holiness desired:

> Among the seven-fold purified, God will sanctify unto himself a sanctuary of eternity and purity among those who are cleansed, and they shall be priests, his righteous people, his host, and ministering (with) the angels of his glory.[36]

---

34. Baumgarten, *Qumrân Cave 4, XIII: The Damascus Document*, 18, writes, "The Qumran view of the imminence of the 'latter days' led, not to what has been termed a 'straining at the leash of the Law,' but to the search for a more rigorous fulfillment of its requirements."

35. Naude, "Holiness in the Dead Sea Scrolls," 189, writes, "members of the Dead Sea sect are often said to enjoy fellowship with the angels. The phrase 'people of the holy ones' refers to Israel in 1QM 10:10 and Daniel 7:27. There is no case, however, where the unqualified word קדושים refers unambiguously to human beings in the scrolls." The phrase usually refers to angels; see J. J. Collins, "In the Likeness of the Holy Ones: the Creation of Humankind in a Wisdom Text from Qumran," in *The Provo International Conference on the Dead Sea Scrolls*, ed. D. Parry and E. Ulrich (STDJ 30; Leiden: Brill, 1999) 613-14.

36. M. Baillet, *Qumrân grotte 4, III (4Q482-4Q520)* (DJD 7; Oxford: Clarendon, 1982) 237.

Thus, the highest stage of holiness that human beings can attain is necessary in order for angels to continue to participate in the camp.[37]

Like the Holy One himself, the angels cannot tolerate impurity in the camp.[38] A menstruant must not mingle with others in the community so as not to pollute the "camps of the holy ones of Israel" (4Q274 1 i 6). The *Rule of the Community* states that physically impaired persons will not be able to fight in this apocalyptic battle because of the presence of the holy angels (1QSa 2:5). The Qumran community aspired to participate in the angelic world.[39]

The Holy Spirit is another term used to portray God's powerful holiness among his people, often in the context of atonement. The Holy Spirit atones for impurity of sin. The humility of the penitent clears the way for atonement, but only the spirit of holiness can actually cleanse the sinner from his "spirit of impurity" (1QS 4:20f; CD 4:20-21; one is purified "by the Holy Spirit from all works of wickedness"; cf. 1QH 16:12). Mercy comes via the Holy Spirit (1QSb 2:24). When the chosen ones become a foundation of the Holy Spirit, they will be able to atone for sin (1QS 9:3). The Holy Spirit is powerful and keeps the Instructor from erring (1QH 15:7 [7:7]).

In addition to the power, both physical and moral, that holiness brings to the community, holiness is also the vehicle for divine revelation. Like atonement, revelation comes through the Holy Spirit. The prophets spoke by the Holy Spirit (1QS 8:16; cf. 2 Pet 1:21). Similarly, the sectarians regarded their interpreters of prophecies as "visionaries (חוזי) of truth" (1QH 2:15) and considered all others who do not interpret "by the Holy Spirit" as "visionaries (חוזי) of deceit" (1QH 4:10) and "falsehood" (4:20).[40] The Holy Spirit reveals those who are the elect to specially chosen anointed individuals (CD 2:19). The Instructor is advised by the Holy Spirit (1QH 20:12 (12:12). Unlike the rabbis who see the Mosaic revelation as final, the Scrolls emphasize that revelation is, in Joseph Baumgarten's words, "a continuing process involving a constant search for new illuminations."[41] The Teacher of Righteousness was expected to present new revelation (1QS 8:12ff; CD 3:13ff). In order

---

37. Naude, "Holiness in the Dead Sea Scrolls," 189, cites also M. J. Davidson, *Angels at Qumran: A Comparative Study of 1 Enoch 1–36, 72–108 and Sectarian Writings from Qumran* (Sheffield: JSOT Press, 1992) 132-342.

38. García Martínez, "Les limites de la communauté," 118. The last stage of thought in the history of this literature is that the community must be so pure because of the angels within it, "exigence de pureté angelique."

39. Naude, "Holiness in the Dead Sea Scrolls," 173.

40. Fishbane, "Use, Authority and Interpretation," 367.

41. J. Baumgarten, *Studies in Qumran Law* (Leiden: Brill, 1977) 29-31.

for the community to receive new revelation, holiness had to be at a maximum level, for only in a holy community could God be revealed.

It is well known that the law was of utmost importance at Qumran. According to the *Rule of the Community*, the sectarians spent one-third of each night studying the Torah (1QS 6:7). Yet mere study and observance of the law was insufficient to bring new revelation from God. For that, more holiness was required. To receive additional revelation to that already given in Scripture was a goal eagerly pursued. The only way additional revelation could be given was in the same manner the original Sinaitic revelation was given, that is, through a state of maximum holiness.[42] This holiness is achieved by purity in its broadest sense. Purity of both body and soul are required. At Sinai Israel refrained from sexual intercourse, set up boundaries upon the holy mountain, and performed special purifications. Moses was in such a state of holiness that he did not even eat or drink for forty days, and when he returned to Israel, his face glowed with God's glory. Under these exceptional conditions, revelation was given and could be given again. Josephus states that the Essenes required ritual purification as a prerequisite to prophecy (*J.W.* 2.159).[43] Nevertheless, ritual purity was not sufficient to bring about holiness. In order to truly be a "kingdom of priests," Israel had to agree to all of the terms of the covenant (Exod 19:3-8). Likewise, in order for the sect to "establish the spirit of holiness in truth eternal," the community had to be pure from every flaw. The Qumranites were attempting to live in a state of perfection so that divine holiness could endow them with both revelation and power. Law played a vital role in turning a worldview into an everyday reality. Only by legislation could the Qumran authors weave their agenda into the daily life and practice of the community.

42. As B. Z. Wacholder says of the *Temple Scroll*, its author's main goal was "to reproduce in the holy land the sacred camp in Israel as it stood before the Lord at Mount Sinai" (B. Z. Wacholder, *The Dawn of Qumran: The Sectarian Torah and the Teacher of Righteousness* [Cincinnati: Hebrew Union College Press, 1983] 16).

43. Cited in J. Baumgarten, "Purification Liturgies," in *The Dead Sea Scrolls after Fifty Years*, 2.207.

Rewriting Rubrics:
Sacrifice and the Religion of Qumran

ROBERT A. KUGLER

Any discussion of the religion of Qumran must account for some peculiar circumstances. The community that resided there revered the sacrificial cult and priests as the means for establishing communion with God. Yet because they rejected the Jerusalem cult as corrupt beyond fair use, they separated themselves from the sanctuary, its practices, and its leadership.[1] How, then, did the residents of Qumran make up for this critical deficit in their religious life?

Some say that the community's prayer and praise, or alternatively its life of Scripture reading and interpretation, replaced sacrifice,[2] while others sug-

---

1. For the community's reverence of the cult and its rejection of the corruption in Jerusalem, see especially 4QpsMos[b] 3 iii 6; 4QpsMos[e] 1:1-2; 1QpHab 9:4; 1QpMic 11:1; 4QpNah 3-4 i 11; 3-4 ii 9. Against Frank Moore Cross, *The Ancient Library of Qumran* (3rd ed.; Minneapolis: Fortress, 1995) 85-86, the evidence of animal bones under ceramic remains may not be taken as evidence that animal sacrifice was performed at the site. As a contrast to Cross, see Georg Klinzing, *Die Umdeutung des Kultus in der Qumrangemeinde und im Neuen Testament* (Göttingen: Vandenhoeck & Ruprecht, 1971) 41-43.

2. For the praise and prayer as a replacement, see, for example, Lawrence Schiffman, "The Dead Sea Scrolls and the Early History of Jewish Liturgy," in *The Synagogue in Late Antiquity,* ed. Lee Levine (Philadelphia: American Schools of Oriental Research, 1987) 33-48, esp. 34-35. On the religious significance of Scripture study, see Steven Fraade, "Interpretive Authority in the Studying Community at Qumran," *JJS* 44 (1993) 46-69, esp. 42, where he writes, "Scriptural and legal studies at Qumran were not simply a means toward the end of covenantal compliance, but religious performances — media of religious expression and experience — themselves."

gest that the group constituted itself as a temple community, thus eliminating the need for oblations.[3] Evidence supporting these claims abounds. 1QS 9:3-6 states that the community's "offering of the lips" replaced sacrificial offerings. 4QFlor 1:6-7 says that God "has commanded that a sanctuary of man (מקדש אדם) be built for him, that there they might offer before him (like the smoke of incense) precepts of Torah." And the community did arrogate to itself priestly roles, requirements, and practices, as if to become a temple community in the desert. The group conceived of itself as having the atoning function reserved to the priesthood (1QS 5:1-7), and it claimed for itself the holy status of priests (1QS 8:5-6, 8; 9:6; 10:4; 4Q511 35). On several occasions community texts make an explicit claim for the group's priestly status (1QS 5:6; 8:9; 9:6; CD 3:18–4:4; 4QFlor 1:3-4). The group's members also imagined themselves to be like the heavenly angels (1QS 11:8; 1QSb 3:25-26; 4:24-26; 4QFlor 1:4). They submitted to priestly purity regulations (1QS 5:13; 6:16-17; 1QSa 2:3-10; CD 15:15-17), and they set the ages for service by priestly standards (1QSa 1:8-17; CD 10:6-8). They may have engaged in prayer and praise intended to take place at the same time as key liturgical rites of the temple cult (see, e.g., 4Q409).[4] Whether they observed them in any way, they preserved priestly rota in their library (4Q317-333).[5] All of this does point to a community intent on mirroring in its day-to-day existence the essential characteristics of the cultic and priestly life.

The *Songs of the Sabbath Sacrifice* provide perhaps the most compelling evidence for the group's tendency toward imaginative reflection of something resembling the temple cult. Yet the *Songs* also reveal the limitations of this strategy for the community, for like the other texts surveyed above, the *Songs* stop short of actually *replacing* sacrifice. Largely a description of the heavenly liturgy undertaken by angelic priests on thirteen successive Sabbaths, the *Songs* "do not speak of actual co-participation in the conduct of the cult in the heavenly temple,"[6] nor do they ever reveal the words of the hymns sung by

---

3. For the community as a temple, see, for example, Klinzing, *Umdeutung*, 50-93; and Devorah Dimant, "*4QFlorilegium* and the Idea of the Community as Temple," in *Hellenica et Judaica: Hommage à Valentin Nikiprowetzky*, ed. A. Caquot, M. Hadas, and J. Riaud (Leuven/Paris: Peeters, 1986) 165-89.

4. On this interpretation of 4Q409, see Elisha Qimron, "Time for Praising God: A Fragment of a Scroll from Qumran (4Q409)," *JQR* (1990) 341-47.

5. For a recent discussion of many of these texts, see James C. VanderKam, *Calendars in the Dead Sea Scrolls: Measuring Time* (London: Routledge, 1998).

6. Carol Newsom, "'He Has Established for Himself Priests': Human and Angelic Priesthood in the Qumran *Sabbath Shirot*," in *Archaeology and History in the Dead Sea Scrolls*, ed. Lawrence Schiffman (JSPSup 8/ASOR Monographs 2; Sheffield: JSOT Press, 1990) 101-20; for the quotation, see p. 117.

ROBERT A. KUGLER

the heavenly angels. In fact, in the second song the single instance of first person speech in the work states, "But [...] how shall we be considered [among] them? And how shall our priesthood [be considered] in their habitations? And our ho[liness — how can it compare with] their [surpassing] holiness? [What] is the offering of our mortal tongue [compared] with the knowledge of the 'ēl[îm . . . ?]" (4Q400 2 2-3).[7] The passage implies that the author of the work and his audience thought themselves able to look in on the angelic liturgy, but never to participate in it. Thus no matter how much "a common experience is generated through the power of the language of the songs to invoke and make present the worship of the heavenly temple,"[8] it in no way replaced the human liturgy that took place in the Jerusalem sanctuary.[9]

So in fact, the community's prayer, praise, study, and priestly-cultic self-definition *did not* replace the act of sacrifice; at best they mimicked or mirrored it. The deficit in the group's religious life resulting from separation from the Jerusalem cult abided. How did they respond to what must have been for them a crisis of faith? Another group of scrolls suggests that the community's solution — only partial in character — lay in rewriting the biblical rubrics for sacrifice through harmonizing and narrowing exegesis. In lieu of actually participating in the cult, the group's members satisfied themselves with redefining it according to their vision, surely in anticipation of their own return to the temple one day.

Exegetically Based Scrolls on Sacrifice and Closely Related Topics: A Survey

A number of prominent scrolls deal at length with the temple and temple sacrifice. They reveal time and again that through the exercise of their exegetical imagination the group, separated from actual practice in the temple, speculated at length on the nature of what *should* transpire there according to biblical precepts.

The *Temple Scroll* provides the most expansive treatment of cultic regu-

7. For the text and a discussion of its larger significance for understanding the *Songs,* see Newsom, "'He Has Established,'" 105-6, 117.
8. Newsom, "'He Has Established,'" 117.
9. Newsom ("'He Has Established,'" 117) theorizes that the *Songs* construct "a realm where adequate cult is maintained" in contrast to the corrupted cult in Jerusalem and the generally inadequate worship rendered by human beings. Thus "[t]he experience provided by the *Sabbath Shirot* serves to authenticate and reward human worship while at the same time allowing for a proleptic transcendence of its limits."

lations.[10] Virtually all of columns 13-30 address the offerings made in the scroll's idealized temple, and most of column 60 treats the dues owing to priests for their sacrificial service. Lawrence Schiffman has proved that this "sacrificial calendar" correlates and reconciles biblical laws on the various sacrifices; as such its author's intention was to "reform the entire temple and the conduct of its ritual . . . to return to what in his view was the true intent of the Torah."[11] Throughout the scroll the aim is to clarify and tighten biblical regulations pertaining to sacrifice and priestly duties. For example, the instructions for the ordination ceremony in 11QT[a] 15:3–17:5 coordinate the consecration accounts in Exodus 29 and Leviticus 8 to develop new instructions for a yearly investiture liturgy to take place in the future, ideal temple.[12]

A number of fragments in the *New Jerusalem* texts also contemplate sacrifice in a future temple, but unlike the one in the *Temple Scroll,* this sanctuary exists in an eschatological aftertime.[13] An Ezekiel-like visionary reports

10. For 11QT see Y. Yadin, *The Temple Scroll* (3 vols. + suppl.; Jerusalem: Israel Exploration Society, 1983); E. Qimron, *The Temple Scroll: A Critical Edition with Extensive Reconstructions* (Judean Desert Studies; Beer Sheva-Jerusalem: Ben Gurion University of the Negev Press, Israel Exploration Society, 1996). See also the recently revised text in translation (German) from Johann Maier, *Die Tempelrolle vom Toten Meer und das "Neue Jerusalem"* (3rd ed.; München: Reinhardt, 1997). For a recent discussion of the contents of and critical issues associated with the *Temple Scroll,* see Florentino García Martínez, "The *Temple Scroll* and the *New Jerusalem,"* in *The Dead Sea Scrolls after Fifty Years: A Comprehensive Assessment,* ed. Peter W. Flint and James C. VanderKam (2 vols.; Leiden: Brill, 1998, 1999) 2.431-45.

11. L. Schiffman, "*'ôlâ* and *ḥaṭṭā't* in the *Temple Scroll,"* in *Pomegranates and Golden Bells: Studies in Biblical, Jewish, and Near Eastern Ritual, Law, and Literature in Honor of Jacob Milgrom,* ed. D. P. Wright, D. N. Freedman, and A. Hurvitz (Winona Lake, Ind.: Eisenbrauns, 1995) 39-48; the quotation is on p. 48. See also Schiffman's numerous essays on 11QT listed in Florentino García Martínez and Donald W. Parry, *A Bibliography of the Finds in the Desert of Judah, 1970-95* (STDJ 19; Leiden: Brill, 1996) 386-95. For further observations on the exegetical strategies evident in the *Temple Scroll,* see Jacob Milgrom, "The Qumran Cult: Its Exegetical Principles," in *Temple Scroll Studies: Papers Presented at the International Symposium on the Temple Scroll, Manchester, December 1987,* ed. George J. Brooke (Sheffield: JSOT Press, 1989) 165-80.

12. On this passage and its use of Exod 29 and Lev 8, see Lawrence Schiffman, "The *Milluim* Ceremony in the *Temple Scroll,"* in *New Qumran Texts and Studies: Proceedings of the First Meeting of the International Organization for Qumran Studies,* ed. George J. Brooke and Florentino García Martínez (STDJ 15; Leiden: Brill, 1994) 255-72.

13. For the Cave 11 *New Jerusalem* texts see Florentino García Martínez, Eibert J. C. Tigchelaar, and A. S. van der Woude, *Manuscripts from Qumran Cave 11 (11Q2-18, 11Q20-30)* (DJD 23; Oxford: Clarendon Press, 1997) 305-55; and for 2Q24 see M. Baillet, J. T. Milik, and R. de Vaux, *Les 'pétites grottes' de Qumrân* (DJD 3; Oxford: Clarendon Press, 1962) 84-89. For the most recent survey of the work's contents and of recent scholarship on it, see Florentino García Martínez, "The *Temple Scroll* and the *New Jerusalem,"* 2.445-57.

on the temple's dimensions, accoutrements, and daily operations. 2Q24 4 and 11Q18 13 and 20 especially show the work's interest in the sacrificial system and its operation in the New Age. According to 11Q18 13 the visionary sees a priest performing a well-being offering (Lev 3:1-17; 7:12-14),[14] and 2Q24 4 and 11Q18 20 report on eighty-four priests consuming the bread of presence (Lev 24:5-9). Here too Scripture-based speculation clarifies and expands on what takes place in a (future) temple.

In addition to the *Temple Scroll* and the *New Jerusalem* texts, a few other compositions deal with transactions in the temple. 4Q156 (4QTargum of Leviticus) reproduces with no significant change Leviticus 16:12-15, 18-21.[15] 4Q264a (4QHalakha B) and 4Q375 1 ii 3-9 (4QApocryphon of Moses[a]) preserve fleeting, Scripture-based reflections on sacrificial acts.[16] 4Q276-277 (4QPurification Rules B[a,b]) expand on the red heifer rite in Numbers 19.[17] All of these texts stay well within the boundaries established by the *Temple Scroll* and the *New Jerusalem* texts by providing occasionally corrective and expansionist exegeses of the biblical rules for sacrifice and related matters. To take a closer look at this habit of rewriting rubrics through Scripture exegesis, we turn now to 4QMMT.

The Case of 4QMMT

4QMMT (4QSome Works of the Law; henceforth MMT) also deals at length with issues related to priestly practice and the sacrificial cult.[18] Like the *Tem-*

---

14. It is also possible that this fragment describes the ritual associated with the ordination of priests, where the mixture of meat and bread sacrifice also occurs (cf. Lev 8:26).

15. R. de Vaux and J. T. Milik, *Qumrân Grotte 4, II* (DJD 6; Oxford: Clarendon Press, 1977) 86-89, 92-93; see also A. Angerstorfer, "Überlegungen zu Sprache und Sitz im Leben des Toratargums 4QtgLev (4Q156), sein Verhältnis zu Targum Onkelos," *BN* 55 (1990) 18-35; and Loren T. Stuckenbruck, "Bibliography on 4QTgLev (4Q156)," *JSP* 10 (1992) 53-55.

16. For 4Q375, see M. Broshi et al., in consultation with J. C. VanderKam, *Qumran Cave 4, XIV: Parabiblical Texts, Part 2* (DJD 19; Oxford: Clarendon Press, 1995) 111-19; and John Strugnell, "Moses-Pseudepigrapha at Qumran," in *Archaeology and History in the Dead Sea Scrolls,* 221-56, esp. 224-34.

17. See J. M. Baumgarten, "The Red Cow Purification Rites in Qumran Texts," *JJS* 46 (1995) 112-19.

18. For the official edition, see E. Qimron and J. Strugnell (in consultation with Y. Sussmann and with contributions by Y. Sussmann and A. Yardeni), *Qumran Cave 4, V: Miqsat Ma'aseh ha-Torah* (DJD 10; Oxford: Clarendon, 1994). The secondary literature on MMT is abundant and grows ever more enormous. For a good selection of essays, see *Reading 4QMMT: New Perspectives on Qumran Law and History,* ed. John Kampen and Moshe J. Bernstein (SBLSS 2; Atlanta: Scholars Press, 1996); and the more recent contribu-

ple Scroll and the other texts discussed in the preceding section, it exegetes and harmonizes Scripture on the topics of cult and priesthood as a means of composing new rubrics for cultic administration, rules that are more restrictive than the ones expressed in the Bible.[19] Moreover, it treats each issue in a clear and orderly fashion, making it the most accommodating text for illustrating in greater depth the community's habit of rewriting rubrics in place of the act of sacrifice.

Most regard MMT as an early group document that nevertheless retained currency in the community throughout the duration of the group's residence at Qumran.[20] John Strugnell and Elisha Qimron divide the work into three parts. Part A is a calendar. Part B is a collection of first-person plural speeches addressed to a second-person party on disputed halakic issues. Part C is a first-person plural hortatory address to a second person urging the addressee to side with the authors in the halakic disputes surveyed in part B. While the supposedly epistolary genre of MMT as a whole is legitimately disputed,[21] parts B and C together do include the elements of

---

tions by George J. Brooke, Lester L. Grabbe, and Hannah K. Harrington in *Legal Texts and Legal Issues: Proceedings of the Second Meeting of the International Organization for Qumran Studies, Published in Honour of Joseph M. Baumgarten*, ed. Moshe Bernstein, Florentino García Martínez, and John Kampen (STDJ 23; Leiden: Brill, 1997).

19. Critics disagree regarding the amount of scriptural citation and exegesis in MMT. The DJD editors say that "the word כתוב . . . [i]n MMT . . . never introduces biblical verses," but that "[i]t sometimes precedes a description or paraphrase of a biblical verse" (*Qumran Cave 4, V: Miqṣat Maʿaseh ha-Torah*, DJD 10, 140). Moshe Bernstein, "The Employment and Interpretation of Scripture in 4QMMT: Preliminary Observations," in *Reading 4QMMT*, 29-51; and George J. Brooke, "The Explicit Presentation of Scripture in 4QMMT," in *Legal Texts and Legal Issues*, 67-88, are likewise rather conservative in their estimates of how much Scripture actually turns up in MMT, even if they do find direct quotations where the editors did not. In what follows I take a much more liberal position, finding even in isolated snatches of biblical rhetoric (that are nonetheless relatively unusual or even unique in Scripture) evidence of probable exegetical activity on the part of the author and certainly testimony to recipients that MMT is engaged with Scripture as a principle witness to proper cultic action.

20. The composition survives in six manuscripts (4Q394-399), dating from 75 BCE to 50 CE (see *Qumran Cave 4, V: Miqṣat Maʿaseh ha-Torah*, DJD 10, 3-42). Because it lacks much of the group's "sectarian" language and seems to presume circumstances in which the disputes between the authoring group and the opponents could still be discussed and perhaps worked out, most regard it as an early group document. Thus the youth of the manuscripts belies the enduring value of the document for the community.

21. See especially John Strugnell, "Appendix 3; Additional Observations on 4QMMT," in *Qumran Cave 4, V: Miqṣat Maʿaseh ha-Torah*, DJD 10, 203-6; idem, "MMT: Second Thoughts on a Forthcoming Edition," in *The Community of the Renewed Covenant: The Notre Dame Symposium on the Dead Sea Scrolls*, ed. Eugene Ulrich and James

a letter.[22] Thus it seems likely that MMT was, at least at an early stage of its development, a memorandum from the community to an external authority encouraging him to accept the community's views and to reject those of another, unnamed group.

Among the seventeen issues addressed in part B, those relating to priests and sacrifice dominate. In what follows I explain the biblical basis for over half of those issues to show in greater detail how the Qumran community went about rewriting rubrics for the temple liturgy by harmonizing and narrowing biblical exegesis.[23]

1. 4QMMT B 11-13; 16-17 (?); 25-27; 82 (?)

Several times MMT warns the priests regarding their sacerdotal practice, saying,

11 [כי לבני[
12 הכוהנ[ים] ראוי להצהיר בדבר הזה בשל שלוא י[היו]
13 מסיא[י[ם את העם עוון

VanderKam (CJA 10; Notre Dame, Ind.: University of Notre Dame Press, 1994) 57-73. Central to the question is whether part A was originally part of the composition known from parts B and C; for the definitive argument in favor of separating the calendar from the rest of the work, see James VanderKam, "The Calendar, 4Q327, and 4Q395," in *Legal Texts and Legal Issues*, 179-94.

22. Or, in Strugnell's words, "a legal proclamation to an accepted ruler" ("MMT: Second Thoughts," 72).

23. I do not treat eight of the seventeen rulings identified by Qimron and Strugnell (see the list in *Qumran Cave 4, V: Miqsat Ma'aseh ha-Torah*, DJD 10, 147). The rulings on the prohibition of Gentile wheat in the temple (B 3-5), the cooking of offerings (B 5-8), sacrifices from Gentiles (B 8-9), and the impurity of lepers (B 64-72) are all too fragmentary or too questionable as restored texts to permit reasonable analysis. (See especially the sharp disagreement between Qimron and Strugnell, *Qumran Cave 4, V: Miqsat Ma'aseh ha-Torah*, DJD 10, 166-70, and Bernstein, "Employment and Interpretation," 41-45, on the reconstruction of B 64-72; see also the dubious view of the editors' reconstruction of B 64-72 expressed by Brooke, "Explicit Presentation," 82.) The rulings on the impurity of hides (B 18-24), the impurity of streams (B 55-58), the impurity of dogs in Jerusalem (B 58-62), and impurity as a result of contact with human bones (B 72-74) are not closely enough connected to the temple and the cult to merit attention here, and in some cases they are also too fragmentary for comment. I do treat as a separate matter the cautionary refrain directed to the priests in MMT B 11-13; 16-17 (?); 25-27; 82 (?).

For the sons of the priests should take care concerning this matter lest they cause the people to bear guilt.[24]

The language of the refrain echoes Leviticus 22:16 and Numbers 18:1.[25]

והשיאו אותם עון אשמה באכלם את קדשיהם כי אני יהוה מקדשם

They cause them to bear guilt requiring a guilt offering when they eat their sacred donations, for I the Lord make them holy. (Lev 22:16)[26]

ויאמר יהוה אל אהרן אתה ובניך ובית אביך אתך תשאו את עון
המקדש ואתה ובנך אתך תשאו את עון כהנתכם

And the Lord said to Aaron, "You and your sons and your ancestral house with you, you bear guilt for defilement of the sanctuary, but you and your sons with you [alone] bear guilt for defilement of your priesthood." (Num 18:1)[27]

However, Elisha Qimron and John Strugnell and Moshe Bernstein agree that the principal relationship is with Leviticus 22:16, which itself is ambiguous when read in relationship to what precedes it.

24. (Translations of MMT are taken from the DJD edition, with only minor adjustments.) Parts of this formula appear in roughly similar fashion after the rulings on when meal offerings must be consumed (B 9-13), when those involved with the ashes of the red cow are properly cleansed (B 13-17), and the disposition of animal hides (B 17-27). It may also have followed the ruling regarding the marriage of priests (B 82).

25. Qimron and Strugnell (*Qumran Cave 4, V: Miqṣat Ma'aseh ha Torah*, DJD 10, 47 n. 11 and 48 n. 13) seem to share this view; but see the following discussion. Bernstein, "Employment and Interpretation," 36, cites only Lev 22:16.

26. עון אשמה is translated here as "guilt requiring a guilt offering" in accordance with the NRSV; literally the phrase is "guilt of a guilt offering."

27. The translation is borrowed in large part from Baruch Levine, *Numbers: A New Translation and Commentary* (AB4; Garden City, N.Y.: Doubleday, 1993) 435, 439-40, who correctly notes that עון plays double-duty here. On one hand it denotes what one does (defile the sanctuary), and on the other it indicates the consequences for one's actions (guilt and its consequences [Levine uses the word "punishment" here]). In any case, the assignment of guilt is clear: acting as a buffer for the laity in matters pertaining to God's holiness in the temple (see the cry of the people in Num 17:12-13, as observed by N. H. Snaith, *Leviticus and Numbers* [Century Bible; London: Nelson, 1967] 64-65), the levitical clan as a whole would absorb any guilt for errors committed; and Aaronites would take the blame for any wrongdoing by the priestly clan. For much the same reading, see E. W. Davies, *Numbers* (NCB; Grand Rapids: Eerdmans, 1995) 185.

ואיש כי יאכל קדש בשגגה ויסף חמשיתו עליו ונתן לכהן את
הקדש ולא יחללו את קדשי בני ישראל את אשר ירימו ליהוה

If a man eats of the sacred donation unintentionally, he shall add one-fifth
of its value to it, and give the sacred donation to the priest. No one shall
profane the sacred donations of the people of Israel, which they offer to the
Lord. (Lev 22:14-15)[28]

After mentioning a lay person and priests in verse 14, verses 15-16 use third-
person plural verbs without supplying specific subjects. As a consequence
there is little agreement among commentators and translators regarding just
who causes guilt and who bears guilt according to verse 16.[29] Qimron and
Strugnell and Bernstein rightly note that MMT resolves the ambiguity by
making the priests responsible for the guilt of the layperson. But MMT goes
this one better, interpreting Leviticus 22:16 even more severely in the priests'
disfavor. In Leviticus the context dictates that the priests' causative power re-
sides merely in *assigning* the guilt to the laity responsible for improperly eating holy food. But MMT has adapted the verse's language so that the priests'
causative power rests in actually bringing about the layperson's guilt through
their own poor stewardship of the priestly office.

There is still more to this formula's relationship with Scripture. It seems
unlikely that the author or audience of this text would not also have thought
of Numbers 18:1 in composing or encountering it. At first that presents a
problem, since Numbers 18:1 assigns all guilt to the priests for cultic misdeeds. Does MMT abrogate Numbers 18:1 by way of clarifying Leviticus
22:16? The answer must be "no" for MMT does not deny that priests and

---

28. NRSV.

29. The range of opinion is surprisingly wide. For example, Martin Noth, *Leviticus:
A Commentary* (Philadelphia: Westminster, 1965) 158, 161-62, seems to think that Lev
22:14-16 is all about priestly administration of cultic food, and that priests cause the one
who offered the donation to bear guilt by mishandling the layperson's gift; Jacob Milgrom,
Cult and Conscience: The ASHAM and the Priestly Doctrine of Repentance (Leiden: Brill,
1976) 63-66, translates v. 16 as, "They [the priests] must make them [the Israelites] bear
the penalty of reparation, if they [the Israelites] eat their holy things," suggesting that the
laity cause their own guilt by misappropriating the sacred donations, but the priests are
the ones who enforce the punishment for the error. Snaith, *Leviticus and Numbers,* 147-48,
understands v. 16 to mean that priests are responsible for restraining the laity from trans-
gression; Roland Faley, "Leviticus," in *New Jerome Biblical Commentary,* ed. Raymond
Brown et al. (Englewood Cliffs, N.J.: Prentice Hall, 1990) 75, insists that the priests must
restrain the laity so that the priests do not incur punishable guilt through the misdeeds of
the laity!

their households would bear guilt for cultic errors; rather, it simply adds to their responsibility by indicating that they are accountable not only for their own righteousness, but also for that of the lay people they serve.

In this first passage we see how MMT clarifies and harmonizes scriptural norms regarding cultic practice to circumscribe in new ways temple procedures and the responsibilities of those associated with them. In this case the result of such harmonizing exegesis is that there are more rigorous requirements for priests than those imposed on them by Scripture.

2. 4QMMT B 9-13

This passage concerns when one should have consumed the last of a meal offering made in the temple. Scripture provides no ruling on the matter, and, apparently to avoid concocting a judgment out of thin air, the author of MMT borrowed the rhetoric and content of Leviticus 7:15 and 19:6 to construct a law that deals with the issue.[30] Both verses deal with the disposition of the meat of the thanksgiving sacrifice of well-being.

ובשר זבח תודת שלמיו ביום קרבנו יאכל לא יניח ממנו עד בקר

And the meat of the thanksgiving sacrifice of well-being, it shall be eaten on the day of its offering, and none of it shall be left until morning. (Lev 7:15)

ביום זבחכם יאכל וממחרת והנותר עד יום השלישי באש ישרף

On the day of your offering it shall be eaten, and on the next day, and what is left over until the third day, it shall be consumed by fire. (Lev 19:6)

These two verses present an interpretive problem. ביום קרבנו, "on the day of its offering," in 7:15 suggests that the meat must be consumed by the first sunset after it was offered, since that is the end of the day on which it was sacrificed. But עד בקר, "until morning," seems to permit continued con-

---

30. For the view that Lev 7:15 and 19:6 inform this ruling, see *Qumran Cave 4, V: Miqṣat Maʿaseh ha-Torah*, DJD 10, 47, 51-52; and Elisha Qimron, "The Nature of the Reconstructed Composite Text," in *Reading 4QMMT*, 9-13, esp. 10. Brooke, "Explicit Presentation," 71 n. 16, also acknowledges the connection between the MMT passage and Lev 19:6, but see the further discussion of his views on the passage below, n. 33; see also Lawrence Schiffman, "*Miqṣat Maʿaseh Ha-Torah* and the *Temple Scroll*," *RevQ* 14 (1990) 436-57, esp. 436-38.

sumption through the night (i.e., into the new day after the sacrifice was made) and until the next morning. ביום זבחכם יאכל וממחרת, "On the day of your offering it shall be eaten, and on the next day," in 19:6 also provides its share of troubles. The last word implies that one could continue to consume the offering until the next day, but ביום זבחכם יאכל contradicts that claim. As Qimron points out, the rabbis took a lenient view in the matter, interpreting עד בקר (and, by implication, ביום זבחכם יאכל וממחרת) to mean that one could continue to eat the food after sunset and into the next day, so long as consumption did not go past midnight (*m. Zebaḥ.* 6.1).[31]

By contrast, the sectarian authors exhibit the opposite attitude. They respond to the ambiguity of Leviticus 7:15; 19:6 by saying

10   ואף [כתוב   [

11 שהמנ[חה נאכלת] על החלבים והבשר ביום זוב[חם

And it is written that the offering should be eaten after the fat and the flesh[32] (are sacrificed), on the day of their sacrifice.[33]

The sectarian authors intended the meal sacrifice to be consumed entirely by sunset of the day of its offering. They left no room for error in the matter. After all, the handling of sacrifices was the means by which the priest established and sustained a relationship between God and people. This ruling, like the exhortation to the priests, harmonizes and resolves a tension produced by ambiguous biblical witnesses, and in doing so opts for a rigorous view of matters.[34]

31. *m. Zebaḥ.* 6:1 reads ליום וללילה עד חצות, "on that day and night until midnight" (cited in *Qumran Cave 4, V. Miqṣat Maʿaseh ha-Torah*, DJD 10, 151).

32. The phrase על החלבים והבשר, though difficult, is best translated "after the fat and the flesh." For an attempted explanation, see *Qumran Cave 4, V: Miqṣat Maʿaseh ha-Torah*, DJD 10, 151, n. 90.

33. The כתוב supplied by the editors is rejected by Brooke, "Explicit Presentation," 71, n. 16; and by Bernstein, "Employment and Interpretation," 39. Brooke especially thinks that the biblical language of this passage is too allusive to think that it was introduced by the כתוב-citation formula. This is somewhat curious given his conclusion that "MMT helps us to see that we should not look for nor expect to find scripture quoted in the form it is known to us in the MT. Nor should citations which contain no major words other than those which are also to be found in the MT be discarded as nonbiblical" (88).

34. Qimron and Strugnell say that the sectarian conclusion is actually a function of substantially more intricate exegetical reasoning. They conclude that the author achieved the stricter interpretation by conflating Deut 24:15 with Lev 7:15 (*Qumran Cave 4, V: Miqṣat Maʿaseh ha-Torah*, DJD 10, 151-52). Deuteronomy 24:15 treats the payment of

3. 4QMMT B 13-17

This expansion on the rules for purifying the participants who prepare the red cow ashes for the water of purification (Num 19:1-10) draws considerable attention because it ostensibly reflects the Pharisaic-Sadducean dispute over the *tĕbûl yōm*.[35] After a period of impurity, when may one participate again in ritual activities and consume sacred food? After washing, or only after sunset of the last day of one's period of impurity? The Pharisees admit the *tĕbûl yōm* — the one who has only washed — to such activities, but the Sadducees insist that only one who has washed and waited until sunset of the last day of impurity is ritually pure again (*m. Para* 3.7).[36] Most agree that this passage takes the Sadducean side in the debate, and that this ruling is directed against opponents who would permit, as do the "elders of Israel" in *m. Para* 3.7, ritual action by a *tĕbûl yōm* in the matter of the red cow rite.[37]

---

wages to a day laborer, saying, ביומו תתן שכרו ולא תבוא השמש עליו, "On the day give him his wages, and do not allow the sun to set upon him (without payment of wages)." The absence of any language from Deut 24:15 in MMT B 9-13 leaves the editors unconcerned because they find a similar ruling on cereal offering in 11QT^a 20:12-13 that echoes Deut 24:15 (השמש) ביום ההוא תא[כל]כל] / [ולוא תבוא עליה] השמש), "On that day it shall be eaten, and the sun shall not set on it"). From this parallel Qimron concludes that the sectarians had a preexisting exegetical tradition that brought the two biblical legal claims together. But genetic connections between MMT, with its peculiarly "mishnaic" language, and the *Temple Scroll*, with its biblicizing rhetoric, are by no means certain. Thus it seems best not to appeal to Deut 24:15 to explain the stringency of MMT's interpretation of the crux in Lev 7:15. Rather the evidence supports taking the document's claim at face value. Echoing the ambiguous biblical passages Lev 7:15; 19:6, MMT solves their ambivalence with a strict interpretation of their language.

35. See *Qumran Cave 4, V: Miqṣat Maʿaseh ha-Torah*, DJD 10, 152-54, Lawrence Schiffman, "Pharisaic and Sadducean Halakhah in Light of the Dead Sea Scrolls: The Case of the *Tebul Yom*," *DSD* 1 (1994) 285-99, esp. 287-90; Avi Solomon, "The Prohibition Against *Tevul Yom* and Defilement of the Daily Whole Offering in the Jerusalem Temple in CD 11:21–12:1: A New Understanding," *DSD* 4 (1997) 1-20, esp. 13-17. See also Magen Broshi, "Anti-Qumranic Polemics in the Talmud," in *The Madrid Congress: Proceedings of the International Congress on the Dead Sea Scrolls, Madrid, 18-21 March 1991*, ed. Julio Trebolle Barrera and Luis Vegas Montaner (2 vols.; STDJ 11; Leiden: Brill, 1992) 2.589-99. By contrast, Lester Grabbe, "4QMMT and Second Temple Jewish Society," in *Legal Texts and Legal Issues*, 90-93, esp. 91, nn. 6-7, and 93, n. 15, has argued that this text is not at all about the *tĕbûl yōm*, and that the concept may not yet have even been an issue at the time of MMT's composition.

36. See also the other rabbinical texts cited by Schiffman, "Pharisaic and Sadducean Halakhah," 290-91, nn. 18-19.

37. So say Schiffman, "Pharisaic and Sadducean Halakhah," 288-90; Solomon, "The Prohibition Against *Tevul Yom*," 14; and *Qumran Cave 4, V: Miqṣat Maʿaseh ha-Torah*, DJD

13 ואף על טהרת פרת החטאת
14 השוחט אותה והסורף אותה והאוסף [א]ת אפרה והמזה את [מי]
15 החטאת לכול אלה להערי[בו]ת השמש להיות טהורים
16 בשל שא יהיה הטהר מזה על הטמה

And concerning the purity regulations of the cow of the purification offering: he who slaughters it and he who burns it and he who gathers its ashes and he who sprinkles the water of purification, all of these become pure at sunset so that the pure may sprinkle on the impure.

One wonders if close reliance on the rabbinical discussions of the *těbûl yōm* has prejudiced the discussion of MMT B 13-17. Indeed, read apart from the *later* disputes a much simpler explanation of what the passage attempts to accomplish presents itself. MMT B 13-17 clearly relies on Numbers 19:1-10, and a look at both texts proves their agreement that only after washing *and sunset* is one pure again. However, the biblical passage addresses only the purity of the priest who oversees the slaughter of the cow, the one who burns the cow, and the one who gathers its ashes. Numbers 19 does not provide for the one who slaughters or the one who sprinkles. At precisely this point MMT makes its advance over the biblical law: it adds the slaughterer and the sprinkler to *its* list of individuals who must wait until sunset to be ritually pure. And to emphasize this as the real point of the ruling the author states אלה לכול, "For *all of these*" purity is achieved at sunset.

So here again we encounter a ruling that interprets Scripture on the correct procedure for cultic activity and in doing so manages to intensify and expand the biblical requirements associated with such activity. Indeed, its closing flourish, "so that the pure may sprinkle on the impure," seems to raise considerably the stakes on proper procedure. It declares that the effect of the red cow's ashes depends on their proper preparation: make a mistake (by ignoring the one who slaughters and the one who sprinkles) and all bets are off on the effectiveness of the rite.

4. 4QMMT B 27-35

Here MMT takes up Leviticus 17:3-4 and its insistence that all slaughter take place at the tent of meeting, and that none be undertaken in the camp or out-

---

10, 154. See also Y. Sussmann, "Appendix 1: The History of the Halakha and the Dead Sea Scrolls," in *Qumran Cave 4, V: Miqṣat Maʿaseh ha-Torah*, DJD 10, 179-200, esp. 187-88.

side the camp.[38] The ruling clarifies what each of those places is: the sanctuary is the tent of meeting and the holy of holies, Jerusalem is the camp, and "outside the camp" refers to the settlements in the land outside of Jerusalem.

27 ‏[וע]ל שא כתוב] איש כי ישחט במחנה או]‏

28 ‏[ישחט]מחוץ למחנה שור וכשב ועז כי] בצפון המחנה]‏

29 ‏ואנחנו חושבים שהמקדש] משכן אוהל מועד הוא וי]רושלי[ם]‏

30 ‏מחנה היא וחו[צה] למחנה] הוא חוצה לירושלים]הוא מחנה‏

31 ‏ער]י[הם‏

And concerning that which is written: if a person slaughters inside the camp, or slaughters outside the camp cattle or sheep or a goat: for . . . in the northern part of the camp. And we think that the sanctuary is the place of the tent of meeting, Jerusalem is the camp, and outside the camp is outside Jerusalem, that is, the encampments of their settlements.

According to this ruling all slaughter must take place at the sanctuary (rendering every act of slaughter an act of sacrifice), a practice apparently not observed by the author's opponents.[39]

To this point the halakah seems relatively unremarkable. It merely identifies its authors' views with the conservative perspective in Leviticus 17. But this changes when the ruling concludes by urging the removal of sacrificial waste to a place beyond the boundaries of Jerusalem (ll. 31-32), saying

---

38. Qimron and Strugnell (*Qumran Cave 4, V: Miqṣat Maʿaseh ha-Torah*, DJD 10, 156) call this a paraphrase of Lev 17:3, as does Bernstein ("Employment and Interpretation," 39). Brooke ("Explicit Presentation," 72) takes issue with the use of the term "paraphrase," noting rightly that the language of MMT is entirely that of Leviticus; thus it is a reordering, not a paraphrase.

39. See MMT B 35, ‏אי]נם שוחטים במקדש‏, "They are not slaughtering in the sanctuary." For the same view of where slaughter should take place, see 11QT 52:13–53:4 and the other passages cited by Hannah Harrington, "Holiness in the Laws of 4QMMT," in *Legal Texts and Legal Issues: Proceedings of the Second Meeting of the International Organization for Qumran Studies, Cambridge 1995,* ed. M. Bernstein, Florentino García Martínez, and John Kampen (STDJ XIII; Leiden: Brill, 1997)114-16; on the treatment of the sacred space in MMT B 35 and in the *Temple Scroll,* see Lawrence Schiffman, "The Place of 4QMMT in the Corpus of Qumran Manuscripts," in *Reading 4QMMT: New Perspectives on Qumran Law and History,* ed. John J. Kampen and Moshe J. Bernstein (SBLSS Z; Atlanta: Scholars Press, 1996) 88 89; idem, "Exclusion from the Sanctuary and the City of the Sanctuary in the *Temple Scroll,*" *HAR* 9 (1985) 308-9; idem, "Architecture and Law: The Temple and Its Courtyards in the *Temple Scroll,*" in *From Ancient Israel to Modern Judaism: Intellect in Quest of Understanding, Essays in Honor of Marvin Fox,* ed. J. Neusner, E. S. Frerichs, and N. M. Sarna (2 vols.; BJS 159; Atlanta: Scholars Press, 1989) 1.267-84.

כי ירושלים [היא המקום אשר 32

33 [בחר בו מכול שבטי ישראל

For Jerusalem is the place that God has chosen from among all the tribes of Israel.

With this the instruction echoes Deuteronomy 12:5 so that Jerusalem — not just the sanctuary — is the place of God's choosing. Even more, it subsumes Deuteronomy's more liberal view regarding slaughter — that only sacrificial acts must be performed at the holy site, and profane slaughter may occur elsewhere in the land of Israel — under the conservative view of Leviticus 17 that eliminates profane slaughter by requiring all killing of animals to take place at the sanctuary.[40]

In this ruling, then, we encounter yet again harmonizing exegesis that sides with the most rigorous biblical rules governing cultic action.

5. 4QMMT B 36-38

This ruling against sacrificing a parent animal and its offspring on the same day echoes Leviticus 22:28.[41] While it is largely reconstructed, and anything said about it must be tentative, the editors and most commentators are confident of the general contours of the halakah.[42]

36 [על העברות אנחנו חושבים שאין לזבוח א[ת האם ואת הולד ביום אחד

37 [ ] ועל האוכל אנח[נו חושבים שאיאכל את הולד

38 [שבמעי אמו לאחר שחיטתו ואתם יודעים שהו]א כן והדבר כתוב עברה

40. Thus Qimron and Strugnell (*Qumran Cave 4, V: Miqṣat Maʿaseh ha-Torah*, DJD 10, 156-57) err in saying that this passage provides nothing new.

41. Brooke, "Explicit Presentation," 73, seems to think that Deut 22:6 also informed this ruling. That is certainly true of the related halakah in 11QTᵃ 52:5-7 (see below), but in this case the only connection with Deut 22:6 would be the word אם, "mother," which probably appears here not because of an exegetical connection with Deut 22:6 but because the halakah applies Lev 22:28 to a particular case that always involves a female animal (see below).

42. However, Brooke, "Explicit Presentation," 72-73, does not share in the confidence others express regarding the reconstruction. As a consequence he resists associating the passage with Lev 22:28.

And concerning pregnant animals: we think that one should not sacrifice the mother and its fetus on the same day. Concerning consumption [of the fetus]: we think that the fetus may be eaten, the one that was in the womb of its mother, after it has been slaughtered. And you know that this is so, for the ruling refers to a pregnant animal.

Assuming that the reconstruction in line 36, **עַל הָעֵבָרוֹת אֲנַחְנוּ חוֹשְׁבִים שֶׁאֵין לִזְבּוֹחַ**, is correct,[43] the first part of the ruling prohibits *sacrificing* a mother and its fetus on the same day, and the second part permits the priests or the one making sacrifice to eat the fetus after properly *slaughtering* it rather than let it go to waste.

Commentators puzzle over this ruling, finding it difficult to relate it to Leviticus 22:28 and especially hard to explain the use of the **כתוב** formula prior to a single, nonbiblical word.[44] However, it may not be all that much of a puzzle. Leviticus 22:28 only rules against *slaughtering* (**שחט**) a parent animal *(gender unspecified)* and its offspring on the same day. By contrast this halakah takes up a narrower form of that problem, asking whether one can *sacrifice* (**זבח**) a *mother* (**אם**) and the fetus of its womb on the same day. In light of Leviticus 22:28 and Deuteronomy 22:6, no one thinks that it was accepted practice, even among the corrupt Jerusalem priests, to *knowingly* slaughter for sacrifice a pregnant beast. Thus the MMT ruling must address the case of a pregnancy discovered only after the beast had been killed for sacrifice. What should be done under those circumstances? asks the author of MMT. The answer, predicated on the biblical prohibition of *slaughtering* both parent and child beast on the same day, is that both certainly may not be *sac-*

43. It is certainly the most likely reconstruction; Qimron and Strugnell (*Qumran Cave 4, V: Miqṣat Maʿaseh ha-Torah*, DJD 10, 157-58), explain that they posit **הָעֵבָרוֹת** because of the same word in the singular at the end of the ruling (l. 38). Moreover, they supply **לִזְבּוֹחַ** because in a similar ruling in 11QT 52:5-7 the text uses **זבח** instead of the **שחט** of Lev 22:28; the previous ruling dealt with matters relating to animal sacrifice and the sanctuary (see **במקדש** in l. 35); and the second part of this ruling — using the word **אכל** — has clearly shifted to the question of nonsacral slaughter.

44. Qimron and Strugnell (*Qumran Cave 4, V: Miqṣat Maʿaseh ha-Torah*, DJD 10, 157-58) think that the halakah only aims to rule against the intentional slaughter and sacrifice of a pregnant mother and its fetus on the same day. They relate their claim to the widespread debate in early Judaism as to whether a mother and its fetus are separate entities (for citations and secondary literature, see *Qumran Cave 4, V: Miqṣat Maʿaseh ha-Torah*, DJD 10, 157, n 115). Schiffman, (*"Miqṣat Maʿaseh,"* 448-51) mentions this passage but deals mostly with 11QT 52:5-7. His view of the MMT passage is apparently similar to that of Qimron and Strugnell. Qimron and Strugnell, Bernstein ("Employment and Interpretation," 41), and Brooke ("Explicit Presentation," 73) all express varying degrees of discomfort with the use of the **כתוב** formula in this instance.

rificed on the same day. But, having gone that far, what is to be done with the fetus that remains? (Apparently the mother would become the sacrificial animal in such circumstances.) MMT says that it should be slaughtered since it cannot survive outside its mother's womb, and it should be eaten (perhaps so that its food value will not go to waste). Thus, when the ruling closes with the words והדבר כתוב עברה, "And the ruling refers to a pregnant animal," the author is likely claiming that Leviticus 22:28 can be understood to refer to precisely this sort of case, namely, a pregnant animal.[45]

If the editors' reconstruction and this interpretation are correct, it appears that the author of MMT and his community rejected the practice of sacrificing the "surprisingly pregnant" animal and its fetus on the same day. The way he articulated his disagreement is in keeping with what we have observed so far in MMT. He interprets Scripture conservatively, settling thereby on the strictest possible understanding of a biblical law related to the cultic practice at issue.

6. 4QMMT B 39-49

This fragmentary halakah interprets the prohibition in Deuteronomy 23:2-4 against admitting Ammonites, Moabites, bastards, and males with genitals damaged by accident or castration into the קהל יהוה, "the congregation of the Lord." That there was a question from early on as to what קהל יהוה means is clear from Lamentations 1:10 and Nehemiah 13:23-31.[46] Some said that the law only prohibits marriage between Jewish women and men of the forbidden groups, while others applied the ban to marriages between male or female Jews and people of the prohibited classes. Only Lamentations 1:10 and Nehemiah 13:23-31 applied the ban to entry into the sanctuary.[47] To these we may add 4QMMT B 39-49.

---

45. Bernstein ("Employment and Interpretation," 40-41) holds much the same view of the ruling but curiously denigrates the author's reasoning, saying with regard to the view that the fetus must be slaughtered separately, "The 'argument' of MMT (if we may dignify it with that name) asserts, nevertheless, that this is the implication of Scripture" (41).

46. See also the texts from Philo, the Karaites, and the rabbis, cited in *Qumran Cave 4, V: Miqsat Ma'aseh ha-Torah,* DJD 10, 158-60.

47. On Neh 13:23-31 see Joseph Blenkinsopp, *Ezra-Nehemiah: A Commentary* (OTL; Philadelphia: Westminster, 1988) 361-66; Joseph Baumgarten, *Studies in Qumran Law* (SJLA 24; Leiden: Brill, 1977) 77, cited in Qimron and Strugnell, *Qumran Cave 4, V: Miqsat Ma'aseh ha-Torah,* DJD 10, 158, n. 118; but see also Z. Falk, "Those Excluded from the Congregation," *Beth Mikra* 62 (1975) 342-51 (Hebrew).

39 [ועל העמו]ני והמואבי[ן ו]הממזר ופ[צוע הדכה וכרו]ת השפכת שהם באים
40 בקהל] ונשים [ל]ו[ו]קח[ים להיו]תם עצם
41 אחת [ובאים למקדש   [
42 [טמאות ואף חושבים אנחנו   ]
43 [שאין   ואין לבו]א עליהם
44 [ואין]להתיכם [ו]לעשותם
45 [עצם אחת   ואין להבי]אם
46 [למקדש   ואתם יודעים שמק]צת העם
47 [וה]   מ   ים   מתוכ]כים
48 [כי לכול בני ישראל ראוי להזהר]מכול תערובת [ה]גבר
49 ולהיות יראים מהמקדש

And concerning the Ammonite and the Moabite and the bastard and him whose testicles have been crushed and him whose male member has been cut off, who nevertheless enter the congregation and . . . take wives to become one bone and enter the sanctuary . . . impurities. And we think that one must not let them be united (with an Israelite) and make them one bone . . . and one must not let them enter the sanctuary. And you know that some of the people . . . and become united. For all Israelites should beware of forbidden unions and be reverent regarding the sanctuary.

According to Elisha Qimron and John Strugnell, Lawrence Schiffman, and Hannah Harrington, MMT understands Deuteronomy 23:2-4 to prohibit both intermarriage with members of the proscribed groups and their entry into the sanctuary.[48] Moshe Bernstein remains less certain, saying that the single unreconstructed occurrence of the word for sanctuary, מקדש (B 49), provides too little evidence to say that the ruling also deals with entry into the temple. He insists, therefore, that it refers only to marriage.

The evidence speaks against Bernstein on two levels. While the apparent echo of Genesis 2:24 in lines 40-41, 44-45 verifies the author's concern with marriage, the closing allusion to Leviticus 19:30 and its concern for the *sanctuary* marks the ban as relating to entry into the temple as well.[49] And an ancient audience well attuned to hearing echoes of known biblical traditions could hardly have heard the ruling without recalling Lamentations 1:10 and its sanctuary-related interpretation of Deuteronomy 23:2-4.[50] Moreover, this ruling

48. Qimron and Strugnell, *Qumran Cave 4, V: Miqṣat Maʿaseh ha-Torah*, DJD 10, 159 60; Harrington, "Holiness," 122; Schiffman, "The Place of 4QMMT," 94.

49. See also Lev 26:2; 11QT 46:11.

50. For instance שהם באים בקהל (ll. 39-40) recalls לא יבאו בקהל לך of Lam 1:10, and if the reconstruction is correct, the occurrences of בוא with מקדש in lines 41 and 45-46 would further connect the two passages in the minds of attentive listeners.

follows three others that express interest in sanctuary-related matters, while a ruling focused on marriage alone appears later in the manuscript (B 75-82).

Taking into account the full scope of the editors' reconstruction deepens the conviction that this ruling refers to marriage with forbidden groups and its impact on who gains access to the sanctuary. And once again we see that interpreting an ambiguous biblical law through harmonizing exegesis composes a new rubric. The ruling begins with a quotation of Deuteronomy 23:2-4 (ll. 39-40) and then draws on Genesis 2:24 at the end of line 41 (and perhaps again in l. 46) to use the creation story's reference to union between man and woman as support for a legal claim regarding marriage.[51] If the reconstructed occurrences of מקדש in lines 41 and 46 are accurate, then the author meant not only to prohibit — as separate acts — certain types of intermarriage and the entry of forbidden groups into the sanctuary, but he also wanted to link the two phenomena. By their marriage into the קהל יהוה, the members of the forbidden groups would gain access to the sanctuary as well. Thus, he closes with an echo of Leviticus 19:30 as an exhortation to his audience. Of course, also lurking in the background because of its verbal resonance with the ruling is Lamentations 1:10 and its concern to bar Gentiles from the sanctuary. Yet again MMT interprets scripture so as to narrow the gate to communion with God.

7. 4QMMT B 49-54

This ruling addresses access to the sanctuary for the blind and the deaf. It denies them entry but permits them a part in the sacred food.

49 ואף ע]ל הסומ[י]ם

50 שאינם רואים להזהר מכל תערו[בת] ותערובת

51 [א]שם אינם רואים

52 ואף על החרשים שלוא שמעו חוק ומשפט וטהרה ולא

53 שמעו משפטי ישראל כי שלוא ראה ולוא שמע לוא

54 [י]דע לעשות והמה באים לטהרת המקדש

And concerning the blind who cannot see so as to beware of all mixture and cannot see a mixture that incurs reparation-offering; and concerning the deaf who have not heard the laws and the judgments and the purity reg-

---

51. For an even more nomistic reading of Gen 2:23-24 (along with Gen 1:27), see Mark 10:6-7, where God's statements regarding men and women in union with one another become God's law.

ulations, and have not heard the statutes of Israel: since he who has not seen or heard does not know how to obey, they have (only) access to the holy food.

This ruling echoes several biblical passages. First, the concern for priestly physical perfection in Leviticus 21:17 resonates with this passage.[52] Deuteronomy 18:13 ("You must remain completely loyal [תמים] to the Lord your God") provides the rationale for applying priestly rules to laity — MMT interprets "loyal" as "perfect, without blemish." The כי clause recalls Leviticus 5:1, where one who can see and hear but does not use those faculties to witness on another's behalf suffers guilt; likewise, says MMT, blind and deaf persons who lack such senses can incur all the greater guilt through inadvertent action born of ignorance of the law or of the nature of objects.[53]

As in other instances already noted, MMT once more concocts a new law — perhaps in response to the actual entry of such folks into the temple — from a concatenation of existing biblical statutes.[54] As a result MMT again intensifies and expands the biblical restrictions on persons associated with the cult.

8. 4QMMT B 62-64

What is to be done with the fourth-year produce and the tithe of the herd and the flocks said by Leviticus 19:23-24; 27:32 to be "holy to the Lord"? This question, too, attracts MMT's attention.

ואף על מטעת עצי המאכל הנטע	62
בארץ ישראל כראשית הוא לכוהנים ומעשר הבקר	63
והצון לכוהנים הוא	64

52. See also 11QT[a] 45:12-14, and Yadin, *Temple Scroll*, 1.66-67, for a similar linkage between a ruling on physical defects in laity with the biblical law requiring bodily perfection among priests.

53. The connections cited here are suggested by Brooke, "Explicit Presentation," 83. See also Deut 4:9; 5:24, cited by Qimron and Strugnell, *Qumran Cave 4, V: Miqṣat Ma'aseh ha-Torah*, DJD 10, 161. Brooke rightly refuses to connect the MMT passage to Deut 4:9; 5:24 because the points of contact are insufficient.

54. This contradicts Qimron and Strugnell (*Qumran Cave 4, V: Miqṣat Ma'aseh ha-Torah*, DJD 10, 162), who say that they "were unable to find any particular biblical passage on which this ruling is based." Anyway their judgment is immediately qualified by their own citation of the passages indicated above! See also Bernstein ("Employment and Interpretation," 32), who says "the laws in B 49-54 . . . show no signs of scriptural derivation in 4QMMT."

And concerning (the fruits of) the trees for food planted in the land of Israel: they are to be dealt with like firstfruits belonging to the priests. And the tithe of the herd and of the flock should be given to the priests.

Using a handful of key phrases from the two biblical passages,[55] the ruling would surely call both texts to mind for the ancient audience. As for the meaning of the phrase, "holy to the Lord," MMT decides that it makes the priests the proper recipients of the fourth-year produce and the tithe of the herd and the flocks. MMT is by no means alone in interpreting the biblical phrase this way,[56] but it is unique in juxtaposing these two particular kinds of offerings.[57] Thus we find yet another example of MMT's predilection for integrative exegesis of ambiguous biblical passages. Again MMT takes, as a result, a conservative view of matters relating to the cult.

9. 4QMMT B 75-82

This passage deals with prohibited priestly marriages. I include it for consideration because, like the refrain discussed first in this section of the essay, it deals with the custodians of the sacrificial cult.

ועל הזונות הנעסה בתוך העם והמה ב[ני זרע] 75

קדש משכתוב קודש ישראל ועל בה[מתו הטהו]רה 76

כתוב שלוא לרבעה כלאים ועל לבוש[ו כתוב שלוא] 77

יהיה שעטנז ושלוא לזרוע שדו וכ[רמו כלאי]ם 78

בגלל שהמה קדושים ובני אהרון ק[דושי קדושים] 79

[וא]תם יודעים שמקצת הכהנים ו[העם מתערבים] 80

[והם]מתוככים ומטמאי[ם]תא זרע[הקוד]ש [ואף] 81

את [זרע]ם עם הזונות כ[י לבני אהרון] 82

And concerning the practice of illegal marriage that exists among the people: (this practice exists) despite their being sons of holy seed, as it is written, Israel is holy. And concerning his (i.e., Israel's) clean animal, it is writ-

---

55. See, for example, עצי מאכל and מעשר הבקר והצון, cited by Bernstein, "Employment and Interpretation," 37.

56. See Qimron and Strugnell, Qumran Cave 4, V: Miqṣat Maʿaseh ha-Torah, DJD 10, 166, for numerous Second Temple period parallels to the view that priests receive one or the other of these agricultural and sacrificial proceeds.

57. Qimron and Strugnell, Qumran Cave 4, V: Miqṣat Maʿaseh ha-Torah, DJD 10, 166.

ten that one must not let it mate with another species; and concerning his clothes, it is written that they should not be of mixed stuff; and he must not sow his field and vineyard with mixed species. Because they (Israel) are holy, and the sons of Aaron are most holy. But you know that some of the priests and the laity mingle with each other. And they unite with each other. And they pollute the holy seed as well as their own seed with women they are forbidden to marry. So the sons of Aaron should. . . .

This ruling already has a long critical history.[58] Most agree that it interprets the meaning of the enigmatic term זנה in Leviticus 21:7, 14 (on priestly marriages) by bringing into the equation laws on prohibited mixtures (Lev 19:19; Deut 22:9) and language regarding the holiness of Israel (Jer 2:3).[59] A critical gap in the text (see l. 80 above) makes it impossible to be certain of the opinion expressed in MMT, but it is at least certain that the halakah prohibits marriages between priests and non-Jews or between priests and Jews outside of the priestly clan.[60] In either case the ruling forbids far more marriages than do Leviticus 21:7, 14 if זנה is taken in its most typical sense, a nonvirginal woman of questionable character. So for one last time we discover MMT alluding to multiple biblical passages to interpret restrictively an ambiguous scriptural law relating to the cult and its leadership.

58. In addition to Qimron and Strugnell, *Qumran Cave 4, V: Miqsat Ma'aseh ha-Torah*, DJD 10, 171-75, see especially Grabbe, "4QMMT and Second Temple Jewish Society," 103; Martha Himmelfarb, "Levi, Phinehas, and the Problem of Intermarriage at the Time of the Maccabean Revolt," *JSQ* 6 (1999) 1-24; John Kampen, "4QMMT and New Testament Studies," in *Reading 4QMMT*, 135-38; idem, "The Matthean Divorce Texts Reexamined," in *New Qumran Texts and Studies*, 149-67; Robert Kugler, "Halakhic Interpretive Strategies at Qumran: A Case Study," in *Legal Texts and Legal Issues*, 131-40; and C. J. Sharpe, "Phinean Zeal and Rhetorical Strategy in 4QMMT," *RevQ* 18 (1997) 207-22.

59. For the list of passages, see, among others, Brooke, "Explicit Presentation," 83. Not everyone agrees that Jer 2:3 plays any role here; see especially Bernstein, "Employment and Interpretation," 46.

60. Qimron and Strugnell (*Qumran Cave 4, V: Miqsat Ma'aseh ha-Torah*, DJD 10, 172-73) take the last view, relying in part on their supposition that 1 Chr 23:13, with its apparent division between priests and laity in levels of holiness, may have played a role in the development of this halakah; cf. 1QS 9:5-6, and the earlier commentators on the latter passage cited by Strugnell and Qimron, *Qumran Cave 4, V: Miqsat Ma'aseh ha-Torah*, DJD 10, 173, n. 190. Even more persuasive is Himmelfarb, "Levi, Phinehas, and the Problem of Intermarriage," 6-12, who marshals a great deal of other external evidence in favor of this reading. However, the text itself remains irreconcilably ambiguous.

Conclusions

What we find in our study of MMT is repeated confirmation of the hypothesis that in lieu of participating in the sacrificial cult the community contented itself with rewriting the rubrics that governed the temple and its operations through harmonizing and narrowing exegesis. No doubt they engaged in such exegetical activity in anticipation of the day when they would return to the temple. Thus, while they did not completely fill the void left in their religious lives by their separation from the temple cult, they did find a way to remain in contact with its operation through their interpretation of Scripture. Indeed, we might wonder just what the community members read and discussed in their long nights of study (1QS 6:7-8a), and what "precepts of Torah" (4QFlor 6:7) they might have offered up to God in their desert habitation. These rewritten rubrics seem as good a candidate as any for the role. That they did not satisfy the group's religious desires, and that the group's members were not restored to the temple as they wished, may account in part for the apocalyptic mood at Qumran.

Apocalyptic Tradition in the Dead Sea Scrolls and the Religion of Qumran

JAMES C. VANDERKAM

In his *The Ancient Library of Qumran & Modern Biblical Studies,* Frank M. Cross Jr. devoted the last chapter to the topic "The Essenes and the Primitive Church." He argued that the "language of the early Christian community, including that of the sayings attributed to Jesus, is shot through with the terminology of the Jewish apocalyptic; and the early Church conceived itself to be precisely an eschatological community."[1] This suggested to him that one should study "the faith and forms of the apocalyptic communities which preceded Christianity."[2] The Qumran or Essene community was one of these. Cross considered "the Essenes to be the bearers, and in no small part the producers, of the apocalyptic tradition of Judaism,"[3] He pointed to the rich apocalyptic literature preserved at Qumran (using "apocalyptic literature" in a fairly wide sense) and found that these sorts of works came from a common tradition:

> The concrete contacts in theology, terminology, calendrical peculiarities, and priestly interests, between the editions of Enoch, Jubilees, and the Testaments of Levi and Naphtali found at Qumrân on the one hand, and the

1. F. M. Cross Jr., *The Ancient Library of Qumran & Modern Biblical Studies* (rev. ed.; Grand Rapids: Baker, 1980) 198. The statement remains unchanged in *The Ancient Library of Qumran* (3rd ed.; Minneapolis: Fortress, 1995) 143. The following quotations are also worded in the same way in the third edition.

2. Cross, *Ancient Library* (1980), 198.

3. Cross, *Ancient Library* (1980), 198.

113

demonstrably sectarian works of Qumrân on the other, are so systematic and detailed that we must place the composition of these works within a single line of tradition.[4]

With the arrival of the discoveries at Qumran, what Cross called a "new factor" entered the picture:

> The Essene literature enables us to discover the concrete Jewish setting in which an apocalyptic understanding of history was living and integral to a communal existence. Like the primitive Church, the Essene community was distinguished from Pharisaic associations and other movements within Judaism precisely in its consciousness "of being already the called and chosen Congregation of the end of days."[5]

It is reasonable to call the group that lived at Qumran and whose views are reflected in the sectarian texts an eschatological community and even an apocalyptic one, but the relationship of the earliest Jewish apocalypses to this group may be more nuanced that Cross suggested. The simple fact is that the Qumran community did not, it seems, write apocalypses. It preserved and apparently made copies of older apocalyptic works but did not compose new ones.

Actually, there is some room for debate about whether members of the community did produce apocalypses. In the volumes published to date in the Discoveries in the Judaean Desert series a number of texts have *apocalypse* or related terms in their titles: *Apocalypse de Lamech* (1Q20); *Texte apocalyptique* (6Q13);[6] *Un apocalyptique en araméen* (?) (4Q489) (4Q490 is called "Groupe de fragments à rapprocher du précédent [?]"); and *Apocalypse messianique* (4Q521). Although he does not do so in DJD 22, Émile Puech has called 4Q246 (Pseudo-Daniel[d]) an *Apocalypse araméenne*.[7] John Collins allows that 4Q246 could be an apocalypse, and the same is true for 4Q243-45 (the *Pseudo-Daniel* works), the *Testament of Amram*, and 4Q385-90.[8] He also mentions the "Treatise on the Two Spirits" in the *Rule of the Community* (although it is not presented as a revelation, "the content is strongly reminiscent

---

4. Cross, *Ancient Library* (1980), 199.

5. Cross, *Ancient Library* (1980), 203.

6. 1Q20 is now known to be the *Genesis Apocryphon*, while 6Q13 is presently called *Priestly Prophecy*.

7. É. Puech, *La croyance des esséniens en la vie future: Immortalité, resurrection, vie éternelle* (2 vols.; Paris: Gabalda, 1993) 2.570.

8. J. J. Collins, *Apocalypticism in the Dead Sea Scrolls* (London: Routledge, 1997) 9-10.

of the apocalypses"),[9] the historical overview in the *Damascus Document* that is reminiscent of the ones in the Enochic apocalypses, and the *War Scroll.* Elsewhere he notes that the *New Jerusalem* text is possibly an apocalypse.[10] If one searches the most recent form of the inventory list of the manuscripts found at Qumran, the word "apocalypse" appears in the titles of two works: 4QpapApocalypse ar (4Q489), and 4Messianic Apocalypse (4Q521).[11] However, not enough of either work is preserved, especially at the beginning, to test whether they have the literary form of apocalypses.[12] 4Q489 is represented by eight fragments, only the first of which has any recognizable text: on it one can read וחזותה (and its vision) and וחזיתה (and you saw) on consecutive lines.[13] 4Q521 has received much discussion in recent times and has now appeared in DJD 25, edited by Puech.[14]

If, as nearly as we can tell, the group living at Qumran produced no or very few of their own apocalypses, why should we call them an apocalyptic community? The answer has been that, while they did not compose apocalypses, they lived according to apocalyptic ideas such as the imminence of the end. Collins, who finds the apocalyptic designation for the group an appropriate one, devotes most of his recent book *Apocalypticism in the Dead Sea Scrolls* to a series of apocalyptic motifs in the Scrolls. The themes he treats are creation and the origin of evil, the periods of history and the expectation of the end, messianic expectation, the eschatological war, resurrection and eternal life, and the heavenly world. As he sees the matter, the Qumran commu-

9. Collins, *Apocalypticism,* 10.

10. Collins, *Apocalypticism,* 59.

11. See E. Tov, "A List of the Texts from the Judaean Desert," in *The Dead Sea Scrolls after Fifty Years: A Comprehensive Assessment,* ed. P. Flint and J. VanderKam (2 vols.; Leiden: Brill, 1998, 1999) 2.669-717.

12. For the definition of an apocalypse that underlies such statements, see J. J. Collins, "Genre, Ideology and Social Movements," in *Mysteries and Revelations: Apocalyptic Studies since the Uppsala Colloquium,* ed. J. J. Collins and J. H. Charlesworth (JSPSup 9; Sheffield: Sheffield Academic Press, 1991) 19: "Apocalypse is a genre of revelatory literature with a narrative framework, in which a revelation is mediated by an otherworldly being to a human recipient, disclosing a transcendent reality which is both temporal, insofar as it envisages eschatological salvation, and spatial insofar as it involves another supernatural world;" it is "intended to interpret present earthly circumstances in the light of the supernatural world and of the future, and to influence both the understanding and the behavior of the audience by means of divine authority."

13. M. Baillet, "4Q489. Un apocalyptique en Araméen (?)," in *Qumrân Grotte 4, III (4Q482-4Q520)* (DJD 7; Oxford: Clarendon, 1982) 10-11.

14. É. Puech, "4QApocalypse messianique," in *Qumrân Grotte 4, XVIII: Textes Hébreux (4Q521-4Q528, 4Q576-4Q579)* (DJD 25; Oxford: Clarendon, 1998) 1-38. See his discussion of the genre of the text on pp. 35-36.

nity did not require new apocalypses: their experience of being in community at present with the holy ones removed any need for apocalyptic descriptions of the heavenly world; and the revelations granted to the Teacher of Righteousness and his successors are found indirectly in rule books and other texts such as the pesharim.[15]

In this paper I would like to approach the issue from a slightly different angle. The Qumran community preserved some older apocalypses, primarily Daniel and the Enoch booklets, and some related works such as *Jubilees*. Perhaps we could include *Aramaic Levi* in this group. How did the Qumran community treat these compositions? What did they do with them? Were they demonstrably important there? When were they copied — in all periods of the sectarian occupation of the site or only in some? What was demonstrably derived from them? With these questions in mind, we should now look at the apocalyptic works that the Qumran community inherited.

1. Daniel

Although the final form of the book of Daniel was prepared not long before the first members of the community of the new covenant took up residence at Qumran, in that short time eight copies of the book made their way to three caves. It is clear from the scripts in which the copies were inscribed that the book continued to attract enough interest to justify reproducing it throughout the first century BCE and well into the first century CE. In other words, there are no appreciable gaps between times of copying the book of Daniel, and no sign of this sort that the book fell into disfavor.

a. Copies (8): 1Q71-72 (classical script)

4QDaniel[a-e]
a 100-50 BCE (Ulrich)
b ca. 20-50 CE (Cross, *Ancient Library,* fig. 18)
c ca. 100-50 BCE (Cross, *Ancient Library,* fig. 19); ca. 100 (Ulrich)
d ca. 25-1 BCE
e ca. 100 BCE
6Q7 (ca. 50 CE)

15. Collins, *Apocalypticism,* 152-53.

b. Cited

The book of Daniel is cited in two places in texts that seem to be sectarian. It has, of course, always been of interest that Daniel is explicitly called a prophet in 4QFlorilegium.

i. 4QFlor 1-3 ii 3: In this manuscript from the late first century BCE, Daniel is cited in an eschatological context. The previous column (earlier Psalm 1 was treated) concludes with a citation of Ps 2:1 (the nations rage against the Lord and his anointed in the last days). The pesher of the verse leads into a characterization of the time indicated by the psalm passage: "This shall be the time of the trial to co[me concerning the house of J]udah so as to perfect . . . Belial, and a remnant of the people shall be left according to the lot (assigned to them), and they shall practice the whole Law . . . Moses. This is the time of which it is written in the book of Daniel the Prophet: *But the wicked shall do wickedly and shall not understand, but the righteous shall purify themselves and make themselves white* (Dan. xii,10). The people who know God shall be strong. They are the masters who understand."[16] George J. Brooke writes that "the intention of the midrash on Psalms 1 and 2 is to identify the good parties in those psalms with the community and to suggest that it is the community who is the remnant that is to survive the trial of the latter days, the period that also looks beyond that testing to a time when the understanding of the wise will be vindicated."[17] 4QFlorilegium dates from the Herodian period and uses Daniel to clarify what the writer understands as an eschatological passage in Psalm 2. The comment that "they shall practise the whole Law" with Moses named after a break is significant in this eschatological connection; it exemplifies how important the Torah was to the sectarian understanding of the last days.

ii. 11QMelch 2:18 (commenting on Isa 52:7): "And the messenger is [the ano]inted of the spirit about whom Dan[iel] spoke" (perhaps referring to something in Dan 9:24-27, probably משיח נגיד [anointed prince] in 9:25). Unlike the Florilegium, the author of the text does not identify Daniel's office,

---

16. This and all translations of scrolls passages are from G. Vermes, *The Complete Dead Sea Scrolls in English* (New York: Penguin, 1997). The passage is cited from p. 494.

17. G. J. Brooke, *Exegesis at Qumran: 4QFlorilegium in Its Jewish Context* (JSOTSup 29; Sheffield: JSOT Press, 1985) 159. As Brooke notes, Dan 12:10 and 11:35 are related with Ps 2 through sharing the root שכל (p. 149, 166). A. Steudel has offered a new edition of the text; in her arrangement, the passage from Ps 2 begins at col. III 18 and the pesher begins on l. 19, continuing into the next column; the Daniel passage is in IV 2-4 (*Der Midrasch zur Eschatologie aus der Qumrangemeinde [4QMidrEschat^{a,b}]* [STDJ 13; Leiden: Brill, 1994] 25-26).

but elsewhere in the work he cites from Leviticus (once from Deuteronomy), Isaiah, and the Psalms. 11QMelchizedek was copied in the early Herodian period, perhaps 50-25 BCE.[18]

c. Related Texts

i. 4QPrayer of Nabonidus ar (4Q242) (75-50 BCE): While it is recognized that the contents of this text are related in some way to Daniel 4, the *Prayer* clearly does not derive from Daniel 4 and is unlikely to have been influenced by it.[19]

ii. 4QPseudo-Daniel[a-b] ar (4Q4Q243-244) (early first century CE) overlap and thus belong to the same work. They picture Daniel before Belshazzar; in this setting he surveys history from the flood to the Hellenistic period, possibly with a reference to eschatological times. Whether this is a sectarian work is difficult to say: "Pseudo-Daniel's relation to the Dead Sea sect may be analogous to that of *Jubilees* or the Enoch literature. It is sectarian in a broad sense, insofar as it culminates in the emergence of an elect group, but it does not refer explicitly to the Qumran *yaḥad*."[20]

iii. 4Pseudo-Daniel[c] ar (4Q245) (early first century CE) refers to an unidentified book, contains a list of high priests and kings, and mentions eschatological times. The editors have concluded that the writer of the text, once the offices of high priest and king were combined by Aristobulus I and Alexander Jannaeus, "anticipated an eschatological restoration in accord with the divine order."[21] They doubt that it is another copy of the same work as 4Q243-244, but it does mention Daniel and apparently a writing given to him. The second fragment has several expressions that sound eschatological.

iv. 4QApocryphe de Daniel ar (4Q246) (last part of the first century BCE; formerly called *Pseudo-Daniel[d]* and at times designated as the *Son of God Text*) refers to a person in the presence of a king to whom he is speaking. He mentions the king's vision, the distress that will come upon the earth, a king of Assyria and Egypt, apparently another king who will become great and whom all will serve, and the special names that he will be

18. So P. Kobelski, *Melchizedek and Melchiresha* (CBQMS 10; Washington, D.C.: Catholic Biblical Association, 1981) 3.

19. See J. Collins, "Prayer of Nabonidus," in George Brooke et al., *Qumran Cave 4, XVII. Parabiblical Texts, Part 3* (DJD 22; Oxford: Clarendon, 1996) 85-87.

20. J. Collins and P. Flint, "4Q243-244: The Combined Text," in *Qumran Cave 4, XVII. Parabiblical Texts, Part 3*, DJD 22, 137.

21. J. Collins and P. Flint, "4Qpseudo-Daniel[c] ar," in *Qumran Cave 4, XVII. Parabiblical Texts, Part 3*, DJD 22, 158.

called (son of God, son of the Most High). After this the people of God will arise with an eternal kingdom. There are a number of phrases in the text that recall passages from Daniel.[22] These similarities with Daniel are obvious and have been noted by commentators, regardless whether they consider the person with the titles "son of God" and "son of the Most High" as a positive or negative character.[23]

v. 4QFour Kingdoms[a-b] ar (4Q552-53) mentions four trees that are apparently symbols for kingdoms. Babel and Persia are mentioned, and another seems to involve rule over the sea and the ports. Someone is discussing the trees with the person speaking in the first person, and the speaker interrogates the trees about their identity. Naturally the language and imagery call to mind the four kingdoms in Daniel and other texts. It is not clear whether this poorly preserved work is sectarian.

d. Other Effects of Daniel

i. It is possible but not demonstrable that the Qumran covenanters took the art of pesher interpretation of mysterious messages from Daniel 2, 4, 5, and 7. At least we may say that the term and such interpretations are amply attested in Daniel's handling of dreams and the inscription on the wall in Belshazzar's palace. As John Collins puts it: "Here again Qumran draws important terminology from the Book of Daniel but uses it freely to express its developing worldview."[24] That is, even if pesher interpretation is derived from Daniel, it is obvious that the covenanters use it not only to interpret difficult texts and relate them to world powers but also to unlock the history of their own group in the last times.

ii. Collins also finds similarities in terminology between Daniel and the Scrolls. He mentions משכילים (instructors), רבים (many), and the similarity of בחלקלקות in 11:34 (in deceit) to דורשי החלקות (the seekers of smooth things) in the Scrolls.[25]

---

22. Vermes includes references to these passages in his translation (*The Complete Dead Sea Scrolls in English*, 577).

23. The text was published by É. Puech, "Apocryphe de Daniel ar," in *Qumran Cave 4, XVII. Parabiblical Texts, Part 3*, DJD 22, 165-84.

24. J. J. Collins, *Daniel: A Commentary* (Hermeneia; Minneapolis: Fortress, 1993) 74. On this point, see also the discussion in M. Horgan, *Pesharim: Qumran Interpretations of Biblical Books* (CBQMS 8; Washington, D.C.: Catholic Biblical Association, 1979) 254-59.

25. Collins, *Daniel*, 73.

iii. Collins detects parallels between the "conception of the eschatologi-cal war" in the *War Scroll* and that in Daniel 11–12. The two share a number of terms and phrases, although the understanding of the conflict is far more dualistic in the *War Scroll*.

iv. Another possible area of influence is the seventy weeks of Daniel 9 that seem to be echoed in 11QMelchizedek (it speaks of ten jubilees) and the *Pesher on the Periods*. It has been argued that the same period of 490 years is reflected in the *Damascus Document*, which deals with units of 390 years, 20, and 40; but to reach the desired total of 490 years one has to assume an addi-tional 40-year span for the career of the Teacher, something that is possible but not explicit in the text.

e. Omissions

The parallels with and borrowings from Daniel should be balanced by the themes of the book that do not surface in the Scrolls: Daniel 7 seems not to have been used, and the passage about resurrection in Daniel 12:2-3 is not employed.[26]

2. 1 Enoch

The four parts of *1 Enoch* that were composed at times before the establish-ment of the Qumran community exercised a noticeable influence on some Scrolls writers. There are more copies of the various Enochic compositions than of most books in the Hebrew Bible. For *1 Enoch* (less the Parables), how-ever, it has been claimed that, in contrast to the book of Daniel, interest dwin-dled as time went on during the sectarian occupation of Qumran so that in the later stages no new copies were made.

a. Copies (11 in Aramaic)

4Q201 En^a ar (200-150 BCE): BW
4Q202 En^b ar (ca. 150 BCE): BW
4Q204 En^c ar (ca. 30-1 BCE): BW [BG?] BD EE
4Q205 En^d ar (ca. 30-1 BCE): BW BD

26. Collins, *Daniel*, 79.

4Q206 En^e ar (ca. 100-50 BCE): BW BD
4Q207 En^f ar (ca. 150-125 BCE): BD
4Q208 Enastr^a ar (ca. 200 BCE)
4Q209 Enastr^b ar (ca. early years CE)
4Q210 Enastr^c ar (ca. 50 BCE)
4Q211 Enastr^d ar (ca. 50-1 BCE)
4Q212 En^g ar (ca. 50 BCE): EE

Józef T. Milik has drawn a set of large conclusions from the fact that, of these eleven manuscripts, only one, 4QEnastr^b, was copied in the first century CE (as were some copies of the *Book of Giants,* which he thought belonged to the original Enochic pentateuch):

> Qumrân scribes and readers must have gradually lost interest in the literary compositions attributed to Enoch, just as happened, though more rapidly and more drastically, in Pharisaic circles. We should note likewise that an early scroll, En^a, had already been withdrawn from circulation and its detached leaves used for other purposes — for example, the verso of the first leaf for a schoolboy's exercise. Equally significant, finally, is the absence of the Books of Enoch from other caves at Qumrân, whose stores formed private libraries. Our copies of 4QEn were no doubt covered with dust on the shelves, in the chests, or in the earthenware jars of the main library, and only a small number of Essene readers consulted and borrowed them, particularly during the first century A.D.[27]

It is not clear that all of Milik's inferences follow from the evidence. If there are several copies from the late first century BCE, there may have been no need to make more of them in the early first century CE; and 4QEnastr^b does show that copying of at least one Enochic work (the most technical and tedious among them) occurred in the first century CE.

To these Aramaic copies of the Enochic booklets we now have to add the admittedly very small fragments of the *Epistle of Enoch* that have been identified in the remains from Cave 7.

7Q4 frg. 1 + 7Q12 + 7Q14 + 7Q8 + 7Q13 = *1 Enoch* 103:3-4, 7-8, 15 (3 successive columns)

---

27. J. T. Milik, *The Books of Enoch: Aramaic Fragments of Qumrân Cave 4* (Oxford: Clarendon, 1976) 7. Milik suggests the dates for the manuscripts on pp. 5, 7 (he acknowledges that "there is a fairly wide margin of error" [7]). The contents of the individual copies are from Milik's chart on p. 6.

7Q11 = *1 Enoch* 100:12 (?)[28]

7Q4 apparently is to be dated to ca. 100 BCE.[29] If that is true, the traditional dating for the *Epistle of Enoch* near the end of the second century BCE is almost certainly excluded, since it would have taken some time for a translation of it to be made.

Exactly what the presence of these fragments means is not clear, other than that there seems to have been someone at Qumran who could deal with the Enochian literature in Greek. Apart from three books of the Pentateuch (Leviticus, Numbers, Deuteronomy), only the *Epistle of Enoch* is attested in its original Semitic form and in Greek among the hundreds of texts found at Qumran. The fragments of *Enoch* in Greek in Cave 7 also show that Milik was incorrect in claiming that Enochian texts were found only in the central library of Cave 4.

b. Cited/Used

The books of Enoch may not be cited verbatim in any of the Scrolls (unless the calendrical scrolls do so), but teachings from various parts of the book are certainly echoed in sectarian texts.

i. The stories about the watchers who sinned: This fundamental Enochic myth, attested in all parts of *1 Enoch* and in no earlier source, is mentioned several times in the sectarian texts of Qumran and in others that may not be sectarian.

α. CD 2:14-21, a section that opens with a direct address by the author to "my sons," warns against "a guilty inclination and lascivious eyes" — a theme that brings the quintessential practitioners of these negative qualities to mind. "For having walked in the stubbornness of their hearts the Watchers of heaven fell; on account of it they were caught, for they did not follow the precepts of God. And their sons, whose height was like that of cedars and whose bodies were like mountains, fell" (2:17-19; see 4QD^b 2 ii 17-19; 4QD^e frg. 1:2-3). These

---

28. See E. Muro, "The Greek Fragments of Enoch from Qumran Cave 7 (7Q4, 7Q8, & 7Q12 = 7QEn gr = Enoch 103:3-4, 7-8)," *RevQ* 18 (1997) 307-12; É. Puech, "Sept fragments de la Lettre d'Hénoch (1 Hén 100, 103 et 105) dans la grotte 7 de Qumrân (= 7Hén gr)," *RevQ* 18 (1997) 313-23. Cf. also G. W. Nebe, "7Q4: Möglichkeit und Grenze einer Identifikation," *RevQ* 13 (1988) 629-33; É. Puech, "Notes sur les fragments grecs du manuscrit 7Q4 = 1 Hénoch 103 et 105," *RB* 103 (1996) 592-600.

29. This is the view of C. H. Roberts, as cited by M. Baillet in M. Baillet, J. T. Milik, and R. de Vaux, *Les 'pétites grottes' de Qumran* (DJD 3; Oxford: Clarendon, 1962) 142, 144.

lines transparently build upon the contents of *1 Enoch* 6–11 and related passages although the wording is not drawn directly from those chapters.[30]

β. 4Q180 (first century CE): 4Q180, at the beginning of a new section, says that "the interpretation concerns Azazel and the angels who [   ] bore them giants. And concerning Azazel . . . and iniquity; and to cause them all to inherit wickedness. . . ." Here the Azazel version of the story is already joined with the one in which the angels mate with women and father giants from them.

γ. *Genesis Apocryphon:* Columns 2:1–5:27 provide a retelling of the incidents surrounding the birth of Noah that are familiar from *1 Enoch* 106–107. The form of the story in the *Genesis Apocryphon* is different (a first-person account by Lamech), but the content is largely the same. Here too Lamech learns with certainty from Enoch that Noah is his son and is not the offspring of the sons of heaven or the watchers. The more recently available material from the text increases the evidence for reliance on *1 Enoch:* in 6:11 Noah mentions the "activities of the sons of Heaven," 6:19-20 refer to the nephilim and to "the Holy Ones with the daughters of men."[31] The Cave 1 manuscript was copied in the late first century BCE or early first century CE.[32]

δ. 4Q227: The text has been labeled *Pseudo-Jubilees*[c] and dates from the early Herodian period. As its name suggests, it belongs more in the orbit of *Jubilees* (see below), but it does indicate an interest in Enoch and summarizes his achievements, including his testifying against the watchers.[33]

ε. *The Book of Giants:* Milik argued that the *Book of Giants* was a part of the original Enochic pentateuch and thinks that 4QEn[c] and 4QGiants[a] are from the same manuscript.[34] Although his theory about the place of the *Book of Giants* in an Enochic pentateuch has not carried the day, there can be little doubt that it was an important Enochic work at Qumran, and it is difficult to imagine that it was not influenced by any of our Enochic booklets. According to the latest form of the inventory list of Qumran texts, the following are the copies of the *Book of Giants.*

---

30. Milik (*The Books of Enoch*, 57-58), however, claims the description of their great height does not come from *1 Enoch* 7:2 but more likely from the *Book of Giants*.

31. The translations of col. 6 are from M. Morgenstern, E. Qimron, and D. Sivan, "The Hitherto Unpublished Columns of the *Genesis Apocryphon*," *AbrN* 33 (1995) 41, 43.

32. J. Fitzmyer, *The Genesis Apocryphon of Qumran Cave I: A Commentary* (BibOr 18A; Rome: Biblical Institute, 1971) 15. Although some have argued that the scroll was a source for *1 Enoch* and *Jubilees*, this seems unlikely; moreover, the Aramaic in the scroll dates from the first century BCE or CE (pp. 16-19).

33. See J. VanderKam and J. T. Milik, "227. 4QPseudo-Jubilees[c]," in Harold Attridge et al., *Qumran Cave 4. VIII. Parabiblical Texts Part 1* (DJD 13; Oxford: Clarendon, 1994) 171-75.

34. Milik, *The Books of Enoch*, 178.

1Q23 EnGiants[a] ar
1Q24 EnGiants[b] ar
2Q26 EnGiants ar (Herodian)
4Q203 EnGiants[a] ar (last third of the first century BCE)
4Q206 EnGiants[f?] frgs. 2-3 (first half of the first century BCE)
4Q530 EnGiants[b] ar (first half of the first century BCE)
4Q531 EnGiants[c] ar (Herodian)
4Q532 EnGiants[d] ar
4Q533 EnGiants[e] ar[35]
6Q8 papEnGiant ar (mid first century CE)

If all of these are actually copies of the *Book of Giants*, it is truly a well-attested work, existing in ten copies distributed over four caves. Moreover, copies were made in both the first century BCE and the first century CE.

ii. 4Q247 *(Pesher on the Apocalypse of Weeks)*: Józef Milik published seven fragmentary lines from a text that he termed "a kind of commentary to the Apocalypse of Weeks in the Epistle of Enoch" and dated to the beginning of the Herodian period.[36] The second line refers to the fif[th] week," the third to the number 400, the fourth to King Zedekiah of Judah, the fifth to the sons of Levi, and the sixth to "the kin[g] of Kittim." As Milik noted, it places construction of the Solomonic temple in the fifth week (if his reconstruction of the number in l. 3 as 480 is correct), just as *1 Enoch* 93:7 does.

iii. Calendar: It can safely be said that the *Astronomical Book of Enoch* is the source for the information that undergirds the calendars of Qumran Cave 4. It can also be said that the Enochian calendar has an eschatological or apocalyptic aspect to it in that it is the law according to which the luminaries move until the end of the creation (*1 Enoch* 72:1). This was planned and known even before the time of the flood, when Uriel disclosed the data to Enoch. The *Astronomical Book*, unlike *Jubilees*, presents both the schematic solar calendar of the 364 days per year and the schematic lunar calendar of 354 days per year. The latter is neither criticized nor compared unfavorably with the solar reckoning, as it is in *Jubilees* 6:32-38. It also provides tables for calculating how many days would have to be added to the lunar calendar in one, three, five, and eight years (although why anyone would need this infor-

35. In his list of the Qumran copies of the *Book of Giants*, L. Stuckenbruck does not include 4Q533 but puts it in his category "Manuscripts Whose Identification with the Book of Giants Is Unlikely" (*The Book of Giants from Qumran: Texts, Translation, and Commentary* [TSAJ 63; Tübingen: Mohr-Siebeck, 1997]). However, he does consider 4Q556 a copy of the *Book of Giants*.

36. Milik, *The Books of Enoch*, 256.

mation is not clear; *1 Enoch* 74:10-17). The Qumran calendars often include both solar and lunar dates and do not disparage any aspect of the latter. Consequently, these calendars are in the Enochian tradition, as far as the astronomical information goes;[37] for the placement of festivals at specific points in the solar calendar the Qumran texts stand in the tradition of *Jubilees*. Alignment with the priestly courses came from other influences.

iv. *Genesis Apocryphon:* In 19:25 Abram reads to some Egyptians from the words of Enoch. What Enochian book this may have been is not said, nor is the reading entirely certain.

3. Jubilees

It is probably inaccurate to classify all of *Jubilees* as an apocalypse because the great majority of its contents do not fit the apocalyptic mold of "a transcendent reality which is both temporal, insofar as it envisages eschatological salvation, and spatial, insofar as it involves another, supernatural world."[38] Those topics do arise, but they are more infrequent than in the apocalypses. Nevertheless, the book is a revelation mediated by a supernatural being to a human recipient. Recognizing that it is a borderline case, as John Collins notes,[39] we may proceed to document its influence on the Qumran sectarian literature.

a. Copies: 14/15

The copies of *Jubilees* from Qumran are:

1Q17 (early Herodian)
1Q18 (late Hasmonean)
2Q19 (Herodian)
2Q20 (first century CE)
3Q5 (first century CE)
4Q176 (Herodian)
4Q216 (ca. 125-100 BCE)

37. For a summary, see J. VanderKam, *Calendars in the Dead Sea Scrolls: Measuring Time* (London: Routledge, 1998) 17-27, 71-90.

38. Collins, "Genre, Ideology and Social Movements," 19.

39. J. J. Collins, "The Jewish Apocalypses," in *Apocalypse: The Morphology of a Genre,* ed. J. Collins (*Semeia* 14 [1979]) 32-33.

4Q217 ? (first half of the first century BCE)
4Q218 (early Herodian)
4Q219 (late Hasmonean
4Q220 (early Herodian)
4Q221 (late Hasmonean/early Herodian)
4Q222 (late Hasmonean)
4Q223-24 (late Hasmonean, ca. 75-50 BCE)
11Q12 (late Herodian, ca. 50 CE)[40]

While Milik believes that 4Q217 is a copy of *Jubilees,* it is not likely that it is because the wording diverges too sharply from the preserved text of the book. Also, in the official edition of 4Q482-483 Maurice Baillet hesitantly advanced the idea that they, too, were manuscripts of *Jubilees,* but the suggestion seems unfounded.[41] The range of the paleographical dates of the fourteen copies of *Jubilees* — from ca. 125 or 100 BCE to ca. 50 CE — give no reason for thinking that the book ever fell out of favor at Qumran.

b. Quotations

Jubilees is referred to explicitly in the sectarian texts and may even be quoted.
    i. CD 16:2-4: The best-known reference to *Jubilees* is in CD 16:2-4, where the writer appeals to it by name. If our *Jubilees* is the one that he had in mind, there can be no question that it served as an authoritative source for him. It is helpful to see the passage in its larger context. It comes after a section about returning to the law of Moses with a whole heart and soul and a treatment of the rule that no defective person may enter the community "for the Angels of Holiness[42] are [in their midst]" (4Q266 8 i 9):

> therefore a man shall bind himself by oath to return to the Law of Moses, for in it all things are strictly defined. As for the exact determination of

40. For these paleographically established dates of the copies, see J. VanderKam, *Textual and Historical Studies in the Book of Jubilees* (HSM 14; Missoula, Mt.: Scholars Press, 1977) 215; and idem, "The Jubilees Fragments from Qumran Cave 4," in *The Madrid Qumran Congress: Proceedings of the International Congress on the Dead Sea Scrolls, Madrid, 18-21 March 1991,* ed. J. Trebolle Barrera and L. Vegas Montaner (2 vols.; STDJ 11; Leiden: Brill, 1992) 2.642.
41. See Baillet, "4Q489: Un apocalyptique en Araméen (?)," 1-2; but he admits that the fragments are too small for positive identification and that they could be from Genesis.
42. These angels are identified as the second highest ranking class of angels in *Jub.* 2:2, 18.

their times to which Israel turns a blind eye, behold it is strictly defined in the *Book of the Divisions of the Times into Their Jubilees and Weeks*. And on the day that a man swears to return to the Law of Moses, the Angel of Persecution [המשטמה] shall cease to follow him provided that he fulfills his word; for this reason Abraham circumcised himself on the day that he knew. (16:1-6)

The author uses the participle מדוקדק twice in the passage, first to refer to something that the Torah specifies, then to something that *Jubilees* defines precisely. The phrase *Book of the Divisions of the Times into Their Jubilees and Weeks* very closely parallels what *Jubilees* calls itself in the Prologue, 1:4, and 1:26 (cf. 1:29). The teaching of *Jubilees* to which the writer of CD appeals is "the exact determination of their times." It seems reasonable to understand these words as pointing to the chronological teachings in the book, although the term קץ is not used in any of the Cave 4 fragments of *Jubilees* (עת is attested frequently). Louis Ginzberg wrote the following about the passage in CD 16:2-4:

> This sentence interrupts the continuity, and its genuineness is very suspect. It probably comes from a reader for whom the Book of Jubilees possessed high authority and called attention to the fact that the words of our fragment, "for everything is exactly given in it (the Torah)," כי בה הכל מדוקדק, are not to be taken literally, for in respect of the "calendar," פרוש קציהם, one must be guided by what is written on this subject in the Book of Jubilees. To the מדוקדק connected with the Torah is opposed the מדוקדק connected with the pseudepigraphon here mentioned.[43]

Whatever one thinks about how well or poorly the sentence fits the context, perhaps the term *chronology* would more accurately define the subject than *calendar*, but both are carefully defined in *Jubilees*. As for the chronology in the book, it does map out the periods of Israel's past and, to a certain extent, of its future; the author also details when certain laws were revealed and thus for the first time became applicable.

Perhaps it is no accident that the angel of Mastemah is mentioned directly after the reference to *Jubilees*. He plays a very active role in the book but has no power over those who obey the Lord. The reference to Abraham's circumcision has puzzled commentators,[44] with Solomon Schechter pointing

---

43. L. Ginzberg, *An Unknown Jewish Sect* (Moreshet Series 1; New York: Ktav, 1976) 94-95.

44. Ginzberg wanted to emend the text from נימול to ניצל ("was saved"; *An Unknown Jewish Sect*, 95) and thought the reference was to when Abram became aware of the one true God.

the reader to *Jubilees* 15:26, 32.[45] The first of these verses is not helpful, but the second notes that God himself, not any angel or spirit, rules Israel and that he guards Israel from the powers. Hence obedience to the law of circumcision, which makes one a member of the pact or covenant, keeps one under God's rule and protects a person from evil forces, presumably including Mastemah, although he is not mentioned in the passage. It is important also to note that the author says that Abraham was circumcised on the day of his knowing. The meaning seems to be that on the very day when he learned of the law of circumcision, Abraham circumcised himself. *Jubilees* 15:24 makes this point ("On the same day Abraham was circumcised"), echoing Genesis 17:23. But it is the reference to Mastemah that makes one think the writer of CD is following *Jubilees* in the larger context. The result is that the entire context appears to be heavily indebted to *Jubilees*.

ii. CD 10:8: Although it is not as frequently noted, CD 10:8 may also allude to *Jubilees*. The line occurs in a paragraph concerning the judges of the congregation, who are to be "learned in the Book of Meditation and in the constitution of the Covenant" (10:6) and are to be between twenty-five and sixty years of age. "No man over the age of sixty shall hold office as Judge of the Congregation, for 'because man sinned his days have been shortened, and in the heat of His anger against the inhabitants of the earth God ordained that their understanding should depart even before their days are completed' (Jubilees xxiii, 11)" (10:7-10). The notion that knowledge or understanding will depart due to old age is in fact shared with *Jubilees* 23:11, but the passage is not quoted from *Jubilees* despite what the translation of Geza Vermes implies.

c. Use and Influence

i. 4QPseudo-Jubilees[a-c] (225-227): For the three manuscripts that Józef Milik placed in the category Pseudo-Jubilees, a case can be made that concepts and even language from *Jubilees* have influenced them. 4Q225 1:6 contains a direct address to Moses, followed in the next line by a reference to the creation and possibly the new creation; these should be compared with *Jubilees* 1:29, which defines the scope of the message contained on the heavenly tablets. The sequel may echo passages such as *Jubilees* 48:9, 18; 49:23. In fragment 2 i-ii one finds a version of the *Aqedah* that, like the one in *Jubilees*, presents the story in the context of a debate between God and the prince of Mastemah.

---

45. S. Schechter, *Documents of Jewish Sectaries*, vol. 1, *Fragments of a Zadokite Work* (reprint New York: Ktav, 1970) 88.

4Q226 in part overlaps with 4Q225, and fragment 7 includes the end of the *Aqedah* and the material directly after it in 4Q225 2. Elsewhere in 4Q226 the language of weeks and jubilees is repeated. 4Q227 fragment 2, as noted above, very closely resembles *Jubilees'* paragraph about Enoch (see 4:17-24). 4Q225-27 are early Herodian in date.[46]

ii. 4QText with citation of *Jubilees* (4Q228) (late Hasmonean/early Herodian): Little of the text remains, but what has survived has some tantalizing references to a work that may be *Jubilees*. In 1 i 9 the phrase כי כן כתוב במחלק'ת ends the line, but the beginning of the next one is lost. The use of a quotation formula that elsewhere is employed to introduce scriptural citations is suggestive, while מחלקות is the first part of *Jubilees'* Hebrew name. A fuller form of the title may have appeared in the first line of the same fragment (מחל[ו]ק[ת העתים; cf. also l. 7).

iii. 4Q265: The text, formerly called *Serekh Damascus* but now known as *Miscellaneous Rules,* has a section that closely parallels *Jubilees'* explanation for why, according to Leviticus 12, a woman remains in her impurity and blood of purification twice as long as a male. Both *Jubilees* 3:8-14 and 4Q265 7 ii relate the phenomenon to the differing times when Adam and Eve were introduced into the garden, and both adduce Leviticus 12 in this context. The facts that 4Q265 speaks of the first week when Adam was brought into the garden and that the garden is here called *holy* make it highly likely that *Jubilees* is the source for mooring this pentateuchal law in the story about the garden of Eden.

iv. 4QCommentary on Genesis A (4Q252) presents an interesting case. Among the varied passages from Genesis that are incorporated into the text, the flood occupies far and away the most space. The commentator's interest, though, does not seem to be so much in the flood itself as in the dates of the events within the flood story. Those dates agree with the ones in *Jubilees* and thus are based on the same chronology, but there are more events dated in 4Q252, and in one case the commentary offers a further specification that corrects a statement in *Jubilees* (another sign that it is the more recent text). *Jubilees* says that the flood waters remained on the earth "for five months — 150 days. Then the ark came to rest on the summit of Lubar, one of the mountains of Ararat" (5:27b-28). Here the writer echoes Genesis 8:3-4: "At the end of one hundred fifty days the waters had abated; and in the seventh month, on the seventeenth day of the month, the ark came to rest on the

---

46. For 4Q225-27, and also for 4Q228, see VanderKam and Milik, "227. 4QPseudo-Jubilees^c," 141-85. If 4Q217 is not a copy of *Jubilees,* it could be included here as a Qumran text influenced by the language of *Jubilees* (see pp. 23-33).

mountains of Ararat." It is one thing for Genesis to say that the period from the seventeenth day of the second month when the flood began (7:11) to the seventeenth day of the seventh month was 150 days, but it is quite another for the calendrically astute author of *Jubilees* to say that 150 days equal five months. In his system, there would be two months of 31 days in that span (months three and six) so that the number of days should have been 152. 4Q252 1:7-10, using the same numbers, says that the 150 days ended on the fourteenth day of the seventh month; the fifteenth and sixteenth are then listed as the time when the waters decreased, but the ark does not rest on the mountain until the seventeenth of the month, that is, 152 days after the seventeenth day of the second month. Here, then, *Jubilees* or its tradition had an influence but one that needed to be improved or rather spelled out in more detail.

v. Although *Jubilees,* by denying a calendrical function to the moon, differs from the Qumran calendrical texts in this regard, its 364-day solar calendar is the one found in the Cave 4 calendars; furthermore, the dates that it assigns to festivals are precisely the ones for the holidays in the Qumran lists. Of particular significance is the date of the fifteenth day of the third month for the festival of weeks and identification of this holiday as the one when the covenant was made and renewed. This seems also to be its role at Qumran, to judge from 4Q266 11:17-18 where the inhabitants of the camps gather in the third month and curse those who depart from the law.

vi. Status of Levi-Judah and the two messiahs: *Jubilees* stands in the tradition of *Aramaic Levi* in several ways, among which we may include its stress on the importance and future significance of Levi and Judah. *Jubilees* 30–32 is in large part devoted to the elevation of Levi and, to a lesser degree, to the blessing of Judah. The place assigned to these two patriarchs in works such as *Aramaic Levi* and *Jubilees* seems to be a preliminary stage to the two-messiah doctrine at Qumran, according to which one messiah is to come from Aaron (not, interestingly, from Levi) and one from Israel (not from Judah explicitly).[47]

vii. Postmortem existence: There is no way to prove the point, but *Jubilees'* understanding of the fate of the righteous after death seems to be similar to the one expressed in a number of Qumran texts. *Jubilees* 23:30-31a says: "Then the Lord will heal his servants. They will rise and see great peace. He will expel his enemies. The righteous will see (this), offer praise, and be very

47. For Levi in these chapters in relation to earlier traditions, see R. Kugler, *From Patriarch to Priest: The Levi-Priestly Tradition from* Aramaic Levi *to* Testament of Levi (SBLEJL 9; Atlanta: Scholars Press, 1996) 139-69. For the relation to Qumran messianism, see J. VanderKam, "Jubilees and the Priestly Messiah of Qumran," *RevQ* 13 (1988) 353-65.

happy forever and ever. They will see all their punishments and curses on their enemies. Their bones will rest in the earth and their spirits will be very happy."[48]

There are other ways in which these texts or traditions exercised detectable influence on the Qumran literature. For example, some terms that are well attested in them also play a role in the sectarian scrolls. Some of these from Daniel were mentioned above; here a few from *1 Enoch* and *Jubilees* should be noted. The heavenly tablets are one such item. They are mentioned as the source of Enoch's revelations in the *Apocalypse of Weeks* (*1 Enoch* 93:2), and in 106:19 Enoch learns the mysteries of the holy ones from them. In *Jubilees* the tablets serve as the celestial source from which the angel of the presence dictates to Moses the contents of the book — whether about the past, present, or future (the tablets contain the account from the first to the second creation). Qumran expressions such as חוק חרות (1QS 10:6, 8, 11) or נצח חרות (1QHᵃ 1:24) appear, and חרות figures in a very predestinarian context in 4Q180 frg. 1:3. The word לוחות does not occur frequently in the Qumran texts but is attested. In 4Q177 frgs. 1-4 line 12 it is used in a deterministic setting (ועתה הנה הכול כתוב בלוחות אשר[). "Eternal tablets" are mentioned in 4Q512 12:4.

Another such term is "plant" or "planting" as a designation for the righteous community that is growing toward a greater future. *First Enoch* 10:16 contains the wish that the plant of righteousness and truth appear, and the expression figures frequently in the Apocalypse of Weeks. In *1 Enoch* 93:2 Enoch says he is speaking about the children of righteousness, the elect, the plant of righteousness. In the third week Abraham is elected as the plant of righteous judgment whose descendants will become the plant of righteousness forever; and verse 10 mentions the elect righteous of the eternal plant of righteousness. Enoch also prays in 84:6 that God will establish the righteous as a plant of the eternal seed (cf. 62:8). *Jubilees* uses the same botanical image. *Jubilees* 1:16 speaks of a future transformation of Israel into a plant of righteousness; Abraham blesses God for the promise that a plant of righteousness would arise from him (16:26); he assures Isaac that God will raise the plant of truth from him (21:24; see 4Q219 2:30 where "plant" must be restored but אמת is preserved); and Isaac exhorts his sons to proper conduct so that God may raise their seed to be an eternal plant of righteousness (36:6). The Qumran community refers to itself, the remnant of Israel, through use of the same expression. In 1QS 8:4-6 one reads: "When these are in Israel, the Council of the Community shall be established in truth. It shall be an Everlasting

48. See Collins, *Apocalypticism*, 110-29.

Plantation, a House of Holiness for Israel, an Assembly of Supreme Holiness for Aaron." Very similar thoughts, but combining the plant image with the idea of communion with the angels, appear in 1QS 11:8-9: "He has joined their assembly to the Sons of Heaven to be a Council of Community, a foundation of the Building of Holiness, and eternal plantation throughout all ages to come [קץ נהיה]." 1QHᵃ 8:5-13 develops the metaphor extensively, speaking of trees with roots going down to the fountain of life. Finally, the historical survey in CD 1 includes (at the end of the 390-year period) the words: "He visited them, and He caused a plant root to spring from Israel and Aaron to inherit his land and to prosper on the good things of His earth" (1:7-8).

Summary

Three texts that are apocalypses, entirely or in part — Daniel, *1 Enoch* (less the Parables), and *Jubilees* — have not only been found in multiple copies at Qumran but have also exercised a demonstrable influence on the sectarian literature of the Qumran community. In that sense we can safely say that there is a strong apocalyptic element in the Qumran texts and the community associated with them. These contributions from older sources were put to new uses as the community formulated its own way of life and belief, but they have left their own stamp on the literature found in the caves.

Can the contributions of the apocalyptic texts and traditions be placed into a larger context having to do with the religion of Qumran? The booklets in the Enochian tradition, which, as we have seen, exercised a distinctive and far-reaching influence on the Qumran sectarian writings, display an interesting pattern of religion for a Second Temple Jewish text. The *Book of the Watchers* and the *Book of Dreams* contain revelations granted to Enoch. These revelations provide information about the cosmos and the heavenly world and/or about the past, present, and future. The *Astronomical Book,* too, is a revelation, although most of its attention is focused on the daily workings of the world. What we find in these works in much smaller measure, if at all, is concern with the Torah of Moses. Naturally, part of the explanation for their reticence about the Mosaic law is the pseudepigraphic setting of the booklets: they are supposed to be revelations from before the flood, long antedating the disclosures to Moses. But there are several places where mention of the Torah would have been most appropriate, and even in them it is weakly represented. For example, the *Apocalypse of Weeks* does mention the law briefly in 93:6 ("a law for all generations"), but nothing more is made of it and it plays no role in the condemnation of sinners or in the judgment. The *Animal Apocalypse* that treats the Sinai episode in 89:29-36 never says a word about the law. Terms such as righteous/sinners and topics such as the judgment are pervasive in the Enoch literature, but the law of Moses is not identified as the standard for defining one's status and for giving rewards and punishments. In the *Epistle of Enoch* we may get a vague reference to it: *1 Enoch* 99:2 mentions transgressing "the eternal law," and Robert H. Charles understood this to be the law of Moses (see also the "commandments of the Lord" in 5:4).[49] Only in a later Enochian text, chapter 108, do we get a clearer indication that the biblical law is in the author's mind as he writes about "those who should come after him and keep the law in the last days" (108:1).

The writings of Enoch do presuppose, of course, that there are laws, but if their several authors meant statutes from the law of Moses, they failed to express the idea clearly. The laws that do receive extended treatment are the unchanging laws of nature. They are emphasized in the *Astronomical Book* and in chapters 2–5, where nature's obedience to the laws assigned to its various components is contrasted with human disobedience to the laws meant for people.

The books of Daniel and *Jubilees* exhibit a different pattern. In Daniel the series of apocalypses in the second half of the book is attached to the court tales in chapters 1–6. In the court tales, Daniel and his friends distinguish themselves by their obedience to the laws that they had inherited, not to the laws of the foreign king. So in the first chapter the young men follow their own rules about food and reject the rich fare offered by the king's appointees. In this way they are obedient to what the author understood to be the implication of the laws of *kashrut* in the Torah. As John Collins writes: "The identity affirmed in the tales is one that found its common expression in the worship of the Most High God and observance of his laws. The life-style proposed for the diaspora, then, was one of active participation in gentile life but without compromising the distinctive requirements of Jewish tradition."[50] In the surveys of the future, the law or the covenant is mentioned in Daniel, and those who are righteous are presumably keeping the law (see 11:30-32), while calamities have befallen the people because they have not kept the law (9:10-11; in 7:25 the "other horn" wants to change the festivals and the law). Obviously more space is set aside for apocalyptic visions than for stories about keeping the law of Moses, but both are present in a significant way in the book.

Jubilees has the same elements as the book of Daniel but in inverse pro-

49. R. H. Charles, *The Book of Enoch or 1 Enoch* (Oxford: Clarendon, 1912) 244.
50. Collins, *Daniel,* 51. See his discussion of the food issue on pp. 141-43.

portion. In *Jubilees* the law plays an overwhelmingly powerful role as the entity at the heart of divine revelation and the center of the covenant. The law defines membership in the covenant by being the criterion for obedience or disobedience, blessing or curse. The law was revealed progressively as the covenant was continually renewed through the generations, and it was finally completed in the revelation at Sinai. Coupled with this emphasis on the law are a few apocalyptic passages, especially in chapters 1 and 23, although eschatological subjects such as the judgment figure elsewhere as well. In the pictures of the future, the law continues to play a central role. *Jubilees* 1:14 predicts that Israel will forget the law, but when they repent they will perform his commandment (1:24). *Jubilees* 23:16, 19 speak of abandoning the covenant and of struggle over law and covenant; the great turning point will be when "the children" start "to study the laws, to seek out the commands, and to return to the right way" (23:26).

We have this same combination of law *and* apocalypse at Qumran as in Daniel and *Jubilees,* although the proportions are more like those of *Jubilees.* There can no longer be any question about the importance of the law of Moses and elaborations of it in the scrolls; and in 4QMMT we now have a good basis for thinking that the initial break of the group from Jerusalem authorities centered around disputes about a series of legal points. A powerful insistence on the law of Moses is present at Qumran along with apocalyptic beliefs about sharing fellowship at present with the angels and about the imminent end. Moreover, in some pictures of the future the laws play a prominent role. A good example is the *War Scroll,* which predicts that in the final conflict laws regarding purity will prevail (7:6-7: sexual purity for the combatants [see Deut 23:11] and separation from the "place of the hand" [see Deut 23:10-15; Josh 3:4]; 9:7-9: priests not coming among the slain [see Lev 21:1-6]). Sacrifices will be offered and priests will officiate at them and at the festivals, firsts of the month, and Sabbaths (2:1-5). The laws about sabbatical years will be in effect (2:6-9). One of the banners — that of Merari — will have the slogan "heave-offering of God" (4:1).[51] In that it combines these elements, Qumran, whatever its distinctive traits, stands more in the Daniel-*Jubilees* tradition than the Enochian one; in that it emphasizes the Torah along with apocalyptic themes, it stands more in the *Jubilees* tradition than the Danielic one.

---

51. Passages from the Pentateuch are quoted in 10:2-5 (Deut 20:2-4) and 10:6-8 (Num 10:9). There are references to the covenant in passages such as 17:7-8.

Qumran's Messiah:
How Important Is He?

CRAIG A. EVANS

The "messiah" I refer to in the title of my paper is the traditionally understood eschatological agent, anointed by God for the redemption of Israel. He is normally understood as Davidic,[1] although there are variations on this theme. I ask about his importance at Qumran because the raw data of the Scrolls themselves at first blush could suggest that this figure was of relatively minor importance. Of the 867 scrolls, some 647 are non-Bible scrolls.[2] Of these only six, or at most eight, scrolls actually refer to an "anointed" personage who is to be understood as the eschatological messiah.[3] These scrolls are the *Damascus Document*, the *Rule of the Community* (1QS), the *Rule of the Congregation* (1QSa = 1Q28a), the *Pesher on Genesis^a* (4Q252), possibly *Non-Canonical Psalms^b* (4Q381),[4] possibly *Paraphrase of Kings* (4Q382),[5] *Narra-*

1. See the summary in G. Vermes, *Jesus the Jew* (London: Collins, 1973) 130-34. In this paper I shall not discuss anointed prophets or heralds.

2. For a convenient catalogue of the Scrolls and related materials, see S. A. Reed, *The Dead Sea Scrolls Catalogue: Documents, Photographs, and Museum Inventory Numbers*, ed. M. J. Lundberg (SBLRBS 32; Atlanta: Scholars Press, 1994). For texts, with English-facing pages and principal bibliography, see F. García Martínez and E. J. C. Tigchelaar, *The Dead Sea Scrolls Study Edition* (2 vols.; Leiden: Brill, 1997, 1998).

3. For "anointed" (or "messiah"), see 2 Sam 2:4; 12:7; Pss 2 and 89.

4. 4Q381 15 7 could be read either "I, your messiah, have gained understanding," or "I have gained understanding from your discourse."

5. 4Q382 16 2 could be read "m]essiah of Isra[e]l," but most of the letters are uncertain and some scholars read "statutes."

tive[a] (4Q458), and the *Messianic Apocalypse* (4Q521).[6] Six scrolls refer to the "Prince" or the "Prince of the Congregation."[7] They are the *Damascus Document,* the *Rule of Blessings* (1QSb = 1Q28b), the *War Scroll* (1QM), the *Pesher on Isaiah*[a] (4Q161), the *Rule of War* (4Q285), and the *Apocryphon of Moses* (4Q376).[8] Four scrolls refer to the "Branch of David."[9] They are the *Pesher on Isaiah*[a] (4Q161), *Florilegium* (4Q174), the *Pesher on Genesis*[a] (4Q252), and the *Rule of War* (4Q285).[10] Two scrolls already mentioned refer to the "Prince" as the "Scepter" *(Damascus Document, Pesher on Isaiah*[a]*)*, alluding to Numbers 24:17: "A star has gone forth from Jacob and a scepter has arisen from Israel."[11] Two other scrolls refer to the "scepter" of Numbers 24 and probably should be understood in a messianic sense *(War Scroll, Testimonia)*,[12] while two other scrolls refer to "scepter" without an allusion to the Numbers 24 or Genesis 49 passages *(Rule of Blessings, Messianic Apocalypse)*. Here too the epithet probably should be understood in a messianic sense.[13] Finally, there are four scrolls that speak of a "son," references that may be messianic *(Florilegium,* the *Son of God Scroll,* the *Prayer of Enosh,* and *Narrative*[a]*)*.[14] Apart from the reference in *Florilegium,* which is a quotation of 2 Samuel 7:14a ("I will be a father to him, and he will be My son") and a comment that "this is the 'Branch of David' who will arise with the interpreter of the Law," the other son passages are disputed.[15]

6. The specific passages are CD 12:23–13:1; 14:19 (= 4Q266 10 i 12); 19:10-11; 20:1; 1QS 9:11; 1QSa 2:11-21; 4Q252 5:3-4; 4Q381 15 7 (?); 4Q382 16 2 (?); 4Q458 2 ii 6; and 4Q521 2+4 ii 1.

7. For "Prince," see Ezek 40:46; 44:15; for "congregation," see Num 27:16.

8. The specific passages are CD 7:20 (= 4Q266 3 iii 9); 1QSb 5:20; 1QM 3:15 (= 4Q496 10 iv 3-4); 5:1; 4Q161 2-6 ii 19; 4Q285 4 2-6; 5 4; 6 2; 4Q376 1 iii 1-3.

9. For "Branch of David," see Jer 23:5; 33:15; Zech 6:12.

10. The specific passages are 4Q161 7-10 iii 22; 4Q174 1-3 i 11; 4Q252 5:3-4; 4Q285 5 3-4.

11. The specific passages are CD 7:20 (= 4Q266 3 iii 9); 4Q161 2-6 ii 19.

12. The specific passages are 1QM 11:6-7; 4Q175 12.

13. The specific passages are 1QSb 5:27-28; 4Q521 2 iii 6.

14. The specific passages are 4Q174 1-3 i 11; 4Q246 1:9; 2:1 (twice); 4Q254 4 2; 4Q369 1 ii 6; 4Q458 15 1.

15. The figure in 4Q246 variously called "the Son of the great God," "the Son of God," or "Son of the Most High" has been interpreted as the messiah, as a Jewish king, or as the Antichrist. The quotation of Zech 4:14 ("two sons of oil") in 4Q254 seems to be in the context of an exegesis of Gen 49:8-12, Jacob's blessing on Judah. If so, the "two sons of oil" may have been understood as the "anointed of Aaron and of Israel," that is, the anointed high priest and anointed king-messiah. The "firstborn son" of 4Q369 has been variously interpreted as the messiah or collectively as Israel. I suppose it might even refer to David in a historical sense. Finally, the "firstborn" of 4Q458 does not actually say "son,"

One will notice that several scrolls were mentioned more than once in this brief overview of the principal messianic terminology.[16] In all, thirteen scrolls contain messianic material: D, 1QS, 1QSa, 1QSb, 1QM, 4Q161, 4Q174, 4Q175, 4Q252, 4Q285, 4Q376, 4Q458, and 4Q521. All thirteen[17] of these scrolls were produced by the men of Renewed Covenant, as the Qumran sectarians are often called today.[18] Thus, the evidence at first glance seems to cut in two direc-

---

though that is probably implied. Whether the reference is to David, Israel, or the messiah is impossible to determine because of the fragmentary condition of the text. In 4Q458 2 ii 6 there is reference to one "anointed with the oil of the kingdom." Even this reference could be to the historical David, not necessarily to the awaited messiah.

16. For a more comprehensive overview of messianic terminology, see M. G. Abegg and C. A. Evans, "Messianic Passages in the Dead Sea Scrolls," in *Qumran-Messianism: Studies on the Messianic Expectations in the Dead Sea Scrolls,* ed. J. H. Charlesworth, H. Lichtenberger, and G. S. Oegema (Tübingen: Mohr-Siebeck, 1998) 191-203. For a recent critical discussion of many of these texts, see F. García Martínez, "Messianische Erwartungen in den Qumranschriften," *JBT* 8 (1993) 171-208; idem, "Messianic Hopes in the Qumran Writings," in F. García Martínez and J. Trebolle Barrera, *The People of the Dead Sea Scrolls* (Leiden: Brill, 1995) 159-89. For a bibliography of Qumran messianism, see *Qumran-Messianism,* 204-14.

17. 4Q458 and 4Q521 may not be sectarian. G. Vermes ("Qumran Forum Miscellanea I," *JJS* 43 [1992] 303-4) and D. Dimant ("The Qumran Manuscripts: Contents and Significance," in *Time to Prepare the Way in the Wilderness,* ed. D. Dimant and L. H. Schiffman [STDJ 16; Leiden: Brill, 1995] 23-58, here 48) contend that 4Q521 is not sectarian. Dimant ("Qumran Manuscripts," 46) also catalogues 4Q458 as lacking Qumran terminology, but certain themes and emphases do suggest that they also are products of the Qumran community. Forms of "piety," "pious," or "pious ones" (חסידים, cf. 4Q521 2+4 ii 5, 7) are found in 4Q171 1-10 iv 1 and 4Q174 1 9, both sectarian. The "poor" (ענוים, cf. 4Q521 2+4 ii 12), a favorite self-designation in Qumran literature, appears in 1QSb 5:22; 1QM 14:7; 1QH 6:3; 13:21; 19:25; 23:14; 4Q161 3:7, 19; 4Q163 18-19 i 1; 4Q171 1-10 ii 8, all sectarian literature. The prophetic passage that is alluded to in 4Q521 2 i 4 ii 8, 12 (i.e., Isa 61:1-2) also appears in 11QMelchizedek and is alluded to in 1QS 9:23; 10:19 ("until 'the day of vengeance'") and 1QM 7:5 ("prepared for 'the day of vengeance'"). "Scepter" (שבט, cf. 4Q521 2 iii 6) appears in CD 7:19-20; 1QM 11:6-7; 4Q161 2-6 ii 19. "Uncleanness" (טמאה, cf. 4Q458 2 i 5) appears many times in the sectarian writings (e.g., CD 7:3 passim; 1QS 4:10; 1QSa 2:3; 1QpHab 8:13). To "swallow up" (בלע, cf. 4Q458 2 ii 4) also appears frequently in the sectarian writings (e.g., 1QpHab 11:5, 7, 15; 17:8; 4Q163 1:3). To "be justified" (צדק, cf. 4Q458 2 ii 5) also finds expression in the sectarian writings (e.g., 1QS 3:3; 1QH 5:23; 17:14). We cannot be dogmatic about this question, but it seems at the very least that 4Q458 and 4Q521 speak in ways quite congenial to the thinking of the men of the Renewed Covenant.

18. This designation is reflected in a recent collection of papers: E. Ulrich and J. C. VanderKam, eds., *The Community of the Renewed Covenant: The Notre Dame Symposium on the Dead Sea Scrolls* (CJA 10; Notre Dame, Ind.: University of Notre Dame Press, 1994). See especially S. Talmon's essay, "The Community of the Renewed Covenant: Between Judaism and Christianity," 3-24.

tions: Not many scrolls are concerned with messianism (fewer than 2 percent of the non-Bible scrolls), but those that are concerned with the topic have been produced by the sectarians. Judgments about Qumran's messianism will have to be mindful of these two observations. What we may say is that the Qumran sect was not a "messianic movement," but neither did the sect entertain ideas of final victory over its enemies without the leadership of a royal messiah.

Before launching into a discussion of the role and importance of the messiah of the Dead Sea Scrolls, a few words on the eschatological setting envisioned by the Qumran sect will be helpful.[19] The men of the Renewed Covenant believed that the end, or eschaton, was drawing near. According to CD 20:14, "from the day of gathering in of the unique teacher until the destruction of all the men of war who turned back with the man of lies there shall be forty years." This is understood to mean forty years after the death of the Teacher of Righteousness, which occurred perhaps in 60 BCE, shortly after Roman occupation of Jerusalem. Some of Qumran's Scripture commentaries, the *Pesharim*, were written before this event, while others may have been written, or rewritten, after and in response to it. But the end did not come. Nevertheless, expectations of its soon coming continued to be held at Qumran, probably right up to the great war with Rome in 66-70 CE.

Qumran's eschatology seems to have been primarily restorative, that is, it was focused on the restoration of Israel. A righteous, "anointed"[20] high priest serving in the temple according to proper interpretation of Scripture, a restored Davidic monarchy, a purified and holy remnant of Israel, at whose core would be the men of the Community of the Renewed Covenant, and a period of divine blessing upon the land seem to be the principal elements of Qumran's eschatological hopes. The end of the world, a general resurrection, and some sort of heavenly, nonearthly existence — which often characterizes Christian eschatology — do not appear to be central ideas at Qumran. Indeed, the doctrine of the resurrection is only weakly attested. Émile Puech has recently argued that the

---

19. I depend here primarily on recent work that has been done by John Collins: see J. J. Collins, "Messianism in the Maccabean Period," in *Judaisms and Their Messiahs*, ed. J. Neusner et al. (Cambridge: Cambridge University Press, 1987) 97-109; idem, "Messiahs in Context: Method in the Study of Messianism in the Dead Sea Scrolls," in *Methods of Investigation of the Dead Sea Scrolls and the Khirbet Qumran Site: Present Realities and Future Prospects*, ed. M. O. Wise, N. Golb, J. J. Collins, and D. G. Pardee (Annals of the New York Academy of Sciences 722; New York: The New York Academy of Sciences, 1994) 213-27; idem, *Apocalypticism in the Dead Sea Scrolls* (The Literature of the Dead Sea Scrolls; London: Routledge, 1997) 52-109; idem, "The Expectation of the End in the Dead Sea Scrolls," in *Eschatology, Messianism, and the Dead Sea Scrolls*, ed. C. A. Evans and P. W. Flint (DSRL 1; Grand Rapids: Eerdmans, 1997) 74-90.

20. See 4Q375 1 i 9; 4Q376 1 i 1. Each text speaks of "the anointed priest."

men of Qumran believed in the resurrection, inspired by Daniel 12, and that this hope is attested in many places in the Scrolls.[21] But apart from 4Q521 and possibly 4QPseudo-Ezekiel[b] (4Q386), there is little evidence for belief in the resurrection, especially resurrection of the body, in the Dead Sea Scrolls. According to 4Q521, God will "heal the wounded, give life to the dead, and proclaim good news to the poor." Here we hear echoes of Isaiah 26:19 ("Thy dead shall live, their bodies shall rise. O dwellers in the dust, awake and sing for joy!") and 61:1-2 ("the LORD has anointed me to proclaim good news to the poor"). 4QPseudo-Ezekiel[b] quotes and paraphrases portions of Ezekiel's dry bones vision (Ezek 37:3-14), but it is not clear that Qumran's version of this vision actually goes beyond canonical Ezekiel's vision of national restoration to that of individual resurrection. In his review, John Collins has rightly questioned Puech's conclusions.[22] 4Q246 may also refer to resurrection. After the warfare described in 2:1-3 the author writes: "Until the people of God arise and they all have rest from the sword" (2:4). The text goes on to speak of an "eternal kingdom," peace, justice, and God's eternal rule (2:5-10). It is not clear, however, that "arise" refers to resurrection. It may, but it may also refer to the ascendancy of the people of God over their enemies.

In my judgment, what the men of Qumran anticipated was a restored Israel, a return to the golden age, as they imagined it to have been. They anticipated that this age would be final and not subject to the vicissitudes that marked Israel's checkered history. This anticipation was based on several Scriptures that were understood in a prophetic sense. The most important of them are Genesis 49:10 ("The scepter shall not depart from Judah, nor the ruler's staff from between his feet, until he comes to whom it belongs; and to him shall be the obedience of the peoples"); Numbers 24:17 ("I see him, but not now; I behold him, but not nigh: a star shall come forth out of Jacob, and a scepter shall rise out of Israel; it shall crush the forehead of Moab, and break down all the sons of Sheth"); and Isaiah 10:34–11:5:

> [34]He will cut down the thickets of the forest with an axe, and Lebanon with its majestic trees will fall. [11:1]There shall come forth a shoot from the stump of Jesse, and a branch shall grow out of his roots. [2]And the Spirit of the LORD shall rest upon him, the spirit of wisdom and understanding, the spirit of counsel and might, the spirit of knowledge and the fear of the

21. É. Puech, *La croyance des Esséniens en la vie future: Immortalité, résurrection, vie éternelle? Histoire d'une croyance dans le Judaïsme ancien*, vol. 1, *La résurrection des morts et le contexte scripturaire* (EBib 21; Paris: Gabalda, 1993).

22. J. J. Collins, "Review of Puech, *La croyance des Esséniens en la vie future*," *DSD* 1 (1994) 246-52.

LORD. [3]And his delight shall be in the fear of the LORD. He shall not judge by what his eyes see, or decide by what his ears hear; [4]but with righteousness he shall judge the poor, and decide with equity for the meek of the earth; and he shall smite the earth with the rod of his mouth, and with the breath of his lips he shall slay the wicked. [5]Righteousness shall be the girdle of his waist, and faithfulness the girdle of his loins.

Genesis 49:10 is seen in the *Pesher on Genesis[a]* (4Q252) fragment 1, column 5:

> [1]A ruler shall [no]t depart from the tribe of Judah when Israel has dominion. [2][And] the one who sits on the throne of David [shall never] be cut off, because the "ruler's staff" is the covenant of the kingdom, [3][and the thous]ands of Israel are "the feet," until the Righteous Messiah, the Branch of David, has come (Gen 49:10). [4]For to him and to his seed the covenant of the kingdom of His people has been given for the eternal generations.[23]

Numbers 24:17 is quoted in *Testimonia* (4Q175) 12-13, though without explicit messianic interpretation. It is reasonable to assume that the passage was understood in a messianic sense, however. The same is probably true in the case of 1QM 11:6-7. Numbers 24:17 is quoted and interpreted in the *Damascus Document* 7:

> The star is the Interpreter of the Law [19]who comes to Damascus, as it is written, "A star has left Jacob, a scepter has risen [20]from Israel" (Num 24:17a). The latter is the Prince of the whole Congregation; when he appears, "he will shatter [21]all the sons of Sheth" (Num 24:17b).

The "Interpreter of the Law," perhaps the eschatological priest, is understood as the "star" of the Numbers 24:17 prophecy, while the "Prince of the whole Congregation" is understood to be the "scepter."

Parts of Isaiah 10:34–11:5 are quoted and commented upon in the *Rule of Blessings* (1QSb = 1Q28b), the *Pesher on Isaiah[a]* (4Q161), and the *Rule of War* (4Q285). These texts will be cited below.

The fulfillment of these scriptures, as well as many others, did not mark the *end* of human history but the *beginning* of Israel's restoration, when the covenant with God would be finally and fully renewed. The era of Gentile oppression, even "exile,"[24] would at last be over.

---

23. Translations of the Scrolls are based on M. O. Wise, M. G. Abegg Jr., and E. M. Cook, *The Dead Sea Scrolls: A New Translation* (San Francisco: HarperCollins, 1996).

24. On Jewish ideas of Israel as in a state of exile, see J. M. Scott, ed., *Exile: Old Testament, Jewish, and Christian Conceptions* (JSJSup 56; Leiden: Brill, 1997).

The subject of Jewish messianism in late antiquity is a complicated and much disputed one. Recent, major books on the subject include those by Antti Laato, John Collins, Kenneth Pomykala, William Horbury, Gerbern Oegema, and Johannes Zimmermann,[25] as well as edited collections of studies by James Charlesworth, Peter Flint, and others.[26] The balance of this paper will treat three aspects of Qumran's messianism: (1) the idea of two messiahs, (2) the royal messiah and his role in the great battle of liberation, and (3) the royal messiah and his relationship to the anointed priest.

Qumran's Two Messiahs

In the wake of the discovery of the Scrolls, a great deal of attention focused on Qumran's expectation of the appearance of two messiahs. Several times the *Damascus Document* speaks of a time when the "anointed of Aaron and of Israel" will appear (CD 12:23–13:1, passim). It is on this basis, though not ex-

25. A. Laato, *Josiah and David Redivivus: The Historical Josiah and the Messianic Expectations of Exilic and Postexilic Times* (ConBOT 33; Stockholm: Almqvist & Wiksell, 1992); idem, *A Star Is Rising: The Historical Development of the Old Testament Royal Ideology and the Rise of the Jewish Messianic Expectations* (USF International Studies in Formative Christianity and Judaism 5; Atlanta: Scholars Press, 1997); J. J. Collins, *The Scepter and the Star: The Messiahs of the Dead Sea Scrolls and Other Ancient Literature* (ABRL 10; New York: Doubleday, 1995); K. E. Pomykala, *The Davidic Dynasty Tradition in Early Judaism: Its History and Significance for Messianism* (SBLEJL 7; Atlanta: Scholars Press, 1995); W. Horbury, *Jewish Messianism and the Cult of Christ* (London: SCM Press, 1998); G. S. Oegema, *Der Gesalbte und sein Volk: Untersuchungen zum Konzeptualisierungsprozeß der messianischen Erwartungen von den Makkabäern bis Bar Koziba* (SIJD 2; Göttingen: Vandenhoeck & Ruprecht, 1994); idem, *The Anointed and His People: Messianic Expectations from the Maccabees to Bar Kochba* (JSPSup 27; Sheffield: Sheffield Academic Press, 1998); J. Zimmermann, *Messianische Texte aus Qumran: Königliche, priesterliche und prophetische Messiasvorstellungen in den Schriftfunden von Qumran* (WUNT 104; Tübingen: Mohr-Siebeck, 1998).

26. J. H. Charlesworth, ed., *The Messiah: Developments in Earliest Judaism and Christianity* (Minneapolis: Fortress, 1992); I. Gruenwald et al., eds., *Messiah and Christos: Studies in the Jewish Origins of Christianity* (TSAJ 32; Tübingen: Mohr-Siebeck, 1992); Evans and Flint, *Eschatology, Messianism, and the Dead Sea Scrolls*; and Charlesworth, Lichtenberger, and Oegema, *Qumran-Messianism*. See also the German collection of studies in E. Stegemann, ed., *Messiasvorstellungen bei Juden und Christen* (Stuttgart: Kohlhammer, 1993). Also important are the monograph by T. N. D. Mettinger, *King and Messiah: The Civil and Sacral Legitimation of the Israelite Kings* (ConBOT 8; Lund: Gleerup, 1976), and the collection of studies in P. E. Satterthwaite et al., eds., *The Lord's Anointed: Interpretation of Old Testament Messianic Texts* (Carlisle: Paternoster, 1995). These two latter works probe the origins of messianism in the Old Testament literature itself.

clusively, that scholars began to speak of a diarchic or binary messianism at Qumran.[27] However, recently some scholars have challenged this near consensus — for example, Michael Wise and James Tabor have argued that Qumran's messianism is monarchic.[28] Yet the diarchic view remains widely held and in my opinion is correct.[29]

The idea of two anointed personages is based on the Hebrew Scriptures themselves, as seen so clearly in Zechariah and Haggai,[30] but also in Jeremiah 33:15-18, where God promises a frightened and beleaguered Judah:

> In those days and at that time, I will cause to sprout for David a righteous Branch; and he shall execute justice and righteousness in the land. In those days Judah will be saved and Jerusalem will live in safety. And this is the name

27. The standard older treatment is K. G. Kuhn, "The Two Messiahs of Aaron and Israel," *NTS* 1 (1954-55) 168-80; reprinted in K. Stendahl, ed., *The Scrolls and the New Testament* (New York: Harper, 1957; reprint New York: Crossroad, 1992) 54-64, 256-59. CD's epithet "Messiah of Aaron and of Israel" (משיח אהרון וישראל) refers to *two* anointed figures, as in 1QS 9:15 (משיחי אהרון וישראל), not to *one* figure. S. Talmon and M. G. Abegg, Jr., point to two examples in the Hebrew Bible where a singular noun form, in construct with two nouns, is functionally plural: "the heads of Oreb and Zeeb" (Judg 7:25, where "head" is singular); and "the kings of Sodom and Gomorrah" (Gen 14:10, where "king" is singular). Examples in the Scrolls include CD 5:3-4; 1QS 6:6; 1QSa 2:18-19; 10:10; 1QM 3:13-14 ("the names of Israel and Aaron"); 4Q251; 11QT^a 43:8-9. It is important that all of these examples are from the sectarian literature. See Talmon, "The Concepts of Māšîaḥ and Messianism in Early Judaism," in Charlesworth, ed., *The Messiah*, 105 n. 64; and M. G. Abegg Jr., "The Hebrew of the Dead Sea Scrolls," in *The Dead Sea Scrolls after Fifty Years: A Comprehensive Assessment*, ed. P. W. Flint and J. C. VanderKam (2 vols.; Leiden: Brill, 1998, 1999) 1.334-35.

28. M. O. Wise, and J. D. Tabor, "The Messiah at Qumran," *BARev* 18.6 (1992) 60-65, esp. 60.

29. F. M. Cross, "Notes on the Doctrine of the Two Messiahs at Qumran and the Extra-Canonical *Daniel Apocalypse (4Q246),*" in *Current Research and Technological Developments on the Dead Sea Scrolls: Conference on the Texts from the Judean Desert, Jerusalem, 30 April 1995*, ed. D. W. Parry and S. D. Ricks (STDJ 20; Leiden: Brill, 1996) 1-13. On p. 2 Cross says: "a consistent doctrine of only two messiahs — one of Aaron and one of Israel — is evident throughout the sectarian Qumran literature." J. Collins agrees: Diarchic messianism is "usually taken to be the norm at Qumran and to be the most distinctive feature of Qumran messianism" (*Scepter and the Star*, 75). Qumran's diarchic messianism has been defended in a recent study by W. M. Schniedewind, "Structural Aspects of Qumran Messianism in the *Damascus Document,*" in *The Provo International Conference on the Dead Sea Scrolls: Technological Innovations, New Texts, and Reformulated Issues*, ed. D. W. Parry and E. Ulrich (STDJ 30; Leiden: Brill, 1998) 523-36.

30. J. C. VanderKam ("Jubilees and the Priestly Messiah of Qumran," *RevQ* 13 [1988] 365) has expressed some doubt about the influence of either Zechariah or Haggai in Qumran's diarchic messianism. However, he expressed this doubt before the publication of 4Q254, in which a portion of Zech 4:14 appears.

by which it will be called: "The Lord is our righteousness." For thus says the Lord: David shall never lack a man to sit on the throne of Israel, *and the levitical priests shall never lack a man in my presence* to offer burnt offerings, to make grain offerings, and to make sacrifices for all time. (emphasis added)

William Schniedewind draws our attention to the way 4QFlor adds a second personage, a priestly one, to the Davidic covenant, as expressed in 2 Samuel 7:13-14.[31] See 4QFlor lines 10-12: "He is 'the Branch of David' who will arise *with the Interpreter of the Law,* who shall arise in Zion in the last days" (emphasis added).

The diarchic nature of Qumran's messianism is clearly presupposed in two of the sect's most important and most authoritative writings: the *Damascus Document* and the *Rule of the Community.* Since these texts explain the sect's origin, reason for being, and requirements for membership, what they say about messianism should be accorded normative status, even if it is mentioned only in passing. No further corroboration should be required, though other scrolls offer additional evidence, such as the passage from 4QFlorilegium cited in the preceding paragraph.

The Royal Messiah and Battle

We expect the royal messiah to play a leading role in the anticipated great war for Israel's liberation, but the priests also assist in the great eschatological battle, as seen in the *War Scroll.* This scroll describes in great detail the duties of the priests in organizing Israel for holy war, a war that was expected to endure for forty years. Part of these preparations involved engraving various names and slogans on shields and other implements. According to 1QM 5:1, "on the sh[ie]ld of the Prince of the whole Congregation they shall write his name, the names 'Israel,' 'Levi,' and 'Aaron,' and the names of the twelve tribes of Israel according to their order of birth." The name of the "Prince of the whole Congregation" joins the names of Israel, Levi (the patriarch of the priestly tribe), and Aaron (the Levite through whom the high priest descends), as well as the names of the other patriarchs. This is quite distinguished company. These names emphasize that all of renewed Israel will be represented by the Prince.[32]

31. Schniedewind, "Structural Aspects of Qumran Messianism," 528.
32. It is analogous to Jesus' appointment of the "twelve" (Mark 3:14), as well as his promise that the twelve will sit on twelve thrones judging the twelve tribes of Israel (Matt 19:28 = Luke 22:28-30). The number twelve signifies the restoration of the "whole congregation" of Israel.

Priestly duties are also spelled out in the great *Temple Scroll*. According to column 58, Israel's king

> must not go to battle prior to coming to the High Priest to inquire of him about the judgment of the Urim [19]and Thummim. The king will go out to battle and return guided by the priest — the king and all the Israelites [20]with him. He must not go out by his own decision prior to inquiring of the judgment of the Urim [21]and Thummim. Then he shall succeed in all his ways because he went out by the judgment that . . .

The high profile of the priests in the *War Scroll* reflects the role Scripture gives the high priest in times of war. We see this in Deuteronomy 20:1-4, where it is the priest who speaks to Israel on the eve of war (see 1QM 10 for the priestly exhortation). In Joshua 6 the priests play a prominent role in bringing down Jericho's walls — blowing trumpets, carrying the ark of the covenant, and participating in the march (see 1QM 8-9 for the priestly trumpeting). The *War Scroll* has greatly expanded and embellished the scriptural teaching pertaining to the priests' duties in wartime.

Although the royal messiah is not depicted in the *War Scroll*, his involvement in the great struggle between the sons of light and the sons of darkness is very probably presupposed. 1QM 11:1-2 alludes to David's defeat of Goliath, while 11:2-3 alludes to David's victory over the Philistines. Allusions to David's great military victories suggest that his anointed successor will also enjoy great victories over Israel's contemporary oppressors. 1QM 11:4-7 quotes Numbers 24:17 and says, "he rules from Jacob." Who is this who "rules"? It is probably the royal messiah. In 1QM 11:11 the author reminds God of his promise to "display the might of Your hand against the Kittim," that is, against the Romans.

The royal messiah may only be implied in the *War Scroll* (and may actually have made an appearance in the original, full text), but he makes unmistakable appearances in other texts. The two most important are the *Pesher on Isaiah*[a] (4Q161) and the *Rule of War* (4Q285), both of which are based on Isaiah 10:34–11:5, and the latter of which may have been part of another version of the *War Scroll*. The first passage reads:

> [5]["Right now, the Lord God of Hosts is pruning the treetops with a hook. The tallest of all are hewn down,] [6][the mightiest are laid low. The forest] thickets [will be cut down] with iron tools, the trees of Lebanon, for all their majesty, [7][will fall" (Isa 10:34). This refers to the] Kittim, who will fall at the hand of Israel and the humble [8][of Judah, who will . . .] the Gentiles, and the mighty will be shattered, and [their coura]ge will dissolve. [9][. . . The

"tallest] of all will be cut down" refers to the warriors of the Kit[tim,] [10][who . . . as for the verse that say]s, "The forest thickets will be cut down with iron tools," they are [11][. . .] for war against the Kittim. "The trees of Lebanon, for [all their majesty, [12]will fall": they are the] Kittim, who will be put into the power of the nobles of [Israel . . .] [13][. . .] when he flees befo[re Is]rael . . . [14][*vacat*] [15]["A rod will grow from] Jesse's stock, a sprout [will bloom] from his [roots;] upon him wi[ll rest] the spirit of [16][the Lord: a spirit of] wisdom and insight, a spirit of good coun[sel and strength], a spirit of true know[ledge] [17][and reverence for the Lord, he will delight in reverence for] the Lord. [He will not judge only] by what [his eyes] see, [18][he will not decide only by what his ears hear;] but he will rule [the weak by justice, and give decisions] [19][in integrity to the humble of the land. He will punish the land with the mace of his words, by his lips' breath alone] [20][he will slay the wicked. 'Justice' will be the girdle around] his waist, 'Tr[uth' the girdle around his hips"] (Isa 11:1-5).

The second passage reads (frgs. 4-5):

[2][. . . the P]rince of the Congregation to the[Mediterranean] Sea[. . .] [3][. . . And they shall flee] from Israel at that time[. . .] [4][. . . And the High Priest] shall stand before them and they shall arrange themselves against them[in battle array . . .] [5][. . .] and they shall return back to the land at that time[. . .] [6][. . .] then they shall bring him before the Prince of[the congregation . . .] frg. 5 [1][. . . just as it is written in the book of] Isaiah the prophet, "And [the thickets of the forest] shall be cut down [2][with an ax, and Lebanon with its majestic trees w]ill fall. A shoot shall come out from the stump of Jesse [3][and a branch shall grow out of his roots" (Isa 10:34–11:1). This is the] Branch of David. Then [all forces of Belial] shall be judged, [4][and the king of the Kittim shall stand for judgment] and the Prince of the community — the Bra[nch of David] — will have him put to death. [5][Then all Israel shall come out with timbrel]s and dancers, and the [High] Priest shall order [6][them to cleanse their bodies from the guilty blood of the c]orpse[s of] the Kittim.[33]

---

33. For defense of the proper restoration and rendering, "[with timbrel]s and dancers," as opposed to "[by stroke]s and by wounds," as in G. Vermes, "The Oxford Forum for Qumran Research Seminar on the Rule of the War from Cave 4 (4Q285)," *JJS* 43 (1992) 88, see M. G. Abegg Jr., "Messianic Hope and 4Q285: A Reassessment," *JBL* 113 (1994) 81-91, esp. 90. Recognition that the text is speaking about women playing timbrels and dancing (as in Exod 15:20 and Judg 21:23, where Israelite women beat timbrels and dance following victories over Israel's enemies) makes all the more implausible the notion that 4Q285 is talking about a slain prince. On the contrary, the prince slays the leader of the Romans,

The image of the militant, victorious royal messiah is consistent with the biblical picture of King David of old, and it is consistent with the imagery of the Davidic messiah in the *Psalms of Solomon* 17–18. This figure is to "destroy the unrighteous rulers, to purge Jerusalem from Gentiles" (17:22). He will "smash the arrogance of sinners" and will "shatter all their substance with an iron rod" and "destroy the unlawful nations with the word of his mouth" (v. 24). Here again we hear echoes of Isaiah 11.

Qumran's expectation of a conquering royal messiah is not distinctive and appears to be entirely consistent with Jewish messianic and eschatological traditions from the time of Qumran, through the New Testament period, and on into the time of the rabbis.

The Royal Messiah and the Anointed Priest

The *Rule of the Congregation* (1QSa = 1Q28a) describes a banquet that will take place "when God will have begotten[34] the Messiah" among the men of the Community. Because the priest enters first and the messiah enters afterward, this is understood by some to imply that the royal messiah is subordinate to the priestly messiah.[35] The pertinent passages read:

> [11]The procedure for the [mee]ting of the men of reputation [when they are called] to the banquet held by the Council of the Yahad, when [God] has fa[th]ered(?) [12]the Messiah among them: [the Priest,] as head of the entire congregation of Israel, shall enter first, trailed by all [13][his] brot[hers, the Sons of] Aaron, those priests [appointed] to the banquet of the men of reputation. They are to sit [14]be[fore him] by rank. Then the [Mess]iah of Israel may en[ter,] and the heads [15]of the th[ousands of Israel] are to sit before him by rank, as determined by [each man's comm]ission in their

---

the women dance, and the priest gives orders pertaining to purification of the land in the aftermath of battle.

34. The most probable reading of 1QSa 2:11 is *yōlîd* ("he will have begotten"), though other readings have been proposed, such as "he will have brought." The reference to a "messiah" who is "begotten" is an allusion to Ps 2:2 ("messiah") and 2:7 ("begotten"). This language, of course, is metaphorical and does not require a literal interpretation. The author of this text and its subsequent readers did not imagine that God would bring about the birth of the messiah through a virgin, as in later Christian theology, as expressed in the Matthean and Lukan infancy narratives. All that is being affirmed in 1QSa is that God will raise up his anointed one.

35. On the royal messiah's subordination to the priestly messiah, see Collins, "Messiahs in Context," 224, 227.

camps and campaigns. Last, all [16]the heads of [the con]gregation's cl[ans,] together with [their] wis[e and knowledgeable men,] shall sit before them by [17]rank.

[When] they gather [at the] communal [tab]le, [having set out bread and w]ine so the communal table is set [18][for eating] and [the] wine (poured) for drinking, none [may re]ach for the first portion [19]of the bread or [the wine] before the Priest. For [he] shall [bl]ess the first portion of the bread [20]and the wine, [reac]hing for the bread first. Afterw[ard] the Messiah of Israel [shall re]ach [21]for the bread. [Finally,] ea[ch] (member of) the whole congregation of the Yahad [shall give a bl]essing, [in descending order of] rank.

The order of blessings in the *Rule of Blessings* (1QSb = 1Q28b), whereby the Prince of the Congregation is blessed last, is also thought to imply a subordination of the royal messiah to the priestly messiah. But the order of blessings may suggest just the opposite. First to be blessed is the Community itself (1:1-7), followed by a blessing for the anointed priest (2:22–3:21), and then a blessing for all of the priests, the sons of Zadok (3:22–5:17). The last blessing is for the Prince (5:20-29). The Prince's blessing at the end could be climactic, perhaps mirroring eschatology itself, in that the royal messiah has not yet appeared. There is no compelling reason to see the order of blessings as proof of the royal messiah's subordination to the priestly messiah.

Is the order of events or blessings in 1QSa and 1QSb evidence of the "subordination" of the royal messiah, or is it only appropriate deference to the high priest, in his capacity as one who consults the Urim and Thummim to ascertain God's will? There seem to be three basic options: (1) the royal messiah is subordinate to the anointed high priest, (2) the royal messiah dominates (as one might suppose in 4Q521, or as in Christian christology), and (3) neither the royal messiah nor the anointed high priest dominates the other, but they serve faithfully side by side, each respecting the other's duties and prerogatives.

In my opinion the third option seems to match the evidence of the Scrolls better than either of the first two. Accordingly, I do not think that Qumran's messianism is distinctive in any significant way. It envisions the restoration of the monarchy and the priesthood and so may properly be described as diarchic messianism, a restorative messianism that is rooted in Scripture and is entertained in other traditions (e.g., the *Testaments of the Twelve Patriarchs*).

Finally, we must take into account Qumran's interpretation of Isaiah 11:3: "He shall not judge by what his eyes see, or decide by what his ears hear." According to the first pesher on Isaiah, the royal messiah "will judge, as they (the priests) teach him," and "according to their command" he will act (the text breaks off) and the priests will be (again the text breaks off) "with him" (4QpIsa^a 7-10 iii 27-29). This text too has been understood to indicate that the royal messiah is subordinate to the anointed priest. The priestly presence and function are accentuated to be sure, but all that this optimistic pesher is saying is that the king will conduct himself appropriately. How else would the royal messiah behave? Instead of being opposed to the high priest and his colleagues, he will be supportive and will follow their instructions. But the royal messiah's cooperation and compliance in matters that fall within the priestly purview need not be understood in terms of subordination. The point of the pesher's understanding of Isaiah 11:3 is that the royal messiah, whom God will anoint with a spirit of understanding (Isa 11:1, cited earlier in 4QpIsa^a 7-10 iii 15-16), will be thoroughly "orthodox" so far as Qumran's priests are concerned. This is the same idea behind 11QTemple 58:18-21 cited above.

It is certainly correct to say that the priestly role in the eschatological drama is enhanced, but I think it goes too far to speak of the subordination of the royal messiah to the anointed high priest. Qumran says little about the royal messiah because his function *was not at issue.* What was at issue was *the role of the priest and the function of the temple cultus.* Here the men of the Renewed Covenant had grave concerns. Accordingly, we should not be surprised that the anointed priest receives so much attention and the anointed king so little in comparison.

Conclusion

By way of conclusion, I would like to make three points:

(1) Qumran is not preoccupied with messianism; the community presupposes it and utilizes it as part of the community's eschatology and hopes of restoration. When God finally "begets" the messiah and raises him up, he will play an important role in Israel's liberation. He will engage the Kittim, that is, the Romans, in battle and quite possibly will himself slay the Roman emperor.

(2) In comparison to Jewish messianism of late antiquity, Qumran's messianism is not distinctive in any significant way.[36] Qumran's temple-

---

36. Christian messianism became distinctive in that the priestly and prophetic dimensions were subsumed under the royal heading. But the royal messianism of early Christianity was otherwise hardly distinctive from Jewish messianism, as has been rightly emphasized by Horbury, *Jewish Messianism and the Cult of Christ.*

related concerns (touching calendar, matters of purity, and other halakic issues) are distinctive in aggregate, but their messianism is not. Of course, Qumran assumes that the awaited messiah, the "Branch of David" and "Prince of the Congregation," will fully endorse and support the Congregation's cultic reforms. However, the messiah is not subordinate to the anointed priest, nor are his functions in any way significantly different from Jewish messianic expectation. The awaited messiah is subordinate only in the sense that his appearance is tied to Qumran's eschatology. Of course, the anointed priest will not be subordinate to the messiah. Neither will encroach upon the duties and authority of the other.

(3) If Qumranian messianism is not distinctive, that does not mean it was not important. The restoration of Israel, and the vindication of the Community of the Renewed Covenant that is a vital part of this restoration, will not and cannot take place until the "anointed of Israel" appears, one whom God will raise up, or in the words of Psalm 2:7 echoed in 1QSa, whom God will "beget" among his faithful remnant, the "poor." The appearance of the anointed Prince of the Congregation will trigger the eschatological events, which will include the defeat of Rome, the purification and reestablishment of proper worship in Jerusalem, and healing and blessings for the faithful.

Selected Bibliography of Recent Writings on the Religion of the Scrolls

Albani, M. "Horoscopes in the Qumran Scrolls." In *The Dead Sea Scrolls after Fifty Years: A Comprehensive Assessment,* edited by P. W. Flint and J. C. VanderKam, vol. 2, 279-330. Leiden: Brill, 1999.

Alexander, P. S. "'Wrestling against Wickedness in High Places': Magic in the Worldview of the Qumran Community." In *The Scrolls and the Scriptures: Qumran Fifty Years After,* edited by C. A. Porter and C. A. Evans, 318-37. JSPSup 26. Sheffield: Sheffield Academic Press, 1997.

Bernstein, M., F. García Martínez, and J. Kampen, eds. *Legal Texts and Legal Issues: Proceedings of the Second Meeting of the International Organization for Qumran Studies, Cambridge, 1995: Published in Honour of Joseph M. Baumgarten.* STDJ 23. Leiden: Brill, 1997.

Beyerle, S. "Der Gott der Qumraniten. Anmerkungen zum Gottesbild der Qumran-Texte aus der Sicht der Mischna, der Talmudim, frühen Midraschim und des Josephos." *Henoch* 20 (1998) 271-89.

Boccaccini, G. *Beyond the Essene Hypothesis: The Parting of the Ways between Qumran and Enochic Judaism.* Grand Rapids: Eerdmans, 1998.

Chazon, E. G. "Prayers from Qumran and Their Historical Implications." *DSD* 1 (1994) 265-84.

Collins, J. J. *Apocalypticism in the Dead Sea Scrolls.* London: Routledge, 1997.

———. *The Scepter and the Star: The Messiahs of the Dead Sea Scrolls and Other Ancient Literature.* New York: Doubleday, 1995.

Davila, J. R. "Heavenly Ascents in the Dead Sea Scrolls." In *The Dead Sea Scrolls after Fifty Years: A Comprehensive Assessment,* edited by P. W. Flint and J. C. VanderKam, vol. 2, 461-85. Leiden: Brill, 1999.

Evans, C. A., and P. W. Flint, eds. *Eschatology, Messianism, and the Dead Sea Scrolls.* Grand Rapids: Eerdmans, 1997.

Falk, D. K. *Daily, Sabbath and Festival Prayers in the Dead Sea Scrolls.* STDJ 27. Leiden: Brill, 1997.

Fishbane, M. "Use, Authority and Interpretation of Mikra at Qumran." In *Mikra: Text, Translation, Reading and Interpretation of the Hebrew Bible in Ancient Judaism and Early Christianity,* edited by M. J. Mulder, 339-77. CRINT. Philadelphia: Fortress, 1988.

Flint, P. W. *The Dead Sea Psalms Scroll and the Book of Psalms.* STDJ 17. Leiden: Brill, 1997.

Flint, P. W., and J. C. VanderKam, eds. *The Dead Sea Scrolls after Fifty Years: A Comprehensive Assessment.* 2 vols. Leiden: Brill, 1998, 1999.

Harrington, D. J. *Wisdom Texts from Qumran.* London: Routledge, 1996.

Hempel, C. "Community Structures in the Dead Sea Scrolls: Admission, Organization, Disciplinary Procedures." In *The Dead Sea Scrolls after Fifty Years: A Comprehensive Assessment,* edited by P. W. Flint and J. C. VanderKam, vol. 2, 67-97. Leiden: Brill, 1999.

Kampen, J., and M. Bernstein, eds. *Reading 4QMMT: New Perspectives on Qumran Law and History.* Atlanta: Scholars Press, 1996.

Lange, A. "The Essene Position on Magic and Divination." In *Legal Texts and Legal Issues: Proceedings of the Second Meeting of the International Organization for Qumran Studies, Cambridge, 1995: Published in Honour of Joseph M. Baumgarten,* edited by M. Bernstein, F. García Martínez, and J. Kampen, 377-435. STDJ 23. Leiden: Brill, 1997.

Lim, T. H. *Holy Scripture in the Qumran Commentaries and Pauline Letters.* Oxford: Clarendon, 1997.

Maier, J. "Zu Kult und Liturgie der Qumrangemeinde." *RevQ* 14 (1989-90) 543-86.

Metso, S. "Constitutional Rules at Qumran." In *The Dead Sea Scrolls after Fifty Years: A Comprehensive Assessment,* edited by P. W. Flint and J. C. VanderKam, vol. 1, 186-210. Leiden: Brill, 1998.

Newsom, C. A. "Shirot Olat HaShabbat." In E. Eshel et al., *Qumran Cave 4, VI: Poetical and Liturgical Texts, Part 1* 173-401. DJD 11. Oxford: Clarendon, 1998.

———. *Songs of the Sabbath Sacrifice: A Critical Edition.* Atlanta: Scholars Press, 1985.

Nitzan, B. *Qumran Prayer and Religious Poetry.* STDJ 12. Leiden: Brill, 1994.

Puech, É. *La croyance des Esséniens en la vie future: Immortalité, résurrection, vie éternelle?* 2 vols. Paris: Gabalda, 1993.

Qimron, E., and J. Strugnell. *Qumran Cave 4, V: Miqṣat Maʿase Ha-Torah.* DJD 10. Oxford: Clarendon, 1994.

Sanders, J. A. "The Scrolls and the Canonical Process." In *The Dead Sea Scrolls after Fifty Years: A Comprehensive Assessment,* edited by P. W. Flint and J. C. VanderKam, vol. 2, 1-23. Leiden: Brill, 1999.

Schiffman, L. H. "The Qumran Scrolls and Rabbinic Judaism." In *The Dead Sea Scrolls after Fifty Years: A Comprehensive Assessment,* edited by P. W. Flint and J. C. VanderKam, vol. 2, 552-72. Leiden: Brill, 1999.

———. *Reclaiming the Dead Sea Scrolls.* Philadelphia: Jewish Publication Society, 1994.

Schmidt, F. *La Pensée du Temple de Jérusalem à Qoumrân.* Paris: Seuil, 1994.

Schuller, E. "Prayer, Hymnic, and Liturgical Texts from Qumran." In *The Community of the Renewed Covenant,* edited by E. Ulrich and J. C. VanderKam, 153-71. CJA 10. Notre Dame, Ind.: University of Notre Dame Press, 1994.

Stegemann, H. *The Library of Qumran.* Grand Rapids: Eerdmans, 1998.

Ulrich, E. *The Dead Sea Scrolls and the Origins of the Bible.* Grand Rapids: Eerdmans, 1999.

———. "The Dead Sea Scrolls and the Biblical Text." In *The Dead Sea Scrolls after Fifty Years: A Comprehensive Assessment,* edited by P. W. Flint and J. C. VanderKam, vol. 1, 79-100. Leiden: Brill, 1998.

VanderKam, J. C. *Calendars in the Dead Sea Scrolls: Measuring Time.* London: Routledge, 1998.

———. *The Dead Sea Scrolls Today.* Grand Rapids: Eerdmans, 1994.

Weinfeld, M. *The Organizational Pattern and the Penal Code of the Qumran Sect.* Göttingen: Vandenhoeck & Ruprecht, 1986.

Zimmermann, J. *Messianische Texte aus Qumran.* WUNT 104. Tübingen: Mohr-Siebeck, 1998.

Index of Ancient Literature

153

Index of Ancient Literature

Index of Modern Authors